GETTING THERE

TV Smith

Punk Rock Tour Diaries: Volume One

Starring!!

The Adverts!
Attila The Stockbroker!
Tom Robinson!
Die Toten Hosen!
Punk Lurex OK!
Santa Claus!
Henry Rollins!
Garden Gang!
The UK Subs!
Sid Vicious (the dog)!

…and a cast of thousands!!

Published 2006 by arima publishing

www.arimapublishing.com

ISBN 1-84549-128-9

© T V Smith 2006

Back cover photo (2006) by Phil Watts

Printed and bound in the United Kingdom

Typeset in Garamond 11/16

arima publishing
ASK House, Northgate Avenue
Bury St Edmunds, Suffolk IP32 6BB
t: (+44) 01284 700321

www.arimapublishing.com

CONTENTS:

PROLOGUE:

TOP OF THE POPS

I was on that Top Of The Pops once. Twice actually, three times if you count the repeat.

I certainly hadn't expected that when I was jumping up and down on the sofa, age eight, playing the tennis racquet and singing along to The Beatles 'She Loves You Yeah Yeah Yeah.'

I didn't see it coming when I borrowed an acoustic guitar from the Sunday School, and kept it.

Or when as a teenager I played my first gig in the school lunch break, then had to go back to Maths lesson with glitter in my hair. Or at the second gig in Belstone village hall on the edge of Dartmoor. No-one came.

Top Of The Pops was far from my mind when I formed my next band while on a year skiving at Torquay Art College and we got booked to play at a school disco—to the kids!— one evening; but it felt like we were doing something right when the headmaster pulled the plugs before the end of the gig, just like a real band.

We hired a studio for £36.00 plus £2.88 V.A.T. and made a record, pressing up fifty copies for family and friends, but we knew it would never get on Top Of The Pops.

It was only when I moved up to London in the summer of 1976 with my girlfriend Gaye and we set about forming a band just as punk rock started to invent itself that I began to get an inkling of what could happen. Not at first, of course. At first it was just the two of us practising the guitar and bass lines in a tiny one-room attic flat in Hammersmith, two steps in any direction and you'd knock yourself out on the sloping roof. When we weren't going out to see the Sex Pistols or the Stranglers we were holed up in there, watching the rain drip down the light cord, over the bulb and onto the bed. A succession of guitarists came in and showed us their stuff, but none of them seemed to have the idea. They reminded me of the bands I'd already been in.

Eventually one of my small ads in the music press was answered by a guy called Howard who lived down the road. He was a down-to-earth Northerner recovering from a self-imposed spell in a mental hospital, a few years older than us and kind of weird looking. He had an interesting choppy guitar style and could play my songs better than I could, almost before I'd finished struggling through the chord sequence myself to show him how it went. He worked in a music shop that also ran a complex of rehearsal rooms. He could get us free rehearsal time. He was in.

Now all we needed was a drummer. A shifty-looking guy who was always hanging around the rehearsal rooms kept saying he'd like to have a go and eventually we agreed to give him a try. We didn't realise he'd never played drums in his life before. The day of the audition he got some quick coaching from a real drummer who worked in the music shop and blagged his way through. The way he played sounded sort of backwards. He was in.

At the tail end of 1976, after we'd rehearsed together a few times, I phoned up Andy Czezowski who I'd heard was intending to open a club called The Roxy to put on gigs by some of these new punk bands. I asked him if we could get a gig there and he asked me what the band was called. I said, 'The Adverts' and he said yes. He didn't ask to hear us or anything.

The real drummer at the music shop got the job playing drums for another new band, Generation X, and talked them into letting us support them at the Roxy a couple of days before the gig I'd already booked. One month's rehearsal, two gigs. The NME came to the second of them and wrote: 'Frankly they were chronic, a parody of inept tuneless buzzsaw guitar and powerhouse *Sturm Und Drang* drumming. There wasn't a hook line or riff in earsight as the singer raged and ranted unhearable lyrics and snarled half-heartedly.'

Our first review!

But the audiences liked us and the other bands liked us, and Stiff records came down to see us and said they wanted us to record a single. We had a whole day in the studio. It seemed ridiculous; I'd made my record in Torquay in an hour. Pretty soon, an awful lot of people liked us, although there was a lingering resentment from the old musos in the press that we couldn't play. We got ourselves a proper manager, a mid-thirties rebel called Michael Dempsey who was working in the publishing business but came down to the Roxy for the thrill in the air and the talent and the creativity. He signed us to a major label, who booked us into a studio in Worthing for the weekend where we recorded a single called 'Gary Gilmore's Eyes' which went into the charts and the next thing we knew we were on Top Of The Pops.

I never saw it coming and I didn't expect what happened next.

The day for our first ever television appearance came and before heading down to the BBC we dutifully turned up to the fake recording session in an expensive central London studio where union rules demanded the re-creation of the song in an hour and tapes were switched while backs were turned. We'd been told that the programme wouldn't countenance anyone playing live so the band would have to mime, but I was determined to sing so we gave the programme a version of the original recording with the vocals removed.

Late afternoon and a small crowd of teenagers pushes past us at the entrance to the television studios, where we are being forced to sign up to the Musicians Union, otherwise we won't be allowed on the show. The stages are ticky-tacky black painted plywood boxes, and cameramen shove the starry-eyed schoolkids dressed in their best disco clothes out of the way as they surge forward for the next shot. The backing tape for 'Gary Gilmore's Eyes' rolls and the cameras swing towards us, but the track is so quiet that none of us realise it has started and we stand there looking lost. The floor manager groans and orders the cameras back into their starting positions.

Take Two. The track is a little louder, but still only just audible over the heavily padded drumkit which Laurie pounds desperately out of time, straining to hear what he's supposed to be copying. As the first verse starts I round menacingly on the microphone to find that I have been given an aluminium replica. I splutter to a halt. The floor manager lowers his clipboard in disgust and glares at me.

'SING! JUST BLOODY SING!!'

'I was singing...it's not a real microphone...there's no point in singing...I'm...it's...' Sir.

Across the studio, Tony Blackburn covers his face in his hands.

The next one was worse. In our first year together, apart from the Roxy gigs, the band had done a gruelling 30 date transit van tour round Britain supporting The Damned, and a slew of gigs on our own, some of them as far away as Newcastle. But the day our second appearance on Top Of The Pops was due to be recorded we were also supposed to start our first headlining tour overseas—a week in Ireland. The first gig in Coleraine University was already sold out. What to do? After our unhappy experience on the programme last time, we were all for ignoring the offer to go on television and carry on with the tour as planned.

The record company came up with the solution. The chart position-boosting potential of an appearance on Top Of The Pops was not to be missed on any account, so they would charter a flight to Ireland for us. The recording was due to finish late afternoon; obviously we'd miss soundcheck but in theory we could make it to Coleraine just in time for the start of the gig.

This time I've learned my lesson and I mime too. We have a dress-rehearsal for the cameras and lights, and by the time we have run through the song a couple of times a clutch of programme staff have gathered by the side of the stage, where they are in deep discussion and glancing in my direction. Word has come through that the decapitated Action Man doll that hangs from my wrist by a chain could be considered an offensive weapon and is not suitable for a family programme. They whisk it off to the wardrobe department and the band whisks off to the bar. Some drinks later and manager Michael is having an animated discussion with the director about the Action Man, which still hasn't been returned to me.

'It's not violence...it's *Duchamp...!*'

Two hours in the bar and we're due back in the studio for the recording, which is supposed to be done in one take without interruptions. Someone from Wardrobe rushes in with the Action Man. They have taped some black plastic around the chain.

The programme begins but Gaye has gone missing somewhere in the maze of corridors in BBC Television Centre. As the intro to our song 'No Time To Be 21' starts up she runs in, breathless, and leaps onto the stage in the wrong place. Someone slings the bass guitar round her neck. In the last six months Gaye has become the face of the band and the 'sex symbol of punk' so we all expect the cameramen to focus mainly on her, but they are confused that she is not standing on the position marked for her and she barely makes it into any of the shots.

The recording ends at six as anticipated and outside is a sleek black limo, which whisks us off to Heathrow. A two engine plane waits for us on the runway, absurdly tiny against the other giants, and we cram into it; band, manager, a recently-hired thuggish 'minder' who used to work with the Sex Pistols, veteran rock photographer Ray Stevenson and 'Sounds' journalist Jane Suck taking up all the seats available. We take off, shuddering and dipping in the February gale.

Ninety minutes later a fierce headwind is still blowing and the trip has taken twice as long as planned. We hang under the stars somewhere over the Irish Sea, ice building dangerously on the wing, and the pilot glances nervously at the fuel gauge.

'We're just about to run out,' he says grimly, then flicks over to the spare tank with a grin. Gotcha punks! But half an hour later he has a map of Ireland spread over his lap and is muttering, 'The airport's got to be around here somewhere.' This time he means it. The plane buffets and bucks. Laurie, our drummer, complains of feeling ill. His face has literally gone green.

With the needle of the spare tank hovering on empty we bump down the runway at Belfast airport and are swiftly hurried through the small customs hut to where a minibus waits. We were due on stage more than an hour ago and still have a sixty mile drive to Coleraine. We know we're not going to make it, but somehow we are urging the van forward down the soaked black roads as if the effort will turn back time.

Bowling out into the venue we find an empty hall, a few roadies starting to dismantle the gear. The floor is littered with glasses and broken bottles. We can't believe it; all this effort and we missed our own gig. What about all those people who came to see the band? What will they think of us?

One of the roadies shakes his head sadly. 'They were pretty annoyed,' he says. 'Someone threw a dead rat onto the stage.'

The next day was Belfast, but the Top Of The Pops effect wasn't over yet. It was being screened that evening and the organisers of the gig were more excited than we were, setting up a TV in the dressing room, where after soundcheck we ritually watched the show surrounded by people from the venue, roadies and local fanzine writers, all of us griping about how ridiculous it all was and laying into the free beer. Somewhat the worse for wear, we retired to our nearby hotel, garrisoned inside barbed wire-topped fifteen foot high security fences. We continued drinking in the cosy hotel bar while locals told us about The Troubles and treated us like tourists who had no idea what it was like. They were right.

Back at the venue, local punk heroes Stiff Little Fingers are finishing off their support set to a packed crowd. A large haul of knives and guns have been confiscated from members of the audience by the doormen on the way in. Quite normal in Belfast, we're assured. We hit the stage to a barrage of spit, which continues to fly up for the first few numbers until Gaye throws down her bass and storms off. The rest of us shrug our shoulders and wander off too. A few minutes of restless booing from the audience follows until Michael takes the stage and, arms aloft, speaks into the microphone:

'Just stop spitting and you can have them back. They want to play for you, but please STOP SPITTING!!'

A hail of gob falls upon him like a soggy blanket.

Leaving the venue in the minibus we take a wrong turning or two and find ourselves crawling completely lost through dangerously dark and deserted areas of Belfast where high walls divide brick-strewn streets down the middle and soldiers with rifles regard us suspiciously from army checkpoints.

We drive down to Dublin the next day, stopping briefly for a quick exploitative photo session in front of the gates of Stormont for the cover of 'Sounds.' The rest of the drive is uneventful, although we spot a succession of unmarked cars parked in gateways at strategic points on the road to the border, tracking our progress. Michael nods in approval when he sees them, but refuses to say who they are, 'You don't need to know.'

The first pub over the border and we pile out to try the real Guinness. Laurie complains frequently of a terrible headache and we all ignore him. Shouldn't drink so much.

In Dublin we pull off a storming gig at Trinity College, and crowds of people flock into the dressing room afterwards to congratulate us. There are no security personnel and the fans walk in and out as they please. Unfortunately one of them walks out with Gaye's treasured leather jacket which she's worn at every gig since the inception of the band. As she erupts with rage, Laurie leans over the waste paper bin next to him and throws up. His skin is a sickly yellow and he is covered with a slick sheen of sweat.

'Get me to a hospital.'

The next morning we leave Laurie, diagnosed with chronic hepatitis, in a hospital run by nuns, cancel the rest of the tour and head for the airport, stopping briefly at a television studio to mime to 'No Time To Be 21' one more time, with the drum seat being filled at the last minute by one of our P.A. crew, who looks like a hippie.

A week later, 'No Time To Be 21' crashes decisively out of the charts, despite the Top Of The Pops appearance. At the end of the year we find the cost of the limo and the charter flight have been added to our debt to the record company.

Many years later I was in a West London pub one evening and got talking to an Irish guy who went to Coleraine that night. He was pretty disappointed about us not turning up at the time, he said, but that was nothing compared to his best friend, a huge Adverts fan who'd been looking forward to it for ages. As soon as the concert was announced he'd bought a ticket and for weeks could talk about nothing else. A couple of days before the gig he noticed a dead rat on the road and took it home, keeping it in a bag in his fridge ready to throw at us while we were on stage. He was sure we'd appreciate it, it was so 'punk.' The evening of the gig came and he successfully smuggled the rat into the venue, tucked inside his jacket, and awaited his moment...

In the end, when we didn't show up he threw it anyway. Shame to waste a dead rat.

Top Of The Pops. Having a record in the charts. Being a pop star. I didn't see it coming and it wasn't what I expected when it happened. The rest of the band agreed and we split up. I carried on writing songs and playing gigs, first in other bands, then solo, forgot about ever getting on Top of The Pops again, and got on with being a working musician.

But it still wasn't what I expected. In the early '90s I reinvented myself as an acoustic singer/songwriter and ended up playing gigs wherever I could find them, often in circumstances bordering on the absurd. I would take my guitar case and as many CDs and changes of underwear as I could cram into a large travel bag, then battle my way through train and bus timetables to get to my concerts, often as not sleeping on some fan's floor, struggling to stay vegetarian, healthy and sane in a world where junk food and junk culture rules.

I needed to be enterprising. I would take whatever opportunities presented themselves, and when you say "yes" to everything, unusual things happen: one day you are invited to play a concert to a class of primary school children in the Pennines, the next you are in a forest on a hillside in the Czech Republic in a thunderstorm playing to three thousand East European punk rockers. One day you are playing in a chalet on the snowy Italian Alps supporting the most famous band in Germany, the next you are in a three day midsummer festival in Lapland where the sun never sets and the audience never sleeps.

A few years ago I started to keep a diary of what it was like to be on tour without the cocoon of fame. Through daily entries, the diaries reveal the mechanics of life for the independent musician, and show how the reward for the indignities and discomfort of the lifestyle come not in financial terms, but in something far more valuable: a chance for self-expression, of course, but also a privileged glimpse into the lives of other people. Perhaps most importantly, through the challenge of making one's way through the world without a map...an understanding of how the world really works.

TV Smith

1. THE PUNK, THE CRUSTY, THE RANTING POET AND HIS MOTHER

9th September

Danny would hate to be described as the Crusty from Hull, but he's worked for a vegan food shop delivering on a converted milk float, been part of an alternative housing co-op, lived in a tree to protest against the new Manchester airport runway, isn't too bothered about changing his clothes on a regular basis, wears a nose ring, and lives in Hull. Face it, Danny. He's also a very nice guy and has agreed to drive me and ranting poet Attila the Stockbroker around Germany on a two week tour. Oh, and Attila's 74 year old mother, who is coming too.

It's going to be interesting couple of weeks. A few years ago Attila was the first to suggest I try playing solo gigs, after watching me struggle with a succession of bands since the break up of the Adverts in the late seventies. Since then I've been playing the odd gig here and there, slowly building an audience, and I've never looked back. But this is the first time I've done a tour of this length on a low budget and I'm a bit apprehensive about what I'm getting into.

Danny and I head out of London early morning, as the rush hour traffic is coming in. We're in Attila's Citroen, which Danny picked up from outside Attila's place near Brighton yesterday after hitchhiking down from Hull. Attila and his mum have been spending a couple of days in Brussels, and we're going to meet up with them tomorrow; meantime I have a gig on my own in Düsseldorf tonight.

Down to the South Coast, onto the ferry, through France, Belgium, Holland and into Germany. We pull up to the venue at about four in the afternoon, ahead of schedule. It's a tiny bar with no stage, just a small area in a back corner where I'm supposed to play. The guy who booked the gig explains that there are no small venues in Düsseldorf any more, and this was the only place he could find. I ask him where I'll be sleeping tonight, and he tells me that there's a mattress at his place, which Danny and I can share. This is not a promising start.

Soundcheck done, we go and get something to eat in a nearby pizza place. Danny is usually vegan, but he orders a pizza too as there's nothing else available. We're joined by some people from JKP, the label who have just released my album in Germany, and when I have a moan about the sleeping arrangements tonight it turns out that Sven, product manager for the label, has two mattresses in a spare room and could put Danny and me up. By the time we head back to the club I'm in a more positive mood.

I had intended to take it easy on this first night, with so many dates still to go, but I belt it out at full power for about one hour fifty, and it goes down well. The tiny room is packed and everyone has a great time. Afterwards I have a chat with Klaus, who runs my website. He's travelled over from Aachen for tonight, one of the few chances he's had to see me play. He tells me he has bought a train pass and is intending to come to every gig on the tour.

It's past two in the morning when Danny and I follow Sven's car back to his place, make quick stop at the bar opposite—always a novelty for an Englishman, finding somewhere to get a drink open at this time of night—and end up dragging all our gear and sleeping bags up three flights of stairs to his flat an hour or so later.

10th September

Sven's out to work first thing, leaving me and Danny alone in his flat. Considering we don't know whereabouts in Düsseldorf we are and don't have a map, we find the road out pretty quickly, and are soon heading east, on the way to tonight's gig in Gottingen. We arrive early, and sit in the car with some high-volume reggae from Danny's cassette collection pumping out until someone turns up.

The venue looks terrible, a youth centre in a dilapidated house covered with graffiti, tattered anarchist banners hanging from the walls. We're warned to keep all doors locked behind us when we load the gear in as anything unattended will be stolen. I go up to the top floor cafe to talk with the organisers and find there's a problem: the guy who was supposed to engineer the sound has gone to a football match and won't be back for a couple of hours. If at all.

An hour later Attila and his mother Muriel arrive. Muriel is a charming lady who is taking the opportunity to see Germany away from the tourist trail, and watch her son perform. She'll be with us for the first week of the tour and is prepared to put up with the rigours of life on the road as long as she can get a bed every night, regular meals (hiatus hernia), and the front seat of the car (bad back).

Attila also had a very good gig last night, but the trip to Gottingen was delayed when the friend he was staying with inadvertently ran over his own cat as they set off.

Despite the lack of sound man, Attila plugs in his gear and gets started but it's soon obvious that a lot of the club's equipment doesn't work. While he attempts to sort himself out on the stage and various people from the club gaze in confusion at the mixing desk, I unpack my bag and find that the sequencer I use to play backing tracks to some of my songs onstage is missing.

Klaus arrives from the train and sees me pacing around looking worried. When I explain why he offers to go and phone Sven to see if the sequencer is still at his place. I don't have his home phone number though, and it's too late to reach him at the office. Klaus says he'll try to find the number through directory enquiries, and leaves me to do a soundcheck.

Attila has just left the stage and gives me a 'what-can-you-do?' look. His mandola, violin, and my guitar are all going to have to be plugged into the same input in the mixing desk, despite the fact that the sound for each needs to be set up differently. It's now clear that the sound engineer is not going to turn up, and no-one else has a clue. Plans Attila and I had to play a few songs together have to be abandoned as we can't plug in more than one instrument at a time. On the positive side, it's a good day to lose my sequencer—I wouldn't have been able to use it anyway.

When you hit the stage you have to put these problems out of your mind. I'm first on, and my set goes reasonably well in front of an audience who know nothing about me. By the time I've finished I reckon I've made a good impression.

Now and then while Attila's performing I go traipsing back and forth up the stairs to the office to try and get through to Sven on the phone. Klaus managed to find a number for him, but his answering machine is on, so I leave increasingly-distressed messages on it. If he hasn't got the sequencer, it must have been stolen—I'd like to know one way or the other.

I'm also a bit concerned about where we're going to stay tonight. Muriel is already settled into the flat of a friend of Attila's and he'll be joining her there later. Danny and I are supposed to be staying with someone else, but at the moment it's unclear who or where. It's now well past midnight and as everyone gets more beer inside them it's getting harder to pin anyone down to exact arrangements. Klaus is also looking for somewhere to stay.

As the club closes up and everyone goes home, we find out that the guy who was going to put us up has just split up with his girlfriend and stormed off somewhere, so it's left to her to reluctantly find space for the three of us in her small flat, while she'll go off to stay with someone else. We trail along behind her through the streets of Gottingen, carrying our sleeping bags and luggage. There's one room with a couch and a mattress on the floor, and a small side room with another mattress, which I grab. The girl stays and chats distractedly for a few minutes, then leaves, saying she's going to bring Attila's group over to us for breakfast in the morning.

11th September

As soon as I wake up I'm on the phone to Sven at the office. Good news, he's got the sequencer. It turns out that he was at home last night, so I must have left all those messages on someone else's answering machine.

We make plans to get the sequencer sent on to Robert, a friend of Attila in Berlin, where we can pick it up in two days time when we play there. We'll also be driving past today on the way to Cottbus, to drop off Muriel so she can get another night's rest and spend tomorrow sightseeing.

We load into the car and find that travelling is going to be rather a different prospect from now on. With guitar, mandola, violin, merchandising, four people and all their luggage, there is barely a square inch to spare. Attila and I squeeze into the back with bags on our laps and under our feet. Pretty soon we're stuck in traffic, and crawling past the derelict guard houses and border posts that marked the line between East and West Germany before the wall fell. As we edge our way along, Attila points out all the sights to his mum like a ranting punk tour guide.

We pull into a rest area to get something to eat. Danny and myself—vegan and vegetarian, respectively—give up after one glance at the menu and sit with a coffee. Attila orders half a roast chicken, and even he seems shocked when he is served with an entire one. The waitress explains that they were only small. Attila shrugs and tucks in.

'I could eat chicken till it comes out of my arse,' he says to me, 'which, of course, it eventually does.'

Bon appetit.

Hours later we're in the outskirts of Berlin, squabbling about how to find Robert's flat. We know we're in more or less the right area, but the map isn't detailed enough to show exactly where. A phone call to Robert gets us closer, then we see him hopping around on the pavement, waving us into a sidestreet. We rest for an hour at his place, settle Muriel in, then hit the road for Cottbus as night falls.

Stress and lack of food and sleep has taken its toll on my voice, so I'm glugging back water during the journey to try and keep my throat hydrated. There's a general air of gloom in the car as the rain starts to fall and we watch the giant featureless blocks of flats on the outskirts of Cottbus slip by. Troubled recently by racial tension and the burning of immigrant hostels, this is hardly a promising area for us, but Attila assures me that the venue is a haven of culture and liberalism. If only we could find it.

After driving up and down identical looking ugly streets without success, we pull up outside a railway station and get a cab to lead us to the venue. We're late, and get straight into soundcheck. It quickly becomes apparent that my voice has all but gone. It's very disturbing—only the third date in and already I'm in trouble. Attila and I try out a few numbers together, then I go back to the dressing room and worry.

We order in some pizza, the only thing on offer, but it's too near the gig for me to eat, so I leave it for later. Danny looks at the mountains of cheese on his with despair, then picks reluctantly at it. Attila lays into his and roars, 'This is the worst pizza I HAVE EVER EATEN!'

Klaus arrives. He's walked over from the station, and couldn't help noticing gangs of skinheads out on the streets chanting *'Deutschland für die Deutschen!'*

Showtime. I can't let myself be beaten by this voice problem, so I belt it out at full volume, and it sounds better than I dared hope. So a few high notes don't make it—so what.

After the gig I meet a fan who has been writing to me recently. I've promised her a copy of one of my albums which she hasn't been able to find in the record shops. I have just one copy left and decide to make it a present.

'Diese ist ein Gift für dich,' I say with a smile. She steps back, horrified. I have just said, 'This is poison for you.' Must work on the German.

Tonight is one of only two nights on the entire tour that we have a hotel, and it couldn't be more welcome. We have two rooms booked. Attila takes the single as he has a cold coming on; Danny, Klaus and I take the other, which mercifully has three beds. Sleep, beautiful sleep.

12th September

I'm first down to breakfast. The manager and his wife chat to me for a while, curious to find an English person who can speak some German. We look out at the rain sheeting down outside. 'Just like London,' they say.

Klaus sloshes off to the station while Danny, Attila and I load up the car and hit the road for Berlin.

Some hours later when we pull up outside Robert's flat, it's still tipping down. Inside, I'm delighted to find that the package containing my sequencer has arrived. We have a coffee then get back in the car and follow Robert to the venue. On the way we pass the site of a nasty crash that has happened in the last couple of minutes; a car and a small van sit dented and smashed in the middle of the road, and sirens are approaching from the distance. The van was carrying some cans of white paint which have been crushed in the impact and are now splattered all over the inside of the windows, somehow even more horrific than blood.

The venue is a large bar with tables and chairs around the stage and standing room further back. We have a good soundcheck and everything feels promising for tonight. Muriel is enjoying herself, but worried about the volume so I give her my emergency earplugs. Lots of people I haven't seen for years turn up. One fan arrives with a cake she has baked for me.

Next door is a semi-legal squat, where Danny and I will be sleeping. We all go over there after soundcheck as the organisers have cooked us a meal. Vegan!

Tonight Attila is going to go on first, and by the time he hits the stage the room is crammed. He does a blistering set, and I join him towards the end for a few numbers. After a short break, it's my turn. Everything sounds great, I get to do a few numbers with the sequencer again and my voice turns out to be in top form. By the time Attila gets back on stage at the end to play violin with me I'm soaked through with sweat and enjoying what has been one of the best gigs of my life.

We're both drained. Robert takes Attila and Muriel back to his flat, and after a couple of beers, Danny and I carry our sleeping bags next door. Klaus doesn't have anywhere to stay so he comes with us again. We're on the third floor of a big old apartment block, in a room next to the club office. There's no heating working, but throughout the flat are some giant archaic-looking stoves, unlit, which Danny regards with some interest—he's very proud of his wood-burning stove at home in Hull and even builds his own out of discarded gas canisters.

Around three a.m. we're just getting off to sleep when people come into the office, switch on the lights and talk loudly for a long time.

At five a.m. an alarm clock goes off in Klaus's bag. He doesn't stir. I roll over and try to ignore it. Maybe I shouldn't have given Muriel the earplugs.

13th September

I'm first up. There's total silence in the house, except for the gentle snoring of Danny and Klaus. First thing I want to do after spending most of last night dripping with sweat is find a shower. There's no hot water, but I get under it anyway. Now I'm awake.

After a while Danny and Klaus stir, then two of the organisers for the venue turn up.

'Well,' says one of them brightly, 'I expect you'd like a shower so I'll get the boiler going.'

Danny has his first shower of the tour just to piss me off. He changes his T-shirt, and for the rest of the day I pretend not to recognise him.

Back to the club for breakfast with Muriel and Attila, then we follow the promoter's car to the outskirts of Berlin, where she drops Klaus off at the station, and the rest of us make our way onward to tonight's gig in Hanover. Attila's cold is coming on apace and his sneezes threaten to lift the roof off the car.

The club in Hanover is larger than we're used to. It's the opening night after a lengthy make-over and no one's sure how many people will turn up. Still, there's a full-on P.A. and lighting rig, and a stage large enough to accommodate a twenty-piece rock band.

After soundcheck we retire to the dressing room where we are served a meal. Danny once again has no option but to partake of the cheese-based veggie lasagne. The first thing he told me when he arrived at my place before the tour was that he'd just read that E.U. regulations now allow a maximum of 15% pus in milk products; now he's having to eat the stuff. Still it does lead to some interesting German conversations. A quick look through the German dictionary tells us that the word for pus is 'eiter.' The pus comes from mastitis in the udders—'euter.' *Milch ist funfzehn prozent Eiter. Wir sind die Euter Eiter Leute.* ("Milk is fifteen percent pus. We are the udder-pus people!")

Multi-lingual Attila knows the word for nipple in about ten languages, including Welsh, and this leads to a lengthy discussion about the linguistic difference between 'udder' and 'nipple,' *euter* and *brustwarzen*—literally, breast-warts.

And so, the gig. We do our best. It's not such a small turn-out as I feared, but the people who are here seem marooned in acres of floor space. The funny thing is, talking to some of them afterwards I get some of the most positive reactions of the tour so far.

Once again we're all staying at friends of Attila's. There's no room for Klaus, so he's going to stay with one of the promoters and meet us in the morning. As Attila's ill and we're all tired, we pack up and leave fairly rapidly, but not before having some foolish photos taken for the club guest book. They manage to take one of my *brustwarzen* as I'm changing.

14th September

Danny's neck is bigger than it used to be. We're eating breakfast at the flat, taking it in turns to go into the tiny kitchen, when Danny comes in, his head looking kind of *lopsided.* It's a bit worrying, but he says he feels fine, and fit to drive to tonight's gig in Hamburg. We're wondering if maybe we should try and find a hospital and have him checked over, but it's not really possible if we're going to make it in time for the gig.

We reach Hamburg by late afternoon and head straight for the St. Pauli club bar—well, as straight as you can go, after getting lost in the one-way system amongst much general bickering about directions in the car. The place is closed. It seems that there's an away match being played today—it's been switched at the last minute to fit in with television scheduling, much to Attila's disgust. He'd been hoping all his mates from the supporters club would turn up tonight, so it's a bit disappointing. It also looks like we have nowhere to stay tonight— one of them was going to put us up.

We get lost trying to find the Knust and end up having to follow a cab again. Miraculously we find a parking space right outside the venue, though, so it's an easy load-in. Klaus turns up and looks curiously at Danny's neck.

It's an excellent concert with plenty of people. It's good playing a small, packed club after last night's warehouse, but by the end exhaustion is starting to kick in. Mercifully the girlfriend of Attila's football-supporting friend turns up and says it's still okay for us to stay at the flat. We leave Klaus to wander the streets of the Reeperbahn and head back there to find an uncomfortable bunk for Muriel and two wooden-floored rooms for the rest of us. Attila takes the room with a half-inch thick sleeping mat on the floor, Danny takes the couch, and I take the other room which actually has a bed in it.

I'm just getting off to sleep when there's a frantic scrabbling outside the room. The door flies open and a large dog bounds in and sits on me. I try and encourage it off, but it's staying put. The girl who owns the flat appears in the doorway and hisses the dog's name a few times but it's not moving. Eventually she pads in and drags it away, whimpering. Something tells me I've got the dog's room.

I get up and wedge the only heavy thing I can find—a metal frog ornament—against the door, and try and get back to sleep. Moments later I hear the scraping of the frog over the floor and the door opens an inch. In the light from the hallway I see a cat's paw batting away at the obstruction until there's enough of a gap to squeeze through. The cat wanders over, looks at me, throws up over my bag, then wanders nonchalantly out again.

15th September

At seven in the morning, I hear the phone ringing persistently in the next room. Finally Attila answers. Through the thin wall I can hear the conversation: our car is blocking the alley and the neighbours need to get to work, so Danny is roused to go and shift it. I pull my sleeping bag over my head and get another couple of hours.

When I wake up again I wash the cat sick off my bag and take a hot shower. Notice a few fleas crawling over my ankles—yep, definitely the dog's room—and studiously pick them off, then go into the kitchen and hunt around for some coffee. Muriel comes in—she woke up some time ago and has been quietly reading in her room—Attila and Danny follow shortly after. That neck is big. We take a photo.

We set off for Bremen with the intention of getting a doctor there if necessary. There are still no other symptoms, and Danny suspects that the problem might be an allergy to milk products. The swelling is probably pure *eiter*.

A miserable journey through the rain and spray gets us into Bremen by late afternoon. The club owners have set out food for us, including a few vegan things, which Danny stows away in his bag so he can avoid the ubiquitous cheese for a few days and hopefully get his neck back to normal.

Downstairs, the venue is still being built. It's opening night, and people are frantically hammering and sawing to get everything ready. The walls are still bare concrete, and the place is freezing cold. Atmosphere—nil. By the time we start the gig there are only about thirty people in, all looking chilly and perched uncomfortably on the benches lined up in front of the stage. But at least the people who are putting us up are there.

Attila and Muriel head off to one house after the gig, Danny, Klaus and I to another. Danny and I are to sleep upstairs in a tiny room with just enough space to fit in two mattresses side-by-side, Klaus is going to have to take his chances in a downstairs room, but might get turfed out in the night if the person who usually stays there comes home.

16th September

We drive over to where Attila and his mum have been staying, and have some breakfast together. The neck is looking better, keeping off the milk products seems to be working. We only have to get to Dortmund today, so there's time to do some sightseeing. We take the tram into the Old Town and wander round a bit. Underneath the old *Rathaus* there's a restaurant which featured in some of the set-pieces in a schools language programme I watched to try and learn German a few years back. I'm tempted to go in and try a few of the, *'Herr Ober, eine Tasse Kaffee, bitte'* routines, but after a glance at the prices decide not to bother.

Industrial Dortmund is considerably less attractive than Bremen, but we're hoping for a good gig: Attila has played in this venue before, and the first gig of the tour for me was only a few miles away, so we should get some audience. The room is a long narrow basement, with a rudimentary little P.A. that we have to set up ourselves. After soundcheck, Sven from JKP turns up. I'm having a meeting with the label tomorrow morning, so I'm going to stay at his place tonight. Klaus will be finally getting a night at home in Aachen. The others will be staying with the promoter, dropping Muriel off at the station in the morning as she's going back to England, and then picking me up from the JKP offices.

It's a good gig, packed with people, and we make up for lack of sophistication in the P.A. system by banging out the songs at extra high-energy.

Afterwards Muriel comes to say goodbye. It's clear she's had the time of her life and I tell her it's been a pleasure having her along. I get in Sven's car and we drive back through the night to his place. I'll be getting a room on my own tonight, so will have the chance to get a good sleep. But by the time we've had a chat and a couple of beers, it's 4:30 when I finally turn in.

17th September

The meeting at JKP is running late and I'm still waiting to go into it when Attila and Danny arrive. There's a problem with the car: a light on the dashboard which has been flickering on sporadically over the last few days is now staying lit the whole time. No-one knows what it means. We ask around the office if anyone knows anything about Citroens, and Sven goes to have a look. He reckons it's something to do with the brakes—bad news when you have a five hour drive ahead of you. While I'm in the meeting, Danny and Attila take the car to the nearest garage to get it looked at. It turns out the light means we're low on brake fluid so there must be a leak somewhere. We don't have the time or money to get a proper repair done, so we opt for filling up the brake fluid reservoir and keeping a regular check on it.

We power down the motorway, and end up driving into Nuremberg in the dark and rain, only a couple of hours late. We have a quick soundcheck, but there are problems with the P.A., which emits constant howls of feedback. Klaus still hasn't turned up. I reckon the strain of all this travelling's finally got to him and he's decided to stay at home.

The gig isn't bad; a small, appreciative audience, and there's the added bonus that we know we have a hotel tonight. We come off stage and get a beer, pleased that the stress of the day is finally over, and two minutes later Klaus walks in. The train he was on derailed and he had to hang around for hours at the site of the accident. Finally he got into Nuremberg, and raced over to the gig only to miss it.

We take pity on him and offer him a place in the hotel with us as we have two double rooms. We all squeeze into the car and follow the promoter. There's a gleaming white modern frontage to the hotel, but inside things are less promising. In a dingy dining room the elderly couple who seem to be the owners are sat slumped in front of a game show on the television and get up only reluctantly to hand us our keys. Danny and I share a room. It's dirty and damp-smelling, with black mould creeping up the walls. I kill a couple of cockroaches, the nearest us vegetarians get to blood sports, then collapse into sleep.

18th September

Down to the breakfast room where the owners are still in the same position as last night, open-mouthed in front of the TV, fags dangling from their lips. A couple of pots of coffee, some dry rolls and anaemic jam is served. The coffee tastes like burnt metal but we all need the caffeine and drink it anyway. After half an hour or so, Klaus pours out the last cup, and is just about to take a sip when a cockroach floats to the top. We call over the owner, and point at Klaus's cup. He looks from it to us, thinks about it, shrugs his shoulders and says finally, 'You want another pot?'

After Klaus leaves for the station, the rest of us take the U-Bahn into the centre of the Old Town. It's very atmospheric, with steep hills stepped with towering gothic buildings, and the narrow pedestrianised streets and squares filled with market stalls. After an uncomfortable moment in a CD shop, where the owner suspects Danny of trying to steal stuff—they've never seen anyone like Danny in posh Nuremberg — we take the U-Bahn back to the car and head off to the next gig.

The venue is in a village some miles out of Munich, and we cut across the back roads through the forests and hop fields to avoid a traffic jam on the autobahn. Attila and I have both played the club before and are looking forward to it, but we're all tense, tired and edgy. Even Danny's getting homesick, he's never been away from Hull for so long before.

When we arrive, my friends in a local band called Garden Gang are onstage soundchecking. Talking to the people running the club, it seems that the long-term prospects for it are looking grim. It's been an important part of the local community for many years, but the brewery has been putting prices up so much that it's becoming impossible to make the place show a profit. It's got to the point where it would actually be cheaper to buy in the beer from a supermarket.

So there's rather an air of despondency, increasingly so when very few people arrive for the gig. Anyway, we go for it and it's not bad, but throughout the evening the attention of the small crowd seems to come and go in waves; one minute they're listening, the next they're chatting amongst themselves. All in all, a disappointment.

Danny and Attila stay upstairs at the venue, I go back to the flat of PamP, who sings in Garden Gang, and his girlfriend Andi. They cook some food, and we relax with a local *Weizen* beer, so good for helping you sleep, as if I needed any.

19th September

Just two gigs left now, and I'm really feeling an urge to get it over with. But I'm still sad to leave Bavaria as PamP drives me back through the countryside to the venue—I've stayed with him and played in the area occasionally over the last few years and feel at home here.

Klaus has already left for the train; today's long haul up to Frankfurt is going to take most of the day. We load the car, top up the brake fluid and head off too. Boring hours on the autobahn. Mid-afternoon we're stuck in a mammoth traffic jam, so we swing off into a rest area and sit it out with a coffee and pastry. We've just pulled back onto the road when I realise I've left my jacket hanging over my chair in the restaurant, so we pull over and I jog up the hard shoulder to retrieve it. That's my exercise for the year.

By late afternoon we're drawing near Frankfurt, still in plenty of time for the gig, which doesn't open until 11:00 p.m. Attila slips one of his 1977 punk compilation tapes into the cassette player, and a few songs in I recognise the opening bars to my first single, 'One Chord Wonders.' Suddenly the music is drowned by a thunderous rumble, and the car starts to vibrate and slew to one side. Danny's fists are white on the wheel as he drags us across two lanes, coming to rest on the hard shoulder. We sit there speechless for a moment, the closing bars of the song the only sound in the car, until I quietly ask Danny to switch off the tape. We climb out to see that the front tyre has blown and is now a mess of shredded rubber and steel wire.

It takes us a few minutes to calm down and figure out what to do. As cars rocket past us, we unload our gear onto the verge and get out the spare tyre and jack, but the Citroen hydraulics that have given us such a smooth ride up until now mean the car sits so low we can't get the jack under it. Attila only bought the car recently to learn to drive in and doesn't know much about it, but luckily he did have the foresight to join a European breakdown scheme—now all we have to do is find a phone.

Leaving Danny with the car, Attila and I walk up the hard shoulder, then hop over the fence and scramble down the steep bank to a small road below. In the gathering dusk we can make out the lights of houses in the distance. A ten minute walk finds us at a tram stop and a bar with a phone. It's only when we get through to the rescue service in Britain that we realise we don't know exactly where we are, which makes it tricky explaining where to come and find us. The rescue service says they'll get on to their German counterparts and should have someone in our area within an hour. Attila and I steady our nerves with a beer.

Clambering back up the bank an hour later, we can see there's no rescue vehicle at the car. Night is falling now, and we're beginning to worry about getting to the gig. After some discussion, Attila heads off back to the bar to call the venue, while I wait it out with Danny. Wrapped up against the cold, we go halfway down some steps leading down the bank to try and get some shelter from the continual noise and buffeting of the traffic.

Another hour passes with no sign of a breakdown vehicle or Attila. I notice that the steps lead down to some tramlines and decide to follow them in the hope it'll be a short cut back to where we made the phone call. Sure enough, it takes only a couple of minutes to get to the pub, where I find Attila sitting on a bar stool by the phone, with another beer and several empty glasses. He's made some calls—the rescue service says a breakdown truck has been out looking but can't find us. The venue aren't particularly keen to sort out our problems, they just say keep them informed. I head back up the tramlines to bring this news to Danny.

Surprise—Danny's loading all the gear back into the boot, and the tyre's on.

'Some Yank from an army base pulled up, said, "Looks like you could do with a hand," got out some super-jack from his car, changed the tyre and drove off.'

In pitch darkness I pick my way down the bank and along the tramlines to fetch Attila.

We're just about to get in the car and set off, when Attila grabs the wheel with the wrecked tyre on it. 'We don't need this any more,' he says, and slings it down the bank, where it bounces off into the darkness. Unfortunately we will still need the wheel rim to put the new tyre onto. With the aid of a torch we finally find it resting against the bottom fence amongst shoulder high weeds. For the rest of the journey it sits next to me in the back seat, dried flower-heads and grasses caught up in the exploded steel threads.

We get lost trying to find our way into Frankfurt, and the brake light starts flashing intermittently until it stays on all the time. We're low on fuel, but there are no garages open as it's now past ten at night. The car's running on vapour by the time we finally reach the venue at 11:30.

Tired, hungry, hands covered with dirt and grease, we carry our gear past the queue of people into the venue, which is a warren of dimly-lit damp-smelling basements. There's no hot water to wash the grease off with.

A rapid soundcheck as people wander into the room. Pizza is ordered but I'm too stressed to eat, and make do with a beer instead. I'm approached by a group of Finnish fans who say they want to organise a tour for me in Finland. This is turning out to be a very odd day.

Attila's set goes well. He has a high percentage of left-wing skinhead fans in the crowd and they're roaring their approval at every joke and political reference. To my relief, they warm to me too, despite the fact I blank on the first song and have to abandon it. By two in the morning when we wind it up, it feels like we've had a good gig.

Now we have to find out where we're spending the night. There's a sleeping room above an anarcho-squat venue somewhere in town that tonight's promoters say we can use, but everyone here is drunk and we can't galvanise them into taking us to it, despite the fact we're dead on our feet. Finally two of the organisers walk with us to a cab rank where we get two taxis to take us to the other venue, which is shut up and in darkness. We're shown into a room almost entirely taken up by six mattresses, with the same again on a wooden platform above. Before they leave, our hosts mention that breakfast has been laid out ready for tomorrow in a kitchen downstairs. They're barely out of the door before we're in there, wolfing down everything we can lay our hands on.

Staking our places in the sleeping area, Danny starts to eye up the wood-burning stove on the floor in the corner. It's reminding him of home. He leaves the room for a moment and comes back with some wood from outside, then starts chopping it down to kindling with a large knife. As he feeds it into the stove he has a hypnotised, happy look in his eyes.

20th September

I'm the first to wake up. Doesn't seem to be anyone else in the whole building. There's also no bath or shower, no hot water. Oh well, only one day to go. I wander downstairs to the kitchen, boil some water in the kettle for a wash, and try and figure out how to make the coffee machine work. It's a large kitchen, presumably usually used to cook for the venue as everything's catering pack size, but the place is filthy. Klaus comes down and wanders around, brushing his teeth. Attila is next. He looks around for a pan smaller than a bucket and can't find one, so puts a couple of eggs in the electric kettle to boil. Quite successful. Danny arrives and we sit around the table picking over the leftovers from last night and figuring what we're going to do.

First we need to get back to the car, still parked outside the venue. The next priority is to find a garage as we have no spare tyre at the moment, and we're not confident about the condition of the one we had to put on. Klaus will have to catch a train again, as the place he could have had in the car is taken up by the exploded wheel.

In the cab back to the car, we realise that it's Sunday so we're not going to find a garage open. We fill up with petrol and take it easy out of town and back onto the autobahn for Mühlheim, trying not to take our speed above sixty. As all the other cars and lorries hurtle past, you feel like the slowest thing on earth.

It would be nice if today, just for our last day, everything was to go smoothly, but of course it doesn't. We get so hopelessly lost in the tangle of roads around Mühlheim that we have to phone up the venue, explain where we are and get them to send a car out to find us. The club is a youth centre in an old cow shed, with concrete feeding troughs still set into the walls. At the moment it looks more like a building site, tools and stepladders strewn around inside, dangerously deep trenches in the ground outside loosely covered over with sheets of hardboard. The P.A. is malfunctioning, and as we soundcheck people are taking apart the stage boxes to try and get them working. As soon as one gets repaired, another one cuts out. Once again I won't be able to use the sequencer tonight, but if we juggle carefully with the inputs, Attila and I might be able to play a few numbers together.

It's not the big end-of-tour gig we might have hoped for—hardly anyone turns up, for a start. We do our best and it goes alright, but there's a definite sense of anti-climax.

Outside, there's a light rain falling. The guy taking us to sleep at his place squeezes into the back seat next to me and the exploded tyre. Klaus has no place to stay, but it's impossible to fit him in the car, so he's given directions to get to the other side of the pedestrianised shopping area. We'll drive around and meet him there.

Klaus doesn't arrive. We wait for a while, then go on to the flat, and while we settle in our host sets off on his bicycle to look for him. Half an hour later he arrives back with Klaus, who had got lost, given up and settled down to sleep in a bush. He says it was quite a comfortable bush.

21st September

Time to go home. Before we leave, we drive around Mühlheim looking for a place to put on a new tyre. When we find a garage, the mechanic reaches in through the driver's window, pulls a lever and, lo and behold, the car rises up on its suspension. If we'd known about that we could have changed the tyre ourselves.

Out of Germany, across Holland, Belgium, France; we're getting near the Channel Tunnel by mid-afternoon and on the lookout for a shop where real ale fan Attila can buy some Belgian beer to take back to Britain. We're so near home, but somehow end up wandering around a French supermarket, feeling very much out of place among the day trippers and duty free shoppers.

By the time we make it to the Eurostar terminal, the day is slipping away. We get waved to one side by the French customs who proceed to pick through the contents of the car, and interrogate Danny, who they obviously see as a potential Mr. Big of the drug world. They finally let us pass just in time to miss our train, so we have to queue up for the next, which gets cancelled.

We hit London for the start of the evening rush hour, and all sit fuming and bad-tempered as the traffic crawls along. Finally back at my place in West London, Danny and Attila decide to wait for the traffic to die down before setting off for the South coast. The first of the Belgian beers is opened.

And that's it, my first two week tour since I was in The Adverts twenty years ago. Touring was one of the things that finished off the band back then, and on this tour too there were times when Danny, Attila and I got annoyed with each other, found ourselves getting on each others nerves, were downright murderously pissed off with each other. Stick three people in a car together for two weeks, deprive them of sleep and food, don't let them get away by themselves even for a moment, and this will happen. By the time I shut the front door behind them I said to myself, never, ever, EVER again.

Then, a week later Attila rings up saying, 'What a great tour, eh? I really enjoyed myself, we'll have to do it again!' and I find myself thinking, hmm, well...*maybe*...

2. THE IRISH PROBLEM

29th October

By the time I get to Gatwick, the flight is closing. Thanks, Connex South Central, it was very relaxing sitting a mile out of the station for twenty minutes watching the seconds tick by while other trains flew past, including the Gatwick Express which went by in a manner I can only describe as 'flaunting it.' Maybe next time I will pay the extra three quid. I run through the terminal with my guitar, merchandising and baggage and make the gate with just minutes to spare.

When we land at Shannon I have to run again for the bus connection to Limerick station so that I can catch the one train that will get me to Killarney in time for tonight's gig, my first in Ireland since the original Adverts line-up disintegrated in Dublin twenty years ago. Back then, we had a tour manager, were driven around in a minibus and stayed in nice hotels. Now I'm travelling by public transport and sleeping wherever I can find a bed.

After a long dreary journey the train pulls into Killarney and I gather my baggage together. A notice on the train door says, *'STOP! Ensure you are at a platform before stepping out.'*

Outside the rain is falling from the skies in black sheets. I stagger across the road to Scott's Hotel and arrive in reception, drenched. I'll be playing—and staying—here tonight. The reception area looks smart enough but my heart sinks when I hear the directions to my room: 'Go up to the first floor, all the way through the new extension, past the fire escape, then just keep on going until you reach the end of the old wing.'

Sure enough, the decor deteriorates through miles of corridors until I reach my tiny, cold room. I look around to switch up the heating, but there isn't any.

Downstairs to soundcheck in the hotel bar, converted to a gig for this evening. It's difficult to imagine anyone coming to a concert here, and I've already heard that the bands who have played in the two weeks since this series of gigs started, have had disappointing turn-outs. The first band played to just the bar staff.

There's still four hours until I'm due onstage so I take a walk around Killarney to pass the time and get a feel of the place. There's no one out on the streets, and it's dark, cold and raining incessantly. When I return to the venue, virtually the only people there are the local promoter, Shella, and a few of her friends. We sit in front of the open fire in a general air of gloom. I suppose I'm not looking too happy—Shella says, 'you must get lonely travelling around by yourself.' I hate to admit it but, yes, sometimes on nights like this, I do.

All the same, the gig itself is pretty good. The thirty-or-so people in the venue come away from the bar, sit right up close to the stage and listen to every song. Afterwards, we all retire to a back bar and drink into the night. As the alcohol flows, everyone seems keen to tell me about why they are here in Killarney. Many are Brits who escaped to Ireland to find new lives for themselves, or felt themselves hounded out by the Poll Tax, the Criminal Justice Act, or - in the case of Don, one old hippy here - Operation Julie. He's now growing clothing-grade hemp and trying to establish it as a new crop to replace the ailing Irish beef industry.

I get to bed in the small hours and try to sleep, huddled in a ball against the cold.

30th October

As soon as I'm awake I get under the shower until I warm up. I don't need to get the train to Cork until midday so there's time for breakfast. When I get to the station, it turns out the 12:00 only runs in the tourist season, the next train to Cork is in two and a half hours. Can I get to somewhere where I can get a connection? The station master looks up at me with exaggerated patience and says firmly, 'There is no way out of here until 2:37.'

Which gives me more time than I need to take another look around Killarney, out-of-season tourist town. I'm back at the station in good time for the train, you bet, and wait. And wait. The platform fills up. Fifteen minutes after the train should have arrived an announcement is made: 'Ladies and gentleman, the train for Cork is running ten minutes late.'

Cork is built on an island surrounded by rivers, and the rain currently seems to be trying to fill in what isn't already water. I check in at the cheap and cheerful hostel where I'm staying and go to find the venue. I have to set up the P.A. myself as no-one else is around. After a while the manager wanders through. 'Must be hard travelling round on your own,' he says. These people are trying to get to me.

The earliest I'm going to be onstage is 11:30, so once again I take a slow walk around in the rain. I arrive back at the gig at 11:15. Uh oh, doesn't feel right. There are five dolled-up office girls dancing to 'Summer Nights' from 'Grease.' The manager says I won't be needing to go on before 12:00. By then the place is starting to fill up with a disco-type crowd and the dance floor empties as soon as I start playing. After twenty desperate minutes the manager calls me over to the side of the stage.

'Why don't you give it a rest for a while so we can play some records,' he suggests, 'come back on a bit later.'

'Walking On Sunshine' by Katrina and the Waves blasts out of the speakers and people literally run onto the dance floor.

At one in the morning I find the manager and ask him when I'm supposed to go start playing again. He says to hang on a bit then we'll have 'a chat,' which presumably means he'll ask me not to play any more and attempt to reduce the fee. It suits me actually; right now I'd pay to get out of here.

Walk back to the hostel in the rain. Bed 3:30.

31st October

Up at 7:00 to take the early train to Dublin, where I have a radio interview, after which I'll head back South for a gig in Waterford. It's still raining.

I've been given wrong directions to the radio station and stagger around for a bit under my baggage, trying to find the way. At one point as I'm puffing and sweating my way up the road a Japanese guy comes up to me, 'Hey, TV Smith—you playing here tonight?' I disappoint him with the news that I'm actually playing a hundred miles away.

The interview is fun, with a couple of guys who used to work on Hot Press, and interviewed me at the Adverts gig in Dublin all those years ago. I get some mileage chatting with them on air about last night's disaster in Cork, and they put it in context when they tell me about a local singer-songwriter who played a gig in Luxembourg on St.Patrick's night. Unhappy that he wasn't playing traditional songs for the occasion, one member of the audience planted himself in front of the stage and began to heckle repeatedly between each number: 'BE MORE TYPICALLY IRISH! BE MORE TYPICALLY IRISH...!'

The train to Waterford stops at Kilkenny because of engineering works. Bus transfer to Waterford. Main road closed due to roadworks. So here we go, rattling down the back roads, skies lowering, rain spattering on the steamed-up windows, those famous green fields dissolving to a thousand greys as dusk falls.

It's Halloween, and as we go through the little villages on the way to Waterford, bands of soaked children in fancy dress roam from house to house. Do they realise, I wonder, that there is still a law on the Irish statute book, unrepealed from the Middle Ages, that says you can be jailed for up to a year for imitating a witch? At the gig in the evening, two revellers get round this by dressing as Arab terrorists, but surely they are missing the point?

After the show a group of people who've just arrived tell me they heard the radio interview and had intended to come to the gig but missed it because they 'got stuck in the pub.' There is a serious amount of alcohol being consumed around me, but I resist the call to get stuck in the pub myself, and carry my gear back to the hostel—no heating again—and catch five hours sleep.

1st November

The rain has stopped. I walk over to the station under a pale blue sky and my spirits lift at seeing some light and colour in the world. Today is the only day off in the week, and I'm going to travel up to Galway and stay with Sean, the fan and would-be agent who booked this tour. The bus transfer from Waterford takes a couple of hours. I rejoin the train at Carlow, then sit there for another half an hour, unable to move because they can't get the doors to close. By the time I get to Galway six hours later, it's raining again.

Sean meets me at the station and tells me that the Galway gig, planned for two days time, has been cancelled. The manager of the venue got nervous about the kind of fans some of the previous punk bands have been attracting and he doesn't like scruffy people in his club. Result! I haven't been banned anywhere since 1977!

However, there is the question of the fee. When we get back to Sean's place a couple of phone calls establish that if I want to get paid I'm going to have to play tonight, unannounced, supporting an Irish covers band. So it's straight back into the car and a forty minute drive back to Galway.

To great satisfaction all round, except to the manager of the venue, the gig is a real stormer. I just wish I could have done it the day I was booked—there are bound to be a few disappointed fans turn up on Tuesday. A few accidentally turn up tonight, including two guys on holiday from Wales who had been singing along to Gary Gilmore's Eyes on a punk compilation CD this morning and could hardly believe it when they walked in tonight and found I was playing.

We drive back to Sean's cottage at two in the morning, and it's raining so hard it sounds like someone is throwing buckets of nails over the car.

2nd November

Tonight I'm playing in Leap, a village about 50 miles down the coast from Cork. The word is that although the venue—and usually the audience—is small, the atmosphere is big. Sean is driving us to this one, and we set off through an early afternoon hail shower for the expected six hour journey. We've been promised somewhere to stay tonight—apparently someone who owns a cottage in the area has offered to put us up—but I'm wondering what to do the next day. It seems pointless to travel all the way back to Galway tomorrow as the gig is off.

Getting pretty travel-weary now, even more so by the time we pull into Leap at around 7:30. The venue is a small, high-ceilinged room behind a pub, with a narrow balcony running round it. Paddy, the musician who runs it, suggests we relax a bit and have a coffee before setting up.

Monday night in Leap; I'm not expecting more than a handful of people, so when about 25 or 30 turn up I'm pretty pleased. I find myself chatting to two German guys who are on holiday and have, like us, travelled down from Galway today for the gig. They had no idea I played there last night, so now they're kicking themselves.

Really enjoyable gig, everyone very tuned in. At one point I see someone leaning out over the balcony to get a better look at the stage and joke with him that I hope he's not about to throw himself off. He calls back down, 'You'd better hope not, you're staying at my place tonight.'

After the gig he introduces himself as Phil, and we follow his van down the narrow lanes to his cottage way out in the countryside, not another house in sight. We sit around with him and his friends until five in the morning, the place just lit by the flames from the open stove and a few candles. A guy called Ross suggests that if I'm not going back to Galway tomorrow night I could play in a nearby pub instead. He reckons he could ring round some friends in the morning and get a decent crowd in, and says he'll ask at the pub in the morning and then give me a ring.

Phil has offered to sleep in an attic room and let me use his downstairs bedroom, which I accept as I'm pretty much out on my feet. He'd mentioned earlier that he had fetish interests—still, it's odd drifting off to sleep surrounded by handcuffs, chains and shackles.

3rd November

Wake up at 10:30. Now it's daylight I can look round the house, which is decorated pretty organically, great lumps of wood everywhere, attached to walls to form shelving and furniture, stacked as sculpture in the garden. Stripped branches form a ladder up to a rough-hewn platform in a tree that looks out over the surrounding fields.

Ross phones to say the pub, which is in nearby Ballydehob, would like to have me play, so Sean and I drive in to see them. It's a beautiful crisp and cloudless day, and the painted houses of Ballydehob are shining like flags in the sunshine. The pub is run by a German couple who are keen to encourage music there, and we agree that I'll play a short acoustic set at around 11 p.m.

Sean and I get some breakfast in a nearby cafe, buy some peat briquettes to replenish the stove, then head back to the cottage. Sean then leaves for Galway to be with his wife and new baby.

I spend the afternoon playing guitar while Phil is outside making the most of the good weather to fix the sewage system. All toilets and sinks are out of action for the foreseeable future until the concrete sets, as they all empty into the one drain. Calls of nature are to be answered in the garden. When Phil eventually comes in he automatically washes his hands in the sink, ruins the concrete and has to start again.

As the sun goes down, Phil cooks some food and talks about his buddhist faith and his repressed childhood which led to him becoming a sexual masochist. He uses this as a theme for art shows he puts on, the next one planned for Berlin in the Spring. A local musician, Paul, helps with the backing music for his shows. After we've eaten, we drive to Ballydehob and pick up Paul on the way. He lost an arm through heroin misuse when he was a teenager but is now cheery and well-adjusted. When we get to the pub and I show him my guitar, he unscrews his hand and puts in another one with a plectrum fixed into it, and has a strum.

There's a great atmosphere for the gig, but as soon as it's over I feel totally exhausted. Phil's letting me sleep at his place again tonight, so we drive back there, a stunning nearly-full moon lighting up the landscape.

4th November

Ross arrives at 11:00 to drive me to Tralee. It's a nice day and we have a beautiful, bumpy ride round the coast in his old van. Here and there rock arches dramatically over the narrow road, roughly hacked out to form rudimentary tunnels. Far below the sea glitters, and you can just make out the dark clusters of oil silos packed onto the outlying islands, not visible from the holiday towns.

We drink a coffee in Tralee, then Ross heads back. I find the pub I'm playing in tonight, and am greeted by Noel, the manager. 'Travelling' light, are ye?'

He expects me to have a P.A. system with me. That's a problem, but after a couple of phone calls we find one to hire in for the night, agreeing to split the cost. It's a fairly large pub and an acoustic gig wouldn't really cut it.

I check in to the hotel a few doors away and get back to the venue at 6:30 to soundcheck. Noel isn't around. The P.A. has been dumped on the stage instead of set up as promised, and the guys who are hiring it out have gone off to another gig. So I spend an hour or so setting it up and trying to soundcheck. This proves to be difficult because a group of lads playing pool right in front of the stage feel it's putting them off their game. They get a lot of fun among themselves by mimicking the 'One, two...' and other soundcheck stuff I have to do—hilarious. Every time someone puts something on the juke box, the barman asks me to stop until the record is finished 'because they've put in their money.' He also tells me I have to be finished by 7:30, when the Manchester United match comes on the television.

I finally get a clear run to try a song and while I'm playing one of the pool lads comes up and throws an empty cigarette packet at me, then shuffles back to his stool at the bar. I get off the stage and go over and ask him what the fuck he's doing. He mumbles something drunkenly about it being too loud and won't meet my eye. His friends have all gone quiet. It's pathetic. I pack up and leave them to it.

Now I have some time to kill, so I use some of it to check how long it will take me to walk to the station. I have to get a 7:20 train tomorrow morning and don't want to get up a minute earlier than I have to. Despite still being furious about the soundcheck I make myself walk slowly, imitating a man who has just woken up and is carrying two bags and a guitar. Fifteen minutes.

With just a few moments to spare before I'm due to start playing, I get back to the pub, plug my gear back up, and begin right on time. There's a decent-sized crowd, but I can see immediately that most are 'regulars,' only a handful are here specifically to see me so I have to work hard. However, it's the last gig and I don't have to worry about my voice so I just let rip and enjoy myself.

One local lad I speak to afterwards seems completely overwhelmed by how good the gig was, particularly as he'd seen me walking round the town earlier and crossed the road to avoid me, thinking, 'this guy looks like trouble'. I would guess this was shortly after soundcheck. He only came in to the pub by chance for a drink, and there I was, his nemesis, getting up on stage. Now he's a fan for life.

Outside at 1:00 a.m. there's a pizza place still open so I go in. Surprised to see somewhere open so late in Traleee, I ask the guy making the pizza what time he shuts.

'Oh, 2:30—3:00,' he says.

'Any trouble?' I ask.

'No, no trouble,' he says, '—just messy.'

Back at the hotel I set the alarm for four hours time.

Musician's tip: a guitar stand balanced on a hotel convector heater makes a good pizza-warmer.

5th November

Wake up from a dream where all the eyelets fall out of my new shoes. When I get out into the street, bleary and dreary, it's still dark. I'm at the station in time for the train and as it pulls away from the platform the sun comes up, blazing gold between the horizon and a bank of cloud, a full moon still hanging in the watery sky. A few minutes later, a rainbow joins in the show.

Tralee to Mallow. Change at Mallow.
Mallow to Limerick Junction.

Short wait at Limerick junction, connection to Limerick.
Make Limerick just in time.
Bus to airport. Ten minutes to go before last check in.
Flight delayed one hour.
Dublin to Gatwick.
Connex South Central to Victoria.
Picadilly line, District line.
Home in time for the fireworks.

3. A LITTLE BIT OF CHELSEA IN VIENNA

19th November

I've lost count of how many times I've been supposed to play Vienna. Last time I was actually in the travel agent booking my flight when I got a call to say the gig was off. I cancelled the ticket I'd booked moments before and had to pay half the fare.

This time a tour of Austria which had been proposed earlier in the year gradually shrunk to two dates, Vienna and Linz, with Linz pulling out a couple of weeks ago. That left just the Chelsea Club in Vienna. This time I will definitely be going; by a complete coincidence German superstars Die Toten Hosen have asked me to support them at the same club in less than two weeks.

Co-promoters Othmar and Rainer meet me at the airport and drive me into the city. Despite never having played here before I'm feeling reasonably confident about the gig, after coming across a good write-up and photo trailing it in the newspaper that I was given on the plane: *Neue Kronen Zeitung*, the Austrian equivalent of The Sun.

In order to get a flight cheap enough for me not to make a loss, I've got to stay in Vienna for two nights. I hate the idea of an evening with nothing to do in a city where I don't know anyone, so when Rainer tells me a band he manages is playing the Chelsea tomorrow I suggest that I could support them. He likes the idea.

Typical. You wait years for a gig in Vienna, then three come along at once.

Down MarieHilfer Straße to drop my bags at the hotel, a gloomy 'old Vienna' style building about five minutes drive from the venue. The room is small and dingy, with a magnificent view of a brick wall out of the window.

At the Chelsea a problem soon becomes apparent: the entire P.A. system has stopped working and nobody can figure out why. At this point it's possible there might be no soundcheck, or worse—no gig. After an hour or so of panic an obscure fuse in the desk is found that no-one knew existed. It's blown. In two minutes they have replaced it and we're up and running again.

Good gig. Turn-out is okay considering it's my first time here and I end up playing for nearly two hours.

I stay late having a drink with the bar staff. Everyone is pleased I came. Othmar explains how it's really important for him to put on good music, not just bands that will make money. I like this attitude—we have another drink to it, then I cab it back to the hotel.

20th November

There are worse places to spend a day off than Vienna. In fact, I'm a bit annoyed with myself that I didn't manage to get out before 11:30, but sitting in the hotel having a slow breakfast and watching the snow falling was good too.

I know I've only really got time to visit one gallery, so I choose the one with the best reputation and head on the U-bahn down to the Kunsthistoriches Museum. It doesn't disappoint.

After a few hours lost in Breughel and Bosch masterpieces I travel down to the Stephansdom to meet Othmar, his wife and their baby. They'd been intending to show me around the old town, but there's now a biting raw wind so we end up taking shelter in a sterile upmarket cafe bar on the top floor of a department store, with only a good view to recommend it. Soon we get out of there, and walk to an old-fashioned Viennese cafe, very traditional and a bit stuffy, but with much more character.

Back to the Chelsea, where Rainer's band is just finishing soundcheck. It's another very nice gig with a mix of new audience and people from last night.

Othmar goes home early, worn out after yesterday's late night. I get the S-Bahn back to the hotel, and it's only then that I realise I haven't eaten since breakfast. Nothing much is open now. I ask at a fast food place outside the station if he's got anything vegetarian, but he says no, then turns his back on me. Well, I can see some bread rolls inside his little kiosk, and there are onions frying on the griddle beside him, but being a vegetarian around here is obviously not acceptable; I move on. Finally I find another place half way along MarieHilfestraße, and set my guitar and bag down on the icy pavement with some relief. I can't feel my fingers.

So here I am, standing at a Schnell-Imbiss booth at one in the morning, eating a microwaved Borek and drinking a mug of warm Glühwein, watching the traffic, temperature minus 6 degrees. *Auf Wiedersehen*, Vienna, I'll be back in thirteen days.

4. LET THEM EAT BISCUITS

23rd November

Six days at Ronnie Scott's, Birmingham, supporting Tom Robinson. Last week Tom phoned and asked if I fancied having a go at playing bass in his band as well. I've never played bass onstage before—I said yes.

Tom's roadie Mark picks me up at one in the afternoon for the drive to Birmingham, while Tom sets off separately with tour manager and sound engineer Glynn. Mark and I are close to Birmingham when we get a call on from Tom. They are only halfway up the motorway. They stopped off at a computer shop on the way out of London, and as they left the shop Tom picked up the wrong coat. Now the hapless woman customer who had the misfortune to have an identical coat to him is on the phone, stranded, without money or house keys. She is furious, and needs her coat back *now*.

Mark and I head back down the motorway towards London to meet up with Tom. As dusk falls, we park at a service station and swap cars. Mark drives the coat back to London, just in time to hit the rush hour.

Meanwhile, Tom, Glynn and I carry on up to Birmingham and load into the club. Drummer Charles is already setting up and guitarist Adam arrives shortly after. I ask Glynn to EQ the bass to a distant rumble so that no-one will know when I hit the wrong notes.

We'd hoped to rehearse during soundcheck but the incident with the coat has put paid to that. There is some frantic revision of the songs in the dressing room, then Tom and band take to the stage for the first set. They go down a storm. I join them for the last couple of numbers and find I'm actually enjoying it. I briefly decide to give up singing and play bass guitar full time.

Next, I play a short solo set, replacing the resident house band who would normally be on now. Then Tom comes and backs me up on guitar and sings some backing vocals. Finally Tom and band play a second set, I join them again towards the end, and it's all over. Until the next five nights.

Back to the hotel at 1:00 to check in. The hotel has both the words 'quality' and 'friendly' in the name, usually a bad sign. When we walk in, I realise with a shock that this is the same hotel I stayed in with The Adverts in 1977, when, accurately, it had neither adjective. However, the rooms have improved in the last twenty years. Mine even has a radiator, although it doesn't work. There's an interesting beefy odour, possibly a room spray they lay on especially to annoy vegetarians like me. There is a kettle and sachets of coffee but in a commendable environment-friendly move the sink is so small that you can't get the kettle under the tap to fill it.

We gather in my room and talk bollox for a couple of hours.

Feel a bit peckish. Eat the two individually-wrapped complimentary biscuits.

24th November

Cold night. Decide to change my room.

Mark is at reception when I get down there. He's just checked out because he has to go back to London after tonight. It's a shame that he'll miss the rest of the gigs; still, I establish that his room has a heater and move into it. Switch the heater up to full.

Adam arrives in reception. The three of us drive into the city and spend some time in a guitar shop, where Adam tries out various rare and expensive guitars with a kind of dreamy expression on his face. We get a parking ticket.

On returning to the hotel, Adam finds that his mobile phone has been stolen from his room while he was out. Mark rings up the number and hears a woman's voice saying, 'You've got the wrong number.'

He says, 'No, I've got the right number—you've got the wrong bloody phone!' She hangs up.

Adam swaps his room.

Glynn swaps his room.

Evening. Good gig.

Later we gather in my room and talk bollox for a couple of hours. Move a chair and find a large unpleasant stain underneath. There is something growing on it. Move chair back.

Feel a bit peckish. Eat the two individually-wrapped complimentary biscuits.

25th November

Audience is down on numbers from the last two nights; midweek blues. Only a speedball 'One Chord Wonders' at the end really sparks everyone into life.

Afterwards we're all tired, but Tom and I slog off to the entrance of the club to do the meet'n'greet. One guy puts his name on my mailing list and tells me that he came down to the gig this evening straight from the Dean Friedman show at the Alexandria theatre just down the road, where he also joined a mailing list. This is probably the only person in the world on both the Dean Friedman and the TV Smith mailing list.

Hotel. Adam goes straight to his room—he has to get up at 8:00 a.m. tomorrow to get down to London for rehearsals and an early evening showcase gig with another band. Glynn and I head for my room for light refreshments, as I stocked the mini-bar from the local off-licence earlier. Unfortunately the mini-bar is now so full the latch has got stuck and the door won't open. Fortunately Glynn has a Swiss army knife.

There is a tap on the door and Tom appears, bounding into the room thrashing an air guitar and singing *'The Wonders don't care—we don't give a damn!'*

We end up talking bollox again for a few hours, and I get to sleep even later than usual. Sod the biscuits.

26th November

Glynn is on the phone to tell me that Tom reckons he is going down with a virus, so he's going to try and get a few hours sleep. The plan now is for the rest of us to go the venue at 7:00, then Glynn will pick up Tom at 9:00, just in time for the show. This would be the night that Adam won't be there for the first set.

So the gig is different again. Tom rearranges his set to leave the songs he does with Adam until later, and I attempt to do some of Adam's backing vocal parts. You wouldn't know Tom was ill, what a trooper.

In the interval we're a bit concerned that Adam still hasn't arrived, but he makes it with moments to spare.

After the gig, Tom, Glynn and I go back to my room. This feels just like old times, when the three of us were on the road together in '92. I'm in a nice warm, large, comfortable room talking bollox with two of my best mates, and getting the chance to play in front of great audiences every night—and getting paid for it. Touring is hell.

27th November

Wake up a bit earlier than usual, but still too late for breakfast. I take a bus into the city centre to have a look at the municipal gallery, which has a reputation for having some good stuff in it, but is rather disappointing after my recent gallery visit in Vienna. Back to the hotel with a couple of hours to spare before the gig.

I can't get over this audience. Every night it's the same—well dressed, apparently well-off, generally middle-aged people file into the venue. It's tables and chairs; some people take dinner during the course of the concert. Everything seems set for a polite, well-behaved evening. Then, when I ask from the stage if there are any other old punk rockers in the audience, the place explodes. I keep on forgetting, I'm middle-aged too— most of these people grew up with the same music as me.

One more gig to go. With the end in sight we relax a little and turn into post-concert monsters. Back at my room a horrible atrocity is done to an innocent foreign language when we spontaneously start to talk bollox in French, and continue for several hours.

28th November

I'm woken at 1:00 by the chambermaid knocking on the door and asking if I want my room cleaned. I shout back 'No', then as an afterthought throw on some clothes and go out and get some sachets of coffee from her trolley, also grab a couple of individually-wrapped biscuits for breakfast.

Leafing through the paper, I see that Henry Rollins is playing a spoken word concert tonight in the Alexandra. I walk down there to say hello. At the stage door there are two bored-looking off-duty ice cream ladies, still wearing their trays. I ask them if the Rollins party is in the theatre yet. They don't seem to know who I mean, so I explain that he's playing this evening. They tell me that there's no-one in for the evening yet, as the afternoon show is still going on. It's 'The Mister Men Show.'

Bus back to the hotel. Can't get hold of any of our group, so I pack up my stuff for tonight, then cab it back to the Alexandra, where I'm let into backstage because I'm carrying a guitar case, so they assume I'm something to do with whatever it is that's going on. Surprise Henry, who is sitting alone in his dressing room listening to jazz.

So—the gig, last of the week's residency, and a triumph. Full house, and people out from behind the tables and dancing in the aisles. Then the anticlimax; packing the gear up, hanging around, saying goodbyes, back to the hotel. Before we even hit my room, it's nearly 4 a.m.

Feel a bit peckish, but there are no biscuits left.

The chambermaids have taken away my 'Do Not Disturb' sign. I think they are trying to tell me something.

29th November

I wake up five minutes before midday, hurriedly pack up my things and dash to reception to meet Adam, who's giving me a lift to London. He's not there yet, so I order a coffee, which comes with a small plate of biscuits. Individually wrapped. An hour later Adam arrives, we load up the car and head back down the M40.

Evening. I check my e-mail for the first time for a week, and find out that a compilation album called 'Just The Best', which has a song of mine, *Generation Y*, on it, has gone to number one in the German charts.

5. TWO DAYS WITH DEAD TROUSERS

2nd December

It's only rock'n'roll—but when you're up at 7:00 on a cold grey December morning to walk down to the tube, it feels just like a normal job.

Mega-successful German band Die Toten Hosen (literally The Dead Trousers) have booked me flights so that I can come and support them on two secret club dates in Vienna and Zurich. At Heathrow I wait in the long line for check-in anticipating the usual argument as to whether I can take my guitar on board with me, then find out when I get to the desk that I'm in Business Class, so it's no problem.

'You can also use the Business Lounge,' says the woman checking me in. 'Free alcohol...I would.'

Austrian Airlines. Seat number 1A. Wide. I've never travelled Business Class before and I think I could get used to it. Do they have the vegetarian meal I booked? 'Yes, we have it,' snaps the stewardess, almost saluting. A tray of Sekt (in real glasses) is brought round. Newspapers. The Sekt is putting a blur on for take-off. As we roll back from the gate, another stewardess is working her way down the aisles. When she gets to me she apologises, 'I'm sorry, we have no menu cards left.'

Menu cards?

Take-off is very quiet sitting in front of the engines, in fact it's a bit unsettling swooping up into the clouds without the usual accompanying shake and rumble. Suddenly a warm towel is tonged at me.

The meal arrives. It's a selection of veggie pakoras and bhajis, paneer and peppers on cocktail sticks, salad with asparagus tips and slices of vegetable pâté enrobed in spinach leaf. Spring water. Mango, melon and pineapple. A real cloth napkin.

I'm offered bread rolls three times. 'More to drink, sir?'

Sir?

My tray is removed moments after I've finishing eating. Economy Class passengers who have sat pinned under the wreckage of their tasteless meal for half-an-hour will appreciate this.

'Cognac to go with your coffee, sir?' If you took every opportunity for free alcohol in Business Class you could fly to your destination without the aid of the aircraft.

Last night I looked up the weather forecast for Vienna on the internet. They forecast five degrees Centigrade, about the same as London, but it's actually minus six. I've been told to get a taxi to the hotel, but I take the train instead—cheaper and probably quicker—and ease into the city past the back streets, the blocks of flats, the graffiti-covered walls and empty lots overgrown with weeds. I needed to get back to the real world.

Not for long. My hotel room is a suite of three, complete with a bar, kitchen area with microwave, two televisions, two telephones, and a complimentary apple, banana, half an orange and half a kiwi fruit (individually wrapped). A card propped up on the bar says, Welcome Mr. Smith, we hope you have a pleasant blah, blah, blah.

Damn—nothing to complain about.

But I have to get moving if I want to get down to the Akademie der bildenden Künste before it closes at 4:00. I'm determined to get to see Bosch's 'Last Judgment' so I throw my bags down and get on the U-bahn.

Gallery closed ten minutes ago.

I wander back through the chilly, busy streets—past the wooden Glühwein stalls, and the seasonal Christkindmarkts, heady scents of mulled wine and roasting chestnuts in the air. I meet with the Hosen back at the hotel and find most of them are suffering from colds. Winter can be a pain when you're touring.

At the Chelsea Club it's great to see the the promoter and all the staff again, feels like we're old friends. No soundcheck for me until the last minute, as the Hosen are making a video for their Christmas single, a tongue-in-cheek punk version of 'Auld Lang Syne,' and have to run through it countless times while the cameraman sets up shots and filler footage is taken to mix in with the film of the actual gig later.

By the time I'm on stage, the place is crammed with Hosen fans. Whenever I play with this band I'm a bit concerned that the notorious 'Hosen! Hosen!' chant that has driven many a support band from the stage will start up, so I don't leave any gaps, and play a very punked-up set. The pace only falters when I lean down in the dark to switch on my sequencer to accompany me for one song towards the end of the set. I start the backing track and try to play along but can't make any sense of it. After the third attempt I notice that I've pressed the wrong button and put the song into 5/4 time instead of its usual 4/4. The trouble with machines is that if you tell them to do something stupid, they will.

After the show someone tells me, 'You are the best—after the Toten Hosen. The Toten Hosen are God, you are Jesus Christ.' Not sure if this is theologically correct.

Back at the hotel by 3:00. Feel I should stay awake longer just to appreciate the room, but don't.

3rd December

I buy a torch at Vienna airport so I can see the screen on the sequencer tonight. Business Class to Zurich, flying with the band. Even though I hadn't put in a request for it, something meat-free is found for me. Probably some poor vegetarian in Economy has just been told that his meal isn't available.

Another top class hotel in Zurich. Two tangerines, monkey nuts and a date. And a pair of individually-wrapped shower slippers.

Most of the Hosen go to get some more sleep to try and get over their colds. I sit in my room and reprogramme the sequencer to put the song back into 4/4, also speed it up a bit—something tells me it will be another high energy one tonight.

We drive to the club and the band get into a lengthy soundcheck. Sometimes it's tough being the support act. You stand around on the sidelines while the main band is being attended to. Often no-one talks to you, or even knows who you are. Even though I'm playing tonight and the gig is totally sold out, the venue makes a fuss when I hand in a couple names for the guest list. My friend PamP from Garden Gang is driving four hours from Munich for this, so I hope they're going to let him in.

The gig is a blast, people clapping, singing along with the ones they know and generally going nuts. It's such fun to play to a reaction like this, you feel you have boundless energy.

The first song with the sequencer goes well—I can see the display with my new torch, it's in 4/4 timing, and running just that bit faster: perfect. Then, when I reach down to move it on to the next song, the screen shows the message, 'Warning! Battery Low!' I've never seen that before. Usually I plug it in but I didn't have a Swiss power adaptor. I have no idea what happens when the batteries run out; will it go out of tune, slow down, or just stop dead?

It stops dead, halfway through the last number in the set. I carry on without it.

Die Toten Hosen take the place apart. Most groups of their size wouldn't dream of playing smaller venues, but they do it to keep in touch with their audience and it works.

At one point in the set, singer Campino complains that he has nothing to drink onstage. While the band continues playing behind him, he crowd-surfs over the heads of the audience to the bar, near to where I am standing with PamP, who seems to be leaning away a little. Campino reaches down and grabs a bottle from the bar, then crowd-surfs back to the stage to great applause.

PamP turns to me and says, 'Yes, but last time I saw him do that, it was *my* beer he took.'

Time to leave the venue. Post gig merriment in the dressing room is somewhat muted by the sound of repeated and violent vomiting from the drum roadie, aptly named Vom, who has just gone down with a virus. While he's taken off to hospital, I cadge a lift back to the hotel with one of the crew.

Someone has been into my room and placed a chocolate on my pillow.

It's only 2:30 and there's no need to get up early tomorrow. There are 43 channels on the television in my room, but the batteries on the remote control are dead, so my only option is to watch the countdown for the space shuttle take-off. Stops at nineteen seconds.

6. SETTING UP THE U.K. TOUR

It's mid-December, I'm finally back at home for a few weeks and I want to tour Britain in February to go with the release of my new album, so that means getting on the phone. The problem is, venues in Britain don't really care if I tour or not and I hate having to try and persuade them.

Monday. No time to start booking the gigs because I'm going down to East Sussex to see my old friend and musical collaborator Tim Cross who's asked me to write some lyrics and sing on a track he's recording. Goes well.

Tuesday. Should get going on the booking, but the bathroom floorboards urgently need repairing. Buy some wood, cut it to size. Phone up a venue in Southampton that's been recommended to me. I've been told I need to speak to Brin or Richard—neither are there. Try tomorrow.

Wednesday. Un-plumb sink and move it out of the way. Rip up old floorboards. Carpet was stuck to them so now it's full of holes. Will need new carpet. Must get going on the tour. Fit new boards, plumb sink back in, grout.

Thursday. Send CD and biogs to a pub in Birmingham who've said they want to put me on. Phone back the Southampton venue. Brin doesn't sound very interested, tells me to send him a CD I'm out of Jiffy bags. Cycle to the post office to buy some more. Get a puncture.

Friday. Still haven't washed my clothes from the last tour so I put a couple of loads on. Get wheel off bike and fix puncture. Send out CD and biog to an agent who once said he wanted to get me gigs, but never did. Drive over to my mate Martin to return the bass I've been borrowing from him for the Tom Robinson gigs. Also ask him if he could fix my guitar pickup, which stopped working after the last gig. Leave it with him. Write to my friend Mick in Manchester to ask if he knows any venues there.

Saturday. Christmas less than two weeks away, must get cards and stuff. Write to a few people around the country who might be able to help get me some gigs. Phone up Danny, the Crusty from Hull, about a gig there—he'd like to organise one, says ring back in the new year when I know what date I want.

Sunday. Off.

Monday. Must get going on the tour. But first, my last gig of the year is in six days and I've got to send the news out to my mailing list. The list, which I'd spent years building up, got lost when my last record company's computer got a virus. Last week they told me they thought they'd managed to rescue it and were going to send it over to me, but it still hasn't arrived. Phone them up, they say it's been sent. Do some shopping.

Tuesday. Mailing list arrives, but it's for the wrong band. I've got about fifty hand-written names collected from recent gigs, so I gather them together and type them into the database on my computer. Print out the newsletters and envelopes, take the bus down to the Cherry Red offices so they can post them. Mick rings with a few names and addresses of venues in Manchester.

Wednesday. Spend a couple of hours practising ready for gig on Sunday. Speak to Chris from Ozit records about gigs in his area. Ring a number Mick gave me. The promoter is leaving in two days and won't have a new place until Spring. Try another venue. The Manager asks where I'm from. London, I say. He thinks about it. 'So how are you going to get an audience here?' Gives me the name of a guy called Chris who promotes gigs around Manchester. I ring him, he's not there. Wife or girlfriend says ring back tomorrow. Ring back Southampton. Brin's not there, ring back tomorrow. Speak to a London promoter, send him CD and biog. Ring up a venue in Glasgow I've played before, get the bloody BT voice saying, 'the number you are calling knows you are waiting.....please try later.' God, someone just give me *one* gig to start me off.

Thursday. Must get some gigs. But first I've got to send off a copy of the new album to Q magazine, I've a feeling it's near the deadline for next month's issue and it would really help the record if there was a review around the time of the release on the 25th January. Phone them up and they suggest sending in some photos as well in case they can use one. Great, except I have only one copy of each shot left from the last photo session. Cycle down to the photo shop to get some more printed. I'd swear that tyre is going down again.

Get home and put together a package to send off, also send off some more old photos I've found to Ozit for the re-release of one of my albums in the Spring. There's a message on the answering machine from the venue in Birmingham; they'd definitely like to put on a gig. Phone them back and we pencil in possible dates in February. At last, that's one! Must get some more, but I'm feeling a bit nervous about the gig I'm playing on Sunday so I spend a couple of hours practising.

Phone up Southampton. Brin's not there, try again tomorrow. Another attempt to phone Chris in Manchester. No-one home. Evening—try again, someone else answers, he'll pass on the message to Chris. Phone Craig, a fan from the North-East who has booked me gigs in Sunderland and Northallerton in the past. An hour later he rings back with both confirmed for February. And that makes three.

Friday. Must work on getting more gigs, but first I must rehearse. But first I must get hold of Martin and pick up the pickup. But first I have to go and buy a new guitar cable for

Sunday's gig. But first—we have some friends coming round tonight so I have to buy some food and cook something.

At 4:30 I phone up Southampton. Brin's not there—he'll be back at 7:00. Try Manchester again, actually get to speak to Chris. He seems quite into the idea of a gig, I tell him I'll send him a CD and give him a call again next week.

Call Southampton at 7:30, actually speak to Brin! He says he doesn't like the record, but then realises he's mixed me up with a dance act. He won't make a decision about a gig now before Christmas. Ring again in new year.

Saturday. A lot of washing up to do after last night. Send off CD to Chris in Manchester. It's the last weekend before Christmas—there's really no point in trying to get gigs now. Go and look at new carpets for the bathroom.

Martin has left a message that he's fixed the pickup, but he's not at home when I ring him. Finally get hold of him late in the evening, will go and get it tomorrow.

Sunday. Pick up the pickup, fit it back into the guitar, change strings, gather all my stuff for tonight and pack it. Good gig—promoter says we'll definitely do it again in February. When I get back home there's a message from Craig on the machine to say he's 99% certain he's found me another gig in the North East.

Monday. Unpack my gear and wire it all back together again in the front room. Pack up a couple of copies of the Explorers CD that have just arrived, and send them off to Colin, the bass player. Ask in the letter about gigs in his area. By late afternoon I try a couple of phone calls. Newport—no reply. York—the person I speak to has never heard of me even though I've played the venue before, says she'll get someone to ring me back. Sure. Leeds—no reply. Four days to Christmas. I'm wasting my time.

Craig rings up in the evening to confirm Hartlepool.

Tuesday. Gotta get that carpet before the shop shuts for Christmas. Drive down there. Shop is shut for Christmas.

Wednesday. Phone Birmingham and we agree to do the gig on the 20th. Phone Chris in Manchester to try and get him to put gig on the 19th, but he only got the package from me today and is going away for Christmas tomorrow, we'll speak again in the new year.

Thursday. Christmas Eve. Nothing else is going to happen this year...except...Colin phones up to say thanks for the CD, and says he knows a gig in Malvern I could play...we'll speak again in the new year...

And out goes 1998.

1999

First Monday of the new year. I got a cold for Christmas and don't feel like doing anything, but the Hartlepool venue needs promo material fast to get it included in its leaflet for February/March gigs, so I ring up photographer Ian Dickson to get some more prints from the photo session, then go down the copy shop to print some more posters and biogs, parcel them up and send them off.

Tuesday. Speak to Chris at Ozit about the re-release of Channel Five, my first solo album, and make a few phone calls to try and track down the master tapes. Buy the bathroom carpet. Phone Mark P, who's left a message asking if I fancy doing a few gigs with his band, Alternative TV. No-one there, speak to his machine. Get a call from a guy in Blackburn: would I like to do some gigs in his area with a punk band he manages?

Wednesday. Still got this lousy cold, really don't feel like getting on the phone and selling myself to try and get gigs. Decide today is the day I will lay the bathroom carpet instead. I'm cutting it to shape when the phone rings. It's Q magazine to tell me that they want to put one of the tracks from the new album on their cover disc next month.

Finish laying the carpet.

Thursday. Phone Cherry Red to get them to co-ordinate with Q. Suggest they might like to pay to get some photo reprints made to help with promotion. They say they'll get back to me. Ring Newport—no-one answering. Ring Manchester—no-one answering. Ring Leeds—get the bloody B.T. voice saying, the number you are calling knows you are waiting...please try later! I'm just about to ring Southampton when a promoter rings back from Leeds. We sort out a date, but he's worried about the turn-out (aren't we all?) so it's for a low fee, barely enough to get me up there and pay for accommodation. Still, it's one more gig; you could virtually mistake this for a tour.

Cherry Red phone back to tell me that the Q compilation is a disc for subscribers only, and we'd have to pay to be on it. They're going to talk to their distributors to see if they think it would be worth it.

Friday. Drive to the dump to get rid of the old carpet. Phill Brown, who engineered Channel Five, phones to arrange delivery of the tapes next Tuesday. Ring Chris in Manchester about the gig—no reply. Ring Danny in Hull and suggest making the gig there Friday 12th, which would give me four in a row. He likes the idea, but is just fitting a thermostatic valve and has his plumbing head on. He'll ring later. Try Southampton—engaged. Still haven't heard back from Cherry Red, so I go and get the reprints done myself. Outside it's a dull wet Friday afternoon. As soon as I'm back in the house, the phone rings. It's Cherry Red: they will need some photos, so they'll be prepared to go in on the cost. Ring back Southampton and get straight through to Brin, but he's in the middle of a soundcheck and can't remember who I am. Ring back any day next week after 3:00.

Weekend.

Monday. Really getting over this cold now, no excuse not to finish off sorting these gigs out. But first I put on a load of washing, get some bread baking and start fixing up some blinds for the front room. At 2:30 I ring Chris in Manchester—no one there. Cherry Red phone to say the mastering company need another copy of the CD as the last one had a fault. Have to get that out to them now or the release date may be put back. They've spoken to the distributors and don't think it's worth doing the Q disc. Package up a CD and cycle down to the post office, then on to pick up the promo photos. It's four by the time I get home. Suppose I'd better try ringing Southampton but I'm really beginning to resent this gig—may just ditch it. Ring up anyway. Brin is discussing it with his partner at this very moment. 'The trouble is it's so difficult to market this sort of thing. I'll ring you back in fifteen minutes.' He rings back to say he doesn't want to do the gig, and gives me the names of two other venues he thinks I should try in Southampton instead. Ring one of the numbers but the venue is booked up for the next three months. Try Manchester again—no-one there. Finish putting up the blinds. Craig phones in the evening, he needs photos to promote the North-East gigs. Ha! I HAVE photos!!

Tuesday. Ring up Alan in Blackburn. He's been trying to get Manchester Star & Garter for the 27th—a week after the date I've been going for. Suggest he holds off on it until I can find out what's going on. Ring Chris in Manchester and get through, but he says he hasn't got around to sorting anything out yet, and I'd be better off doing it through Alan. Call Alan back to tell him to go ahead with it after all. 'The person you are calling knows you are waiting...please try later!' Package up the photos for Craig and send them off. Call Colin about the Malvern gig, but his wife tells me he won't be in until evening, will call back. London venue rings and we fix up a date for March 7th. Phill arrives with the tapes of Channel Five. Mark rings about the track I'm giving to a benefit album he's compiling, Colin rings with some phone numbers to try for the Malvern gig, and Alan rings back to tell me that the Manchester gig told him, 'TV Smith seems to be trying every way he can to get a gig here, but we're just not interested.'

Wednesday. Package up tape for Ozit and promo material for Leeds, cycle to the post office to send them off. Raining. Brake cable breaks. Danny phones to confirm Hull gig. I phone Malvern and we confirm that. Buy new brake cable, mess up fitting it, have to get another one. Call up Mark P to say 26th is free if he still wants me to play it. He says he'll tell the venue, call back tomorrow. Call Newport TJs get the phone number of the promoter. Ring him, he's not there. Think I could get this gig if I persevere, but time is getting short now.

Thursday. Get more posters photocopied and make up promo packages for all the remaining gigs. Cherry Red phone to say they've decided to do the Q disc after all. We arrange to meet Monday so I can give them a newsletter announcing the tour dates.

Time's up.

7. THE U.K. TOUR

9th February.

Yesterday Craig rang from Sunderland to warn me that it was 'hoiking it down' with snow, but by the time I get off the train, there are just a few flurries in the air. It is bloody cold though. I hang around outside the station for an hour or so until Craig gets a chance to break off from his job delivering car parts and pick me up. Back at his place, Dean and Daniel, his two hyperactive kids, are all over me. They seem fascinated by everything I do and follow me all over the house, including the toilet.

As soon as Craig has finished work, we head off to Hartlepool for tonight's gig in a pub called the Brewer and Firkin. The manager of the pub has taken away the tables and chairs from a raised area in front of the bar, and this is to be the stage. It's surrounded by a waist-high railing with one small gap, which is where I'll have to stand when I play if anyone is going to be able see me.

The P.A. arrives and turns out to be a good one, so at least I can be confident about the sound. I unpack my gear and find I've forgotten my guitar lead, have to borrow one from the sound engineer.

The gig is going to be quite late, so we kill time by going around the corner, slipping and sliding along the icy streets, to see the 'proper' venue in Hartlepool, the Studio, which is an old Church, tastefully converted into an arts centre, with a good stage and in-house P.A. and lighting. A quick drink there, then back to the Brewer and Firkin. A reasonable amount of people are there, and the gig is fine.

Back to Craig's place in Sunderland. Sharon, his wife, goes straight up to bed while Craig and I sit around for a while in front of the fire, having some pizza and a few beers before turning in. The kids are sleeping in their parents room, and I'm to have theirs, which has a bunk bed in it. I dump my bag against the door and squeeze into the bottom bunk, my feet hanging out over the end of the bed, where a line of cuddly toy animals gaze across at me.

10th February.

'Mum, where's Tim?'

'He's still asleep, Dean!'

'I want to see him. I want to see him sleeping!'

The bag shifts a little.

'Dean, man! Come downstairs and leave him alone!'

I shuffle downstairs eventually and two pairs of young eyes are on me. Both kids are off school with chicken pox. They want to show me their Sega Megadrive.

Checking through my bags, I see I've left my guitar strap and mailing list forms in Hartlepool. Craig has taken the day off work, so after some lunch he runs me back down to the Brewer and Firkin to pick them up, then we head for Newcastle to do an interview for B.B.C. local radio to help promote tonight's gig in Sunderland. Craig is looking forward to seeing what it's like at Radio Newcastle—he often listens to it when he's out delivering in the van. We tune in now. It's a very middle-of-the-road station, bland music interspersed with phone-ins from locals. Once when Craig was listening while on his delivery round, he heard a woman ring in to complain about Sunderland being dirty. He listened for quite a while before he realised it was his mother.

The presenter does a surprisingly informed interview with me, and I play a song live. In the side room beforehand I had a quick discussion with the programme assistant about what song would be suitable—'Not Gary Gilmore's Eyes, no.'

On the way back we park up for a few minutes at the 'Angel of the North' sculpture that stands above the motorway between Newcastle and Sunderland. We walk around it for a bit, the biting wind howling over the outstretched steel arms. Critics say it looks like a ditched aircraft but I like it.

At the Sunderland gig in the evening the room has filled up nicely by the time I get on stage and my set goes well, although most of the chat between numbers seems to fall flat. The only real laugh I get is when I describe going to see the Angel of the North that afternoon, then add, '...nice arse!' Later, Craig explains that the only sure way to get a laugh around here is to say something rude or swear a lot.

11th February.

It's Craig's birthday, but he's already out at work by the time I rouse. Dean and Daniel help me change my guitar strings by twanging them violently and snipping the dangerously sharp pincers at each other.

Dean watches the video of 'Titanic' almost every day and now he wants me to watch it with him. I've never seen it, and reluctantly agree, knowing full well I won't go for this Hollywood rubbish. He starts the video from his favourite part where the ship hits the iceberg, and switches it off an hour later, moments after it sinks, just as I was becoming riveted. I have a hot bath. When Craig arrives back from work, harassed and exhausted from a particularly busy day, there's no time for birthday celebrations. We gulp down something to eat, then load up the hired P.A. that's been sitting in the hallway for the past couple of days and head off for tonight's gig in Northallerton.

An hour later we reach the venue, The Tanner Hop, and carry the equipment up to the first floor bar. I've played this one a couple of times before and it's usually a good crowd. Funny where you find them. Tonight is no different. Afterwards a girl who has been whooping joyously throughout the gig comes up and says 'TV, you are singing what we're all thinking!'

Then we break down all the gear and carry it back downstairs to load back into the van. At two in the morning, Craig's birthday party consists of a couple of cans of lager and a sandwich.

12th February.

I say goodbye to Sharon and the kids, and Craig drives me down to Durham station, where I take the train to Hull. Danny meets me there. It's good to see him again, feels like we're old friends since he drove me and Attila round Germany a few months ago.

The gig's a blast. Nice room, nice P.A., nice crowd—the best I can remember having in Hull—what a pleasure.

We drive the P.A. back to the warehouse and unload it, then drive back to Danny's place, where various Hull oddballs have gathered, and drink and talk into the night. I chat to a descendant of the Huegenots, and fill in a few more gaps in my knowledge of history. 100,000 Huegenots persecuted and killed by the French Catholics 280 years ago.

Last time I stayed here, the evening ended with me spending ten minutes blowing up an airbed. This time there's a pump!

13th February.

Just getting into the touring frame of mind and suddenly part one's over and I'm on the train back to London.

20th February.

I'm on the train to Birmingham. One of the doors doesn't work. Whatever happened to good old *Out Of Order* signs? This one says, *Sorry, this facility is temporarily out of service.*

I'm at the venue in plenty of time for soundcheck. The two guys who own the P.A. and are in the process of setting up, will also be the support act. They bear an uncanny resemblance to Cheech and Chong. When I test the microphone it sounds like I'm speaking through a mouthful of cotton wool. 'Any chance of cleaning it up a bit?' I ask. They think about it as if this possibility hadn't occurred to them. 'Yeah...good idea!!'

When they play their set, it's actually pretty energetic and includes a storming version of Iggy's 'Isolation' which I certainly never expected to hear performed by a couple of old hippies in Digbeth. On the last number, one of them jumps up in the air and goes straight through the stage.

From the next bar I watch someone hammering planks over the hole ready for my set. He says he is John Otway's roadie, but somehow this does not fill me with confidence. Every now and then he gets up and jumps up and down on the stage to see if the planks are holding. While the repairs take place I chat to Chris and his partner Angela who have driven down from their home in Northwich, near Crewe, for tonight's gig and will be driving me back to stay there tonight. It's the first time we've met, even though over the phone we've arranged for a couple of my albums to be released on Chris's label, Ozit Records. I also have a chat with Miles Hunt, from local heroes The Wonderstuff. He's a bit unhappy because he ran over a rabbit on the way here. At least he didn't leave it wounded, though—definitely killed it outright; over with both sets of wheels...*ka-thunk, ka-thunk.*

Just before going onstage I nip into the toilet. Someone follows me into the cubicle waving a copy of 'Crossing The Red Sea' and says, 'Hey, T.V! Would you mind signing this for...oh, um...I'll just let you finish that first.'

Well, the pub's pretty horrible, the sound is atrocious, there's no lighting, and everything on the makeshift stage sways around every time I move so that the microphone is continually smacking me in the teeth, but it's a fun gig with a rowdy, good-natured audience.

Afterwards, I pack up my gear and climb into Chris' big old van which has half a ton of stuff-you-might-need-one-day thrown into the back, and we trundle at a leisurely pace up the motorway. The van heater doesn't work and we're freezing by the time we get to Northwich a couple of hours later, and pull into the housing estate where Chris and Angela live. Chris warns me that the van tends to backfire at neighbour-waking volume when the engine stops; we wait, and sure enough a huge BANG rocks the van and cannons around the houses. We climb out, giggling like naughty schoolchildren.

In the house, as in the van, Chris uses the put-it-in-a-big-pile filing system. There are bits of musical equipment and loudspeakers all over the floor. His talkative fifteen year old son Thomas is still up and wants to grill me about music and equipment and guitars. I'm sleeping in his room tonight, below him on his bunk bed. I pick my way across floor which is strewn with bits of Thomas' musical equipment and more loudspeakers, move a few more loudspeakers off the bed and squeeze into it. As I lie there trapped Thomas shows me everything in the room item by item, including a signed photo of a guitarist called Joe Satriano, until I pretend to fall asleep.

21st February.

Someone comes to fix the backfiring engine, then mid-afternoon Chris, Angela and I head off for Leeds in the big van, which rocks and groans alarmingly in the battering wind. There are warning signs all over the high bridge over the Manchester Ship Canal, and at the far end a police car is parked by a lorry which has had its roof peeled off like a sardine can. We drive to Bacup to drop off a loudspeaker at the home of a guitar maker, then on over the Pennines to pick up Steve, who used to drum in a band called Tractor. When Q magazine reviewed a recent Ozit re-release of a Tractor record and called Steve 'a dropout,' he showed it proudly round every pub in town. We pull up outside his house and the van shudders to a stop.

BANG!!

Not such a good repair job.

Steve climbs in and we head over the hills in a light snowfall to the remote home of a loudspeaker builder. It's dark by the time we get there, and through the lighted windows of his workshop we can see shelves and shelves of...loudspeakers. Chris turns off the engine with a glint in his eye.

BANG!!

The snow really is coming down quite heavily now. We have to take it easy the rest of the way to Leeds, shivering and huddled against the cold. Angela says, 'Never, never, never again.' By the time we get to the venue, we're running late, and the engineer is standing in the doorway looking out for us.

BANG!!

Soundcheck goes quickly, then I go upstairs to the dressing room to record an interview and a couple of songs for a local radio and internet station, don't finish until the support act is halfway through his set. Through the windows at the front of the room I can see the snow starting to lay in the street, and it's still coming down heavily. I'm beginning to worry about the trip back.

Nice gig, everyone sitting at tables listening attentively, no talkers. Despite the weather, some people have travelled from Wigan and Manchester—we'll probably see each other stuck on the side of the road later.

It is a pretty unpleasant journey back and takes us over three and a half hours. Eventually we reach Northwich, no lights on in any of the other houses in the estate.

BANG!!

22nd February.

Just getting into the touring frame of mind and part two's over.

26th February.

I drive up to the Dublin Castle in Camden to play a support slot to a revamped Alternative TV.

The gig is packed out. Afterwards I talk to some of the audience who haven't seen me since 1977 and assumed I was dead. I hand out some flyers for my London gig next week and loads of people say they are keen to come.

At the end of the night, the promoter hands me my fee — 'ere you go mate, fifty quid,' and scurries quickly away. I get home and count it—it's £45.

6th March.

On the phone in the morning Colin tells me that it's a glorious sunny day in Malvern, but by the time I've driven halfway up the M40 snow is starting to sweep down.

Colin is my old bass player from the Explorers. He's helped me set up tonight's gig and is going to be guesting with me on a few numbers. If it goes well, we'll do the same thing in London tomorrow. When I arrive at his house, he's got the bass strapped on and is running through some of the songs. We make our way through the wet snow into town to set up the P.A., soundcheck, and rehearse. It's a worryingly small room, but—no problem!—only about twenty people turn up.

Back at Colin's place we sit around and moan about how difficult it is to get people to come out to gigs. What can you do? Those who come get all fired up about it, the rest never know.

We get to bed late. I leave Colin trying to catch a tiny mouse that has been running terrified around the hall and is now hiding among the shoes.

7th March.

I'm first up and slip quietly out of the house, keen to get on the road so I'll have a few hours at home before tonight's gig. Slashing down with rain all the way back, car behaving a bit erratically. Get caught up in a horrendous queue coming into town because a water main has burst and flooded the North Circular.

Colin arrives at my place about five, after getting stuck in the same traffic jam. We make our way up to the Weavers and soundcheck.

About thirty people turn up. They're a great audience, and listen in rapt attention while I do my stuff, but...all the work that's gone into it, the flyers, the newsletters, Colin travelling all this way...*and* I've got a new album out...

13th March.

So, back to Northwich. At Chris and Angela's house there are lots of new loudspeakers lined up along the hallway. Chris is sitting on the kitchen floor holding a soldering iron, a large monitor speaker box in pieces around him. The morning started inauspiciously when the head gasket on his car blew up. Also in the kitchen is Foggy, who'll be engineering tonight and re-mastering my 1983 album Channel Five with me tomorrow on Chris's computer.

We take the van—no longer backfiring, sadly—crammed with P.A. gear, Foggy, Chris, three kids, and me—and a loose speaker box sliding about on the roof—over to the gig, a pub called The Farmer's Arms, and load in, everyone helping haul the gear.

Looks like a typical pub audience, half of them have probably never heard of me. I talk with some of them about the tourist potential of Northwich. Well, there's the salt museum.

Things improve by the time I get onstage. I recognise quite a few familiar faces from my mailing list, and it's a pretty good, reasonably packed gig.

Midnight, and we're loading all the gear back into the van. I'm cringing inwardly as a group of lads at the other end of the car park hang out of the sunroof of their car, music pounding, headlights blazing, and wave their arms in the air shouting 'Smack my bitch up!' I make a face at Chris.

'They're coming back to our place,' he smiles. He's not joking.

14th March.

It's a late start and well into the afternoon before computer problems are sorted out and Foggy can start work on the mastering. We break for something to eat early evening, then Chris and Angela decide they're going to turn in—they're both exhausted and Angela's got to work tomorrow. Foggy and I carry on for a while at ultra-low volume, then as it gets later we switch to headphones. In a house full of loudspeakers.

15th March.

Chris drives me back to the station and suddenly this rag-bag tour is over.

8. LAND OF MILK AND HONEY. AND MONEY.

31st March

It's Switzerland, so I pack extra jumpers and a big coat and stagger around the airport under the weight of my luggage only to arrive in Zurich to find the sun blazing and Mediterranean temperatures. Spend the afternoon basking in a T-shirt on the balcony of René and Mariann's flat in Winterthur.

Late afternoon we head for the venue, the Gaswerk, run by a group of young volunteers. There's a quick soundcheck, then we sit amiably around a long table with the staff, who chat in a hybrid Swiss German that I can't understand.

Half an hour before the gig and there are only eight people in the venue. And I thought I was big in Winterthur. By showtime it's up to about thirty, if you include the crew and the people running the place, but there's a good atmosphere and it turns into a very nice and very long concert.

1st April

Breakfast with René and Mariann, and it's time to learn a few words of Swiss German. Now I can confidently order breakfast wherever I go in Switzerland, and also understand anyone who happens to be talking about breakfast.

Spend some time sunning on the balcony then René drives me into Zurich to soundcheck for tonight's gig. Get caught in the Easter weekend traffic and only just make it for 3:30 soundcheck.

There's no sound engineer, so I sort out the P.A. myself, then we head back to Winterthur, where Rene whips up an asparugus strudel you'd kill for in a restaurant.

We're back at the club shortly before nine. There's just time for one of the locally-brewed 'Voll Mond' (Full Moon) beers before I start. Plenty more people than last night, and a good gig.

Afterwards a German guy gives me a fanzine from 1981 with The Explorers on the cover, playing in Mannheim. I remember this gig—there were only five people in the audience. Who says things aren't getting better?

Get back to Winterthur dead tired. It's full moon, though, and I can't sleep. Maybe I should have knocked myself out with a few more Full Moon beers. At about seven in the morning I drift off into a bad dream where no-one is quite who I thought they were, and wake up twenty minutes later.

2nd April.

Before leaving for Thun, we load the rented P.A. into the car for the Basel gig in two days time so we don't have to return to Winterthur for it tomorrow. After a couple of hours we stop off to visit René's brother and sister-in-law, a few miles outside Thun. We get an effusive welcome and I'm treated like a member of the family. I'm coming to realise that the Swiss are nothing like the stereotype I have of them. Then I discover René's brother is a watchmaker. Hah!

We unload the P.A. into these nice people's living room, then head off for Thun. On the way into the town we drive past the hotel I'll be staying in tonight, *Hotel Emmental*—hah!— then find ourselves passing it a few more times until we finally locate the club, Café Mokka.

The club is a quite a place. Above the outside alleyway hangs a rowing boat with two dummies in it waving cheerfully. Inside, every square inch is crazily decorated with art, dolls, plastic flowers, candles, coloured lights and collected bits and pieces. Every corner is a grotto to spend hours staring into.

Club manager Beat knows what it's like for groups on the road. After soundcheck he lays out the exact schedule for the night: when we will eat, when I can check into the hotel, when I play. It helps.

After the gig, René, Mariann and I sit for a few hours in the dressing room while Beat regales us with tales of the history of the club and the bands that pass through it. He is particularly contemptuous of bands who travel in Nightliner buses.

'The way it happens is: the Nightliner pulls in and one of the roadies gets out; he's been stuck on this thing for hours and the first thing he wants is a quality shit, so he goes down to our nice comfortable toilets and stinks the place out, then another ten roadies go down there for the same thing. Then the sound engineers. Then the rest of the crew. Some nice young ladies arrive at the club from work ready for their evening out, go down to the ladies room to do themselves up and it's, '...*oh my GOD!!*'

He also describes how he solved the problem of drunken youths urinating in the alleyway. First he put up the rowing boat to give it an arty environment. Then he strung up some daylight bulbs overhead so it always feels like daytime. Then he fixed up some large mirrors on the walls so that as the offenders stagger towards them, they look up and see a drunken idiot about to piss in an alleyway staring at them, think, 'Is that really me?' and move on to a less challenging location.

We also talk of more salubrious subjects. I've been having this urge to go up an Alp while I'm here, and René and Mariann pump Beat for information on which one is best. We look over some maps and he recommends a couple to us — one quite a long drive from here which is usually clear, and another—the Stockhorn—which is nearer but often cloudy. He tells us about an American rock band who came over recently with the same request: he sent them up to an Alp to do the tourist thing, but within moments of arriving a paraglider took off from in front of them. The flier had forgotten to attach his gear properly and plunged straight over the edge. His body was brought up by helicopter and laid out in front of the restaurant.

Had been hoping to catch up with some sleep tonight, but turn in at about 4 a.m. Have to get out of the hotel by 10:30 if we're going to get up an Alp.

3rd April

A good breakfast and a quick walk around the picturesque Middle Ages town centre then meet up with René and Mariann. Yes, we're going to do the Alp thing.

I'm prepared. I have the thick coat and wooly hat borrowed from Beat, and gaze at the summit with the look of a seasoned climber. We get into it the cable car with three skiers who regard us with suspicion. They get out at the first station and head off to the slopes, while we make our way round to the lift up to the summit. A man takes our tickets and lets us into the car, then hops nimbly out and shuts the door saying, 'I'll leave you to it, it's a bit too dangerous for me.'

Ho-ho. The Swiss sense of humour.

These things really go high. It's thrilling watching the wall of rock drop below us, the snowy slopes on either side as we clank into the top station. There's no-one else around. We wander leisurely up the zig-zag path to the summit but within minutes thick bands of swirling mist sweep up over the mountain and completely block out the view. We throw a few snowballs and shuffle back down to the restaurant, where we sit with cups of coffee under a giant panoramic photo of what we had hoped to see.

Drive back to Thun to give Beat back his coat and hat. 'Which one did you go to?' he asks me.

'Stockhorn, but it was covered in clouds.'

'HA!' he roars, 'HA-HA!! What did I tell you?' He slaps his palm into his inner elbow, 'Fuckin...TOURISTS!!'

We stop off at René's brother's place to pick up the P.A. then drive to Basel and set it up in the club, only to find it gives out a lengthy ear-splitting whine everytime a tram goes by outside, which is often. There's nothing to be done, apart from knock out the Basel tram network central power supply, so we shrug our shoulders and go out with the owner of the club to get something to eat.

At the start of the gig I plug my guitar cable into the desk but there's no sound coming through the system. I stare dumbly at it, twiddling with various knobs while the audience look on, bemused. René and the club owner come and stare too. I just knew there was going to be a problem with this P.A. system. After what seems a very long time we see what it is: I have forgotten to plug the other end of my guitar cable into my guitar.

Play a two hour set, then we drive back to Winterthur.

4th April

René and Mariann lay on a fantastic breakfast with Swiss muesli—hah!—bread and coffee, orange juice and sparkling wine. They gather together some Swiss chocolate—hah!—eggs to take back to Britain, then take me to the airport where they buy me some Swiss mountain cheese—hah!—and give me a present to open on my birthday tomorrow.

5th April

It's Swiss honey. Hah!! What a very pleasant few days in Switzerland—I shall return.

I am 43 years old.

9. A RIDICULOUS IDEA.

13th April.

There are instructions on my hotel room door that are difficult to follow: *It is forbidden to drink alcohol or stay drunk everywhere else but in your room.*

A ridiculous idea that started when a group of Finnish fans approached me after a gig in Germany has become a reality: I'm in Finland. Last night one of the organisers, Tommi, e-mailed me to say, 'it's a shame you missed the wonderful winter. This year Lapland reached a new Finnish record of minus 52 degrees Celsius.' He's concerned how I'm going to spend my free afternoon in Tampere and has a suggestion: 'you could try a swim in one of the ice holes.' Or I could hit myself over the head with a brick.

At six in the evening Jukka, who runs a local record label, takes me to meet one of his bands, Punk Lurex O.K., at their nearby rehearsal room. They're going to be the support band for the tour, and we're going to practice three Adverts songs together to finish the gigs with. The band have learned the songs faithfully from the records, which means they're far too slow. We try them again faster and they sound great.

While Punk Lurex carry on with their rehearsal, Jukka and I go for something to eat. Chatting with him is a good chance to get an introduction to Finland. He explains some of the curiosities of the language: there are no prepositions, no articles, and no distinction between genders. This explains why people here keep saying things to me like, 'I am going home to my wife. He is expecting me.' Tampere is just a small town compared to London, Jukka tells me. The big headline news today: 40 kilos of potatoes stolen!

Jukka tells me about a festival that happens every summer under the midnight sun in Lapland. Sounds interesting. I feel another ridiculous idea coming on.

We go to a bar with the band and I make the mistake of trying to keep pace with Finnish drinkers. Later. shrugging off offers to walk me back to my hotel, I set off confidently on my own but soon get completely lost. I set down my guitar case and bag of cables to consult the map I have in my inside pocket, but as I unfold it a gust of wind whips it out of my hand and propels it under a barred gate. As it flies along the dark alleyway out of sight I realise I don't know the name or address of my hotel.

After tramping around for a while I finally recognise the street, and then with some relief the hotel, but when I get to the room I realise I have left the bag of cables by the alley and have to dash back out to get it.

I have forgotten to pack any toothpaste.

14th April.

Sleep late, then go and get a coffee and leaf through a guide book to see what I'm going to do today. So much choice: there's the Coffee Cup Museum, for example ('more than 1200 coffee cups. Also old bicycles.') or the Finnish Refrigeration Museum ('History of the refrigeration business, unique objects.') I'm most tempted by the Milk Churn Platform Museum ('Always Open!') but it's too far away and I head off instead to Särkäniemi park, which boasts the highest observation tower in Finland. Halfway there I reach the edge of one of the lakes surrounding Tampere. It's a breathtaking view, a vast grey expanse of ice stretching out to dark bristles of forest on the horizon.

The observation tower, a concrete monstrosity looming over the park, is shut for the winter.

Back at the hotel I put new strings on the guitar and watch a few minutes of an old black-and-white Finnish film drama on T.V. that involves lots of people tramping around log cabins in snow shoes and chopping down trees. Then I make my way over to a record shop a few streets away where Punk Lurex are going to present their new album by playing a few songs acoustically. They've asked me to play a couple too.

After this little concert, some local delicacies are handed round. There seem to be a lot of reindeer balls left by the time I leave.

The venue for tonight is the old customs house, the front wall still pocked with bullet holes from the battles between the Reds and Whites earlier this century when Finland was still part of Russia. People come trickling in while the first band play, and there's a couple of hundred there by the time Punk Lurex O.K. get onstage. I play around midnight. It goes well, and the three Adverts numbers the band play with me at the end are great fun and get everyone up on their feet.

At two-thirty in the morning we're thrown out of the club and wander around the rainy streets of Tampere trying to find somewhere to get a drink. We end up in a dreadful disco lifted straight out of the seventies discussing how far we have to travel to the gigs on this tour. I discover an interesting fact: in Lapland there is a measurement system based on the distance between where a reindeer pisses. Lapland is calling.

15th April.

I'm walking around in the rain trying to find Jyrki's flat. Jyrki used to be in a band whose first album contained a song about how the Adverts were the greatest punk band, and whose cover showed them posing in front of the poster for 'One Chord Wonders.' These days Jyrki's an artist and I'm going to see some of his stuff in the Tampere art gallery and look around the town with him.

We take a walk to Tampere cathedral, built in the bizarre 'National Romantic' style in and decorated by local artist Hugo Simberg. Inside he has painted a huge mural stretching around three walls, showing a procession of young boys struggling under the weight of a vast garland. In a smaller picture, hooded skeletal figures representing death tenderly pick flowers from a flourishing bush. High above the church, in the exact centre of the roof is a painting of a giant coiled snake, its jaws stretched around an apple bearing Simberg's initials.

Next stop is the Lenin Museum. Lenin attended the Tampere conference in this very building in 1905, and there are still historical links between the city and him. Tampere is very proud of the connection. Recently, when communism began to lose favour in Russia and it was proposed that Lenin's fast-decomposing body should be taken off display, Tampere said, 'we'll have it!'

The museum is very kitsch; anything with even the most tenuous link to Lenin gets in— a chair he once sat in, a map of the route he took from his lodgings to the conference, a hologram of a camera that was used to take a photo of him. In the gift shop you can buy a plastic Lenin comb.

There's just time for a quick look at Jyrki's constructions in the art gallery before I have to rush back to the hotel to meet Punk Lurex for the drive to Helsinki. It's a long trip past miles of frozen lakes and forests, pockets of snow lying by the road, and we get to the club late afternoon.

Tommi is celebrating his 40th birthday, and arrives with a cake iced with the words 'No Time To Be 41'. When I get back from checking in to my hotel, the cake is up on the bar of the club. A few slices have been eaten and it now reads, 'No Time To Be'.

The gig is a crowded, steamy, full-on success, made slightly uncomfortable by the fact that the band and I all have to cram into one of the more uncomfortable dressing rooms I've experienced—a short flight of stairs at the side of the stage, blocked off at ceiling level.

Before we leave, the promoter thanks me for the gig and asks where we're playing tomorrow. I tell him it's Turku. He looks at me with a steady gaze and says, 'Four words— The. Arsehole. Of. Finland.'

16th April.

After turning in at 4:30 last night, it's a severe effort to get out of bed, but I want to see at least a bit of Helsinki before we leave for the arsehole of Finland.

Great globs of sleet are dropping out of the sky as I wander up to the imposing white cathedral set high up on steps looking out over a large square, then I head down to the harbour, and take a look at the Russian Orthodox-style church with its fairy-tale onion domes, once used to stand in as Russia for the filming of Gorky Park. Get back to the hotel at midday and Punk Lurex pick me up and we drive over to the state-run radio station, where we're going to be interviewed. The presenter tells us that it will be two separate interviews, 'Punk Lurex will be for our punk programme, TV Smith will be for our culture programme.'

Then back to a bar in the centre of town for an interview with Marcus, who writes for a music magazine. He promises a rave review of last night's gig. His questions come from a slightly odd angle, though: 'If your music was a building, what sort of building would it be? Would you become a stand-up comedian instead of a musician if, say, your left hand got chopped off?'

It's a three hour drive to Turku, and we see an awful lot of forests and frozen lakes by the time we pull up to the venue at about 7:30. Depressing kind of place: dingy linoleum floor, low ceiling, no stage, big pillar in front of where we're going to play.

While we wait for soundcheck, the venue prepare something vegetarian for us to eat. It's small round greasy potato cakes, accompanied by large flat greasy potato cakes.

Meanwhile the first members of the audience are coming in. Tommi, his friend Hessu and more of the Helsinki crew arrive, and present me with 'something to prepare me for my forthcoming Lapland concert' (this seems to be a definite now, although I still haven't been told anything about it)—a Finnish dictionary. Naturally, the first thing I look up is 'Fuck Off!' and I'm able to regale everyone in earshot with the phrase *'Suksi Suolle!'* This seems less effective when I'm told that the literal translation is, 'Go ski to the swamp!'

The gig is good, but when it gets to the songs with the band at the end of the set, we're told we're out of time and are only able to play one. Bit of an anticlimax.

Boy, it's a long drive back to Tampere. I mention that I have a desire to see a moose while I'm here, but drummer Sami tells me that you have to go into the forest at sunrise to stand any chance. He's come across them a couple of times while out on early morning runs, and says it was an awesome sight.

As we drive down the dark, snowy roads the band start up singing some Finnish folk songs in the back of the van. It's all very atmospheric — though less so when the choice of songs moves onto the Rubettes, the Mamas and the Papas, Johnny Logan, Simon and Garfunkel, and a Finnish version of the old Brian Hyland classic, *('I'll send you all my love every day in a letter...sealed with a fish.')*

Back at the hotel at 5:30. I'm never going to get up in time to see a moose.

17th April.

The first attempt at breakfast involves an U.M.M.—an Unexpected Meat Moment—when an apparently innocent cheese roll turns out to contain the unthinkable. Must learn the Finnish for 'meat.'

The band arrive with Tommi for the long, long drive to Vaasa.

Forests, frozen lakes, fields, forests, forests, frozen lakes, fields, forests. Arrive 6:30.

Riitta lives in Vaasa, not far from the club, so we go to her place to relax for a couple of hours before the gig. We have some coffee and beer, then Riitta picks up her accordion and plays a waltz, a mazurka, a polka and a polska.

Back at the club someone comes into the dressing room claiming he is my biggest fan in Finland. 'Do you have ten Marks?' he inquires.

'Er—yes.'

'Will you give them to me?'

'Er—no.'

'O.K. But it was punk to ask.'

Tommi edges him out of the dressing room.

Punk Lurex play and the sound is a dreadful mush. A Mohican punk who has been blowing a hooter all the way through the gig gets up on stage and rips up a prayer book page by page in front of the band.

The trip back seems to take forever. A hideous mixture of drinks is swilled and all manner of bollox talked. But as we reach Tampere, those of us still awake are rewarded with the magical sight of a fuzzy golden sun rising over eerie mists hanging above the melting lakes. I'm back in the hotel at 7:30. Too late and too early to sleep.

18th April.

Jukka knocks on the door just as I've finished packing my stuff ready for the afternoon flight. We go and sit outside in the sunshine at a bar next to the venue, the temperature a startling 21 degrees, and chat about the possibility of me playing the Lapland festival. 'Ah, Lapland,' he sighs, 'home of the lap-top.'

Before I head for the airport we walk over to the old brick Pyynikki observation tower, much lower than the one I failed to go up on my first day here, but with much more character. We stand on top of it in the warm breeze, looking out over the lakes, and Jukka points out a small island of ice in the centre of the fast-thawing water. 'In an hour, that will be gone,' he says. 'Spring has arrived.'

10. THE USUAL

25th May. Gütersloh.

I'm standing in the back bar of a tiny venue in Gütersloh on the first day of a three week tour of Germany, looking through the contracts with PamP, the singer in Garden Gang, who will be touring with me. On every contract under the heading 'Accommodation,' the word 'hotel' has been struck out and replaced with the phrase *wie üblich* ('the usual'). From my tour here last year I know that often means sleeping on the floor of some stranger's flat, usually uncomfortable and cramped—and this time there are seven of us to find space for: myself, the four members of Garden Gang, sound man Tommy, and Klaus who runs my website.

'Except for here,' says PamP, drawing out the Berlin contract, 'we've got a hotel for this one.'

'That doesn't say "hotel",' I point out, 'that says "hostel."'

Even though the flyers for tonight's gig were accidentally printed with tomorrow's date on them, the bar is still packed by the time we play. Afterwards we load all the gear into the back of PamP's van, he and I get in the front, and everyone else squeezes into the Garden Gang car. We follow the guy letting us sleep at his place to a small town a few kilometers away where he lives in an attic flat. Once we've cleared some of the cassettes, C.D.s, old fanzines, plates with leftover food stuck to them, and empty bottles out of the way, there's just enough room for us all to lay out our sleeping bags.

26th May. Hamburg.

By the time we wake up, the guy who owns the flat is already out to work. We start a monumental clean-up operation, clearing out the rubbish into recycling sacks, tidying up, and doing all the washing and drying up. By the time we've finished the place is sparkling. When the owner gets back tonight he is going to be really pissed off.

I always enjoy playing Hamburg: usually the venues are packed with enthusiastic audiences, and last time I was there I was supporting Die Toten Hosen so I'm expecting a good turnout again. But after negotiating endless miles of roadworks on the autobahn and finally arriving at the Molotov club in the late afternoon, we soundcheck and wait for an audience that never comes.

After playing to a near-empty club I sit in the cramped dressing room with my friend Holm who has driven up from an airfield in Oppershausen where he spends his free time building and flying gliders. He has offered to fly me to tomorrow's gig in his two seater motor glider, and we are studying the possible routes on a large plastic-covered map spread out over the table in front of us. We find the nearest airfield and agree a time to meet up there in the morning.

27th May. Braunschweig.

It's a glorious, cloudless day. We spent the night with PamP's uncle in the suburbs and he's now driving us out through the countryside to the Uetersen airfield which is already shimmering in the heat. We pull up at a small cafe and watch Holm's red and white B-Falke plane swoop giddily down out of the sky and bounce gently over the grass towards us.

Close up, those planes are flimsier than they look. If you press the panels along the side, they bend. I try and look confident as I climb in, and find myself sitting on an uncomfortable cramped wooden bench. Holm squeezes in next to me, helps strap on my safety belts, sticks a sun hat on me, then slips an old headset over that so we can communicate above the noise of the engine once we're in the air. He pulls the clear perspex hood down over us, makes a few checks, then starts the engine. PamP and his uncle retreat back to the car.

Interesting. You feel much more exposed in these things than on a commercial flight, but it's very exhilarating. Mind you, I'm taking a lot of care not to touch the joystick in front of me, or the pedals at my feet. We're up in the big blue sky, and Holm has the map open, showing me the intended route once more, explaining how we have to climb to certain altitudes in specific airspaces, and make detours around military training areas. Most of the navigation is done by referring to the map and looking out for landmarks below: 'We fly above this autobahn as far as the canal, then follow that to the third bridge, where we bear left over the railway line...' It takes about ten minutes to climb to 4,000 feet, and when we get there it looks like the ground is a HELL OF A LONG WAY DOWN.

We're only travelling at around 80 miles an hour. 'Loud, slow, and uncomfortable,' laughs Holm, over the roar of static in the earphones. Half of the stuff he says to me I can't make out, and I simply nod idiotically, hoping he hasn't just asked me to press the 'Don't Crash' button.

An hour later we make an impressively smooth landing at Oppershausen for a short break before the final leg to Brunswick. We climb out and Holm shows me round the workshop. I nervously point out a glider with a smashed-up wing. 'Yeah,' he says, 'we were towing it up the autobahn on a trailer and a car hit it.'

We take off again for a twenty minute flight to Braunschweig, then I say goodbye to Holm and take a bus into the town. Nothing's happening at the venue yet, and my guitar and bags won't be here until Garden Gang arrive, so I pass the time by taking a long walk in a nearby park where hundreds of people are out sunning themselves. When I get back to the club, the Garden Gang van is parked outside and the band are in deep discussion with Markus, the promoter. They're not sure if they're going to be able to play tonight because the club is so small they can't fit their gear on the stage. Eventually they agree on using only some of their equipment and playing a more acoustic set. We soundcheck, and hang around in the backstage room while the bar fills up.

The gig is cramped, hot and energetic. Afterwards we go back to Markus's house, where we split up into two rooms to sleep. After only three days, manoeuvring for floor space is already well-advanced and mental notes are being taken about who snores.

28th May. Berlin.

Markus leaves early, the rest of us hang around and linger over a breakfast of bread and cheese and coffee. Some hours later we finally close the door on the flat, and at that moment bass player Mick realises his stage suit is still inside. Too late.

Hours spent sitting in traffic on the autobahns. The sun beats down so the car is like a furnace, and we're soaked through with sweat by the time we reach Berlin, late for soundcheck.

The Pfefferburg is a huge club and the contrast between the vast empty floor space as we walk in and the crowded beer garden outside is worrying. Luckily the small amount of people that eventually arrive react extremely enthusiastically. I give everything and come off stage dehydrated and barely able to stand.

This heat is phenomenal. Even at 3:30 in the morning, on the way back to the hostel, it's still 22 degrees. Surprise: the hostel is clean, welcoming, and has beds, although the fitted sheets are so small that the thin mattress adopts a banana shape when you put them on. We have a drink in the reception area and by the time we head upstairs it's getting light outside.

29th May. Herford.

It's happening again. A nice club but virtually no-one in. I elect to go on first as the only people in the club are a few teenage girls dressed up for a disco and I don't reckon they'll think much of my solo set. Good decision: they sit around looking confused while I play, but when Garden Gang come on at least they get a chance to dance.

I didn't get time to eat before the gig, but the band say the food was really good. I'm ravenous now so I wander downstairs to the bar to look for something. Food is no longer being served. Instead, twenty people are watching a festival of Monty Python films dubbed into German. It's the one where Terry Jones eats so much he explodes.

Back at promoter Rudolph's large, clean, and comfortable house I'm told that I have a room of my own up on the top floor, the chance to catch up on some sleep. Except we open a bottle of wine and sit around chatting until the sun comes up.

30th May. Regensburg.

We breakfast out in the garden. It's already hot and sunny, looks promising for today's open-air gig in Regensburg, but it means another sweaty and uncomfortable journey.

The gig is a curiosity—a battle-of-the-bands contest held on two stages in a shopping centre car park. Garden Gang have played it twice before; once PamP won the 'best dressed' prize, next time the band came second in the best band category. This time they're hoping to win. I'm along to play ten minutes as a 'special guest.' PamP and I get totally lost trying to find our way into Regensburg and when we eventually pull up into the shopping centre under the giant Toys R Us sign there are just ten minutes left before Garden Gang are due to start. The rest of the band arrived ages ago and are standing around looking anxious. PamP bowls out of the van and straight onto the stage.

At the end of the day Garden Gang don't win, but I'm asked to stand on the stage while the prize-giving and endless speeches go on, then I'm presented with a certificate from middle Bavaria thanking me for being a special guest in the category ROCKMUSIK. I am so proud.

Tomorrow and the next day are days off, so we decide to head back to the Munich area now. A couple of hours later I'm sitting with PamP and Andi in their flat in a village in Bavaria, drinking the delicious local Weizen beer and talking bollox long into the night, until the sun comes up and the birds are singing.

May 31st.

Day Off

June 1st.

Day Off

June 2nd. Zwiesel.

On the way out of the village PamP and I stop off to buy some bottles of liquid fennel honey, made by the monks in the local cloisters, and great for the voice. We're in the pretty town of Zwiesel by mid-afternoon, sitting round a table in the youth centre where the gig will take place, eating some good vegetarian food. The heat is stifling and I feel my energy level falling, even though I've caught up on some sleep over the last two days. I drink a lot of coffee and then feel tired with a jittery edge. Someone comes up and asks me if I'm from Augsburg, as I'm speaking with an Augsburg accent. When I tell him, no I'm from London, a glimmer of recognition comes into his eyes and he says, 'Aah, you must be the guy from that punk band, The Antwerps.'

Garden Gang will headline again tonight as they have played here a few times before and have a following in the area. Unfortunately the guy they usually stay with is away, so the only clue to where we'll be sleeping is the phrase 'wie üblich' in the contract. How I hate those words.

To stave off the pre-gig boredom, PamP and I go for a walk through the town, famous for its glass-blowing and steam brewery, then along the riverside and up the hill to a church that looks out over the surrounding countryside. In a hall by the town square a Bavarian band in lederhosen is pumping out some tunes to smartly-dressed old folk on fold-up chairs. We can hear it drifting through the air as we make our way back down to the youth centre.

The gig is painfully hot. No air moving, and I'm on the point of collapse by the time I get offstage, but I seem to have won quite a few new fans.

Garden Gang play to a hero's welcome and much dancing. A couple of numbers into their set I go outside and sit under the veranda to get some air. The weather has just broken, and rain is shafting down, lightning flashing around the sky and the wonderful fresh wind switching around all points of the compass. I sit there for a while just gulping down air and feeling the sweat dry tinglingly cool on my skin.

Back in the hall the gig is over, but most of the band are still pumped up on adrenaline and keen to keep partying. They make plans to go to Zwiesel's only disco, The Colosseum, to wind down. I pass, and sit at the bar of the club with sinking heart as I watch seven mattresses being dragged out of a side room and spread out across the stage and the floor.

PamP and Tommy also decide they can live without the disco. We sit round a table with the venue organisers for a while with a Weizen, grumbling about the prospect of being woken by the rest of the band's noisy return later in the night. Eventually the promoter comes up with an alternative — there's floor space in a rehearsal room just down the hill. At 3:00 PamP and I shoulder a mattress each and head down there in the rain, but Tommy has to stay to make sure only the band get back into the youth centre, 'otherwise,' the promoter tells us, 'half the disco will end up here.'

We close the double sound-proofed doors behind us, move some speakers out of the way, and lay out our sleeping bags. When the light goes out, the place is as still and silent as the grave.

3rd June. Vienna.

There is a banging noise and the creak of heavy doors being opened, then a shaft of sunlight falls across me. The silhouette of a woman appears against the sun. 'Eine Frage...ist da irgendwas los?' (*Is there anything happening here?*)

For a moment I don't know where I am and think it's the maid come to clean the hotel room, then I see the speaker cables and drumkit next to my head. I stare groggily at the mystery woman, unable to speak, and she retreats with an apology, heaving the double doors shut behind her. I go back to sleep.

At 10:30 I get up and carry my mattress back up to the club, leaving PamP sleeping. Tommy is there alone, brewing coffee. He stayed up until 5:00, but none of the others came back. The promoters arrive shortly after and lead me up the hill to a house where I can use the shower. By the time I get back to the club the rest of the band are there. They had a hilarious time at the disco, which played non-stop seventies rock classics, and met someone who invited them all to sleep at his place afterwards.

Tonight we play Vienna. It takes about an hour winding through the hilly roads through the forests of lower Bavaria before we hit the autobahn and cross the border into Austria. The heat is building again and it's another uncomfortable three hour journey. By the time we get to Vienna we have clocked up over 3,000 kilometres on the tour so far. At the Chelsea club I say hello to all my friends there, and start asking around to see if anyone knows where I can stay tonight.

Worried about the turnout again—it's a public holiday, and great weather, which is bad for attracting people into clubs. I go for a walk and there's no-one in the bars or cafés, Vienna is like a ghost town.

People trickle in as Garden Gang play, then later, as the evening cools, enough arrive to add up to a decent turnout — still less than hoped for, but what quality! Favourite gig so far.

And now, as it approaches two in the morning, we have to figure out where to sleep. Drummer Henrik's staying with a friend. Co-promoter Rainer will let me stay at his flat, and reluctantly agrees to let PamP stay there too—he can't put up any more or his girlfriend, who doesn't know they'll be having guests, will kill him. That leaves four. Eventually it's arranged that they can sleep on the floor of an office in town, but PamP has to drive Rainer there to let them in. There's only space for two in the van, so when they return to pick me up I swap places with Rainer and he takes a taxi back to his place, with PamP and I following. There's nowhere to park, so we have to leave the van outside a garage with a note on the window saying where we're staying.

It's late, very late. Already the two days off seem like just a dream.

4th June. Rosenheim.

I'm vaguely aware of the phone ringing around 6:00 and PamP struggling downstairs to move the van, but manage not to come fully awake until a pressing urge to use the loo gets me up two hours later. In the hallway I bump into Rainer's girlfriend, who I've never met before, on the way back from the shower. We both stand there awkwardly for a moment, semi-dressed, then mumble a hello and carry on.

At 10:30 it's time to leave. We phone to check on the rest of the band, then set off. PamP and I are both really feeling the fatigue now and getting a bit foolish, slugging down the Fennel Honey like secret drinkers, talking endless rubbish and offering up polite rounds of applause to good bits of scenery along the way. A small cheer as we re-enter Bavaria, now my second home. I have the certificate to prove it.

The venue is a small bare room with a low stage, on the outskirts of Rosenheim. We drink some coffee at the tables and benches outside while waiting for the rest of the band to turn up, then carry the gear in and set up.

After soundcheck we're all famished and sit down in the bar for one of the Bavarian specialities on offer from the venue — Kässpatzl, kind of baked noodles with cheese and onion. Dessert is elderflower sprigs deep fried in batter and dusted with sugar.

This fatigue can be a good thing. I'm in a loose mood by the time I get onstage and talk a lot between the songs which seems to get everyone on my side. Cooling down outside afterwards, I'm taught a few new Bavarian expressions by the promoter and repeat them liberally to everyone's amusement. This is almost as much fun as the gig; in fact, with half the audience now sitting around us on the benches tuning in and cracking up with laughter it almost *is* the gig.

We drive back to PamP's place and spend another hour talking bollox. Get to bed at 5:00.

5th June. Munich.

Dreamed I was playing a gig with a jacket on that was so big I couldn't reach the guitar properly and kept playing the wrong chords.

Everything I own smells of beer and sweat, so the first thing I do after I wake up and shower around midday is throw some things into the washing machine. Then PamP, Andi and I sit outside and have a leisurely breakfast of organic muesli and strawberries. Feel almost fit again, although if I lay down I would be asleep in seconds.

As we drive out of the village, PamP points out that it is one of the rare days when you can see the Alps far off past Munich. Here they call these special weather conditions *Föhn*, literally 'hair-dryer,' and that's what it feels like: so hot and heavy you can hardly breathe, no sign of a storm coming to break it down.

This is the big one for Garden Gang, a home town show at an all-night festival in the well-known Backstage club. Important for me too, of course, but I'm so tired I'm beyond nervous. We get to the Backstage mid afternoon and I take a look around. There's a large room where we'll be playing, and an even bigger club across the courtyard where there'll be a performance of The Rocky Horrorshow. They're rehearsing it now and it sounds pretty dire. Outside there's a lot of space for the ubiquitous benches and tables, and various stalls, food areas, and a space with reggae coolly pumping out. Looks good.

Worried about people staying out in the beer garden, but by the time I get onstage the place is packed with a very excitable audience, who immediately start dancing, cheering and singing along. Great concert.

In the backstage area I'm joined by the promoter from yesterday who's driven up for the gig. 'It was great,' she says, 'but you should have talked more. Yesterday it was spilling out of you *like a fountain!*'

After the gig, the venue turns into a horrendous thrash death punk metal disco and the night gets long. Eventually the gear is loaded and we have to thread the car through throngs of people who are slow to get out of the way. Outside, the exit is blocked by police taking down the numbers of illegally parked vehicles.

Back at PamP's place, the bloody birds are singing. It's 4:44 when I crawl into my sleeping bag.

6th June.

Day Off

7th June. Stuttgart.

Supporting a band called Citizen Fish tonight. We had been booked to play separate gigs, but fearing small turnouts the promoters decided to cut their losses and combine the two.

As we pull in to park the car outside the venue, Citizen Fish are lurching out, all with the same shellshocked 'band on three week tour' expressions that we're wearing.

The gig's fun, and finally a bit cooler than the previous nights. I feel fit and in good form now I can breathe again onstage.

Accommodation is 'wie üblich.' Tonight that means following the promoter through the streets of Stuttgart, spending half an hour trying to park, then being taken up to a flat he used to live in, which now lies empty while the landlord looks for a new tenant.

Seven of us are crammed into two small rooms. At 4:30, I'm the last to turn in and feel my way in the dark to a sofa bed that creaks and groans every time I move. Trying not to wake the others, I lie frozen in one position and attempt to sleep.

8th June. Koblenz.

Just before nine in the morning someone comes along in the loudest lorry in the world, drives a bulldozer off the back of it and proceeds to scrape the surface off the pavement, while a colleague rolls a shopping trolley full of broken bottles up and down a cobbled street for ever. Well, anyway, that's what it sounded like.

I get a quick shower before the rush, then we slowly gather for a cramped breakfast around the kitchen table. At one point the landlord turns up with a prospective tenant for the flat. He's rather surprised to find us there.

PamP and I get in the car, and toast with the Fennel Honey bottles.

We've been warned that tonight's gig in Koblenz is very small, so it might not be possible for Garden Gang to play. We arrive to find it's basically the back room of a bar, no stage, tiny P.A. Theoretically there's room for the band to set up, but the promoter tells us that an old lady who lives upstairs phones the police if it gets noisy, so they can't risk it. Tommy gets me a decent sound sorted out in soundcheck, then I go for a walk around the old town and sit by the banks of the Mosel for a while.

Back at the venue, I put out some tables and chairs, and light some candles to try and give the cold stone room a bit of ambience. People gather, and the gig is very nice, more of a relaxed and intimate acoustic feel than the recent frantic ones.

The bar closes at 2:00, then we follow Dirk, who usually does the sound here, back to his student lodgings where we all have to find space to bed down in the common room.

9th June. Düsseldorf.

People are stamping through the room at some unearthly hour, slamming the doors and talking loudly. And it's the coldest room in Germany. We all wake up shivering, then have to battle to bag a place in the scuzzy lock-less bathroom and shower stall.

It's a picturesque, and mercifully short, drive along the Rhein, past the Lorelei to Düsseldorf, and we arrive at the Q-stall—first gig on my last German tour—early. We get straight into setting up the gear, then walk through the old town with Opa, the promoter, to a comfortable restaurant where we sit for a while and get something to eat. Guitarist Tom and I do a mock-up of the soundcheck on the table using anything to hand, and have the salt and pepper pots saying 'one, two...' and complaining about the monitors. Just four gigs to go.

Great vibe about tonight; the Q-stall is packed to the seams with people, including three of Die Toten Hosen. Garden Gang play the gig of their lives and lots of people come up to me while they're on saying how much they're enjoying it. By the time they've finished I'm gagging to get going myself, and start at the earliest opportunity.

The gig's a thrill.

And then afterwards we have to arrange the bloody 'wie üblich.' Most of the band are going to squeeze in with Opa. I'd been hoping that PamP and I could stay with Sven from JKP, but at the last minute it turns out he can't take more than one, and we can't really split up because we're travelling in the same vehicle. End up having to ask Campino, the singer in Die Toten Hosen, if it's O.K. to sleep at his place. He says, sure, no problem.

There's a celebratory party mood in the air: it's been a good night, and now they're playing some classic old punk records over the sound system and everyone's feeling good. Campino tells me how much he enjoyed the gig and says, 'I'd really like to hear those songs recorded with a band—maybe with the Toten Hosen.' Yeah, ha-ha.

We're turfed out of the Q-stall eventually and end up in the bar over the road. Uh-oh, I've just realised Campino is getting very drunk indeed. He's charging up and down the club, talking to loads of people, and disappearing outside for long periods. Beginning to wonder if we're going to get back to his place tonight. Minutes turn into hours, then suddenly Campino's hand is on my shoulder and we're swaying through the streets towards a taxi rank. Impressively, he gets us to his place and manages to point out mattresses, bathroom and kitchen before becoming suddenly and decisively horizontal.

10th June. Aachen.

Campino wakes us up around midday, apologising profusely, 'Tim, have you ever, *ever,* seen me that drunk before?'

He prepares some coffee, fruit and muesli, and we chat for a bit about last night. 'You know, even though I talked a load of rubbish yesterday,' he says, 'I was serious about that idea of you making a record with the Toten Hosen.' Over the next half hour the rest of the band wander in, ready for a rehearsal, and they all say that they'd like to do it too. Hmm. Seems like I'm going to be making a record with the million-selling, stadium-playing, most famous band in Germany.

PamP and I head on to Aachen. Clink the Fennel Honey. Sip. Gargle. Mmmmm. 'One, two...check...' Start engine. Spend an hour trying to find the way out of Düsseldorf. I'm the only one who giggles at the road sign to 'Titz.'

It's hot.

We have to back down a frighteningly steep and narrow alleyway to get to the load-in for the Autonomes Zentrum in an old wartime bunker in Aachen. We load the gear through a warren of concrete underground rooms with submarine-type doors, each with a locking handle the size of your arm. Past the haven of the dressing room with bread, cheese and crisps laid out, to a bare black room with a stage, then on to the bar in the next room, where a hot meal is being prepared for us. The toilets off to the side of this room are particularly grisly. On one wall is a large trough for a urinal, on the opposite wall an identical trough with a couple of taps above it and a scrawled handwritten sign, 'Washbasin.' One has to assume that as the night wears on these two troughs become interchangeable.

While Tommy battles with a P.A. system that doesn't work, I take a walk up into the town. Hanging round the railway station are quite a few drunks and junkies, old needles lying in the gutters. Kind of edgy atmosphere. Go back to the bunker.

Tommy has managed to get the P.A. running in mono, at least, so we try a soundcheck. It sounds terrible, but I'm beyond caring. Garden Gang go on to a wary audience backed up in a huddle away from the stage. Halfway through the set Klaus' girlfriend faints in the stifling heat and has to be carried up into the fresh air to revive. Half the audience follows to see what's going on, and Garden Gang look on uncomprehendingly as the room clears mid-song.

My turn. I think I play O.K. Drop two plectrums.

In the dressing room, Tom and I make things talk—cigarette packets, bottles, paper cups; they all have a voice tonight. Tommy kills jelly babies in various ways before eating them. He saves one to kill later.

Klaus is putting some of us up for the night, the rest are staying with his brother. It's great to get back to a clean, comfortable flat, open a couple of bottles of wine and sit around talking bollox. Next thing you know it's seven in the morning, it's light and the bloody birds are singing.

Klaus has reserved me a bed. Luxury.

11th June. Dortmund.

There's something lumpy under the sheet, I realise, as I shift about sleepily, trying to wake up. I reach under it and pull out a remote control for a television. Joke or accident?

T-shirt still wet from last night.

We have a slow breakfast, get in the cars, clink the Fennel Honey, one...two...check...hit the road for Dortmund. I notice the list of gigs for the venue on a poster in the window as we go in: it says 'TV Smith is an English Singer/Songwriter God, Garden Gang are a Speedfolkband.' In three weeks time Nothing But Puke and Aerobitch are playing.

Later, weary but exhilarated after a good gig we sit in the backstage room knocking back beer and talking rubbish. Ben, the promoter, comes back and gives us the directions and a spare set of keys to his flat, as he has to go now. 'At least you know you'll be comfortable there, your own room, same as last time,' he says.

I'm confused; I didn't stay with him last time. 'Yes you did,' he insists, doubt beginning to show in his face. Then the penny drops: tall, thin, grey hair—he has mixed me up with Attila The Stockbroker's mother.

Finally back at the flat, we open some more beer and talk more bollox until PamP puts a finger to his lips and we hush for a moment. Outside the birds are singing.

12th June. Iserlohn.

Last gig, a three day open air peace festival, and it's rumoured that there could be 1500 people there. As we drive up early afternoon there are perhaps a couple of hundred milling around the site and casting the occasional glance at the dreadful band on the stage, lazy tuneless music with some awful hippy woman joining in on bongos.

We hang around for long hours in the backstage tent, dip into the backstage fridge full of organic beer, and pick carefully at the backstage bread and cheese. Note to promoters: if you stack an open cheese roll on top of an open meat roll, it is no longer vegetarian.

It had been planned that I could only play for thirty minutes tonight, but as start time approaches the anarchist who was going to make a speech before my set says he hasn't managed to prepare anything, so could I play for ten minutes longer?

Enjoy the gig. Great sound, loud, lots of room onstage to bounce around, and I manage to cajole most of the reasonably large crowd into enjoying themselves. Then when I get offstage a bout of hay fever hits me. All the power-breathing during the set has filled my system with pollen and I'm streaming from nose and eyes, and exploding with sneezes. Garden Gang go on and I stagger out to watch them from the front. People are doing that festival thing where you join hands and dance around in the dust hippy-fashion, preferably without shoes on, and get some small raggedy-clothed children to join in, smiling all the while because life is so wonderful.

A girl who has travelled up from Vienna for the gig tries to talk to me and I sneeze all over her.

Garden Gang come off, and the main band for the night limber up, a kind of tepid ska group with about twenty members on the stage. While they're on, our party take shifts at sitting in the tent they've just vacated, zipping up the flaps to try and cut down the noise and keep out the cool night air. We try and make light of it, but we're awkwardly aware that this is the last night, and everything feels a bit forced. I hate this; I'm ill and I'm getting cold and I just want to be home *right now*. The headline band self-indulgently play way past curfew time, to the distress of the organisers who could lose their licence because of it.

Midnight and it's freezing and we don't know where we're staying except it's bloody 'wie üblich.' After the heat of the last three weeks no-one has enough clothes for this late night out of doors, so we're all huddled up and shivering. My head's blocked, my teeth are chattering, and my lungs are wheezing.

'It would be nice to go somewhere and have a drink and a chat to celebrate the last night,' says Tom brightly, 'unless you are feeling totally dead, of course.' One glance at me confirms the answer.

So it's two in the morning, there's this drunken hippy woman with a pushbike—*exactly the same woman* who was playing bongos onstage when you arrived—leading you to a flat with no toilet or shower working where half of your party are going to stay. The rest of you will stay with her friend a few doors away, who has three cats. When you finally get to sleep on the kitchen floor the cats will jump over you all night and your hay fever will be boosted by your cat allergy, which is similar but with interesting and unpleasant variations. You will come to in the morning with cat hairs in your mouth and find the skin from your sunburn has been peeling off into your sleeping bag and your towel is still wet from yesterday so you can't have a shower. You will get up and eat bread and cheese for breakfast and drink coffee and drive to the airport to get caught up in a traffic jam in the multi-storey car park that leaves your van stranded on the ramp so that you have to get out and drag your guitar case and bruisingly heavy bags full of unsold C.D.s and t-shirts and wet handkerchiefs and three-week-dirty clothes down four flights of stairs and out through the exhaust fumes and raging motorists who can't and won't get out of your way because they're all stuck and late for their planes too, until you arrive at the check-in desk dripping with sweat, your heart pounding.

You will wonder why you do this.

11. FAR NORTH

31st July/ 1st August

One in the morning, and as we take off from Oulo for the last leg of the flight to Rovaniemi in Lapland it's getting light again. Maybe not midnight sun as it's a couple of months past the shortest day, but midnight twilight at least.

Tommi and Hessu, two of the Helsinki crew responsible for my last tour in Finland, are at the airport to meet me, and we drive into town, drop my bags off at the hotel, then go to check out the Tivoli where I'll be playing tomorrow night. There's a band onstage and a good crowd in the hall. I'm introduced to the people running the event, a handful of music fans who have taken it into their heads to invite bands to the polar circle for this annual three day festival, now running into something like its fifth year.

When the gig finishes at 4:00 a.m., a bunch of us hang around outside under the wan sunlight chatting and drinking. My friend Jukka, who runs a Finnish record label, and is here 'on holiday' points me to the hotel at around 5:30.

I just make it for the hotel breakfast before they pack it away at 11:00, then take a walk by the Kemijoke river. A suspension bridge passes across from the small island of low modern houses that make up the city of Rovaniemi to the vast expanses of forest beyond. A few small boats chug up the river. There are blue skies and it's uncharacteristically warm. Feels like you're by the sea, the air is so fresh and clean.

I wander over to the Irish Times pub, where in a couple of hours I'll be starting the first of my two concerts for the festival, and find the Helsinki crew there. They will be on before me as a band called Ujo-Konserni, playing Finnish-language versions of T.V. Personalities songs. Things are moving slowly, though. The bar is just opening up for the day, and the band are in the process of wheeling off an old iron plough from the courtyard at the back of the pub to make room for a stage.

Enjoy the gig; a nice intimate feel, with the place filling up slowly during the hour or so I play. Afterwards I talk to a few guys who are big fans. One claims he learnt all his English from the first Adverts album. He scrapes a living going out onto the marshes and picking berries. He reckons it would take him two days picking to be able to buy one of my CDs. I slip back to the hotel to shower and change strings ready for the next gig, due to start at 1:30 in the morning at the Tivoli.

Jukka has arranged for us to take a short drive up to cross the polar circle and at 5:00 I go to meet him at the Rio Grande pub. I've barely got through the door before the berry picker is by my side and asking me to sit with him. I tell him I'm meeting some friends, and he says he'll come too. I get the impression he's been drinking all afternoon. He keeps interrupting as I chat with the Helsinki crew, and I only shake him off when I slip outside to meet Punk Lurex O.K., who just arrived after an eight hour train journey from Tampere. On the way back in to the pub I get waylaid by a photographer who was at the gig just now and took loads of pictures, but forgot to put any film in the camera and wants me to pose for some more now. While he's taking them, Berry Picker reappears.

'TV, the gig was great,' he slurs.

'Thank you.'

'So you went back to your hotel.'

'Yes'

'To shower.'

'Yes.'

'And change your clothes.'

'Yes.'

'Your underwear?'

'Er, yes.'

'What's your real name, TV?'

'It's Tim.'

'Tim, do you have a flat or a house? Tim, how many rooms has it got? Tim, are you rich?'

Oh dear, he's going all intense and weird on me. Suddenly Jukka grabs me and says the driver's here so we can leave. Berry Picker looks furious.

'No, stay here!' he erupts. 'Where they are trying to take you is...is...CRAP!! Don't go!!'

We go.

Twenty minutes later we are in a Santa theme park. I mean, *the* Santa theme park, a tourist village of fake log cabins spread around the official post office for the thousands of letters that get sent each year simply addressed to Santa. Outside, a prominent white line shows the position of the arctic circle so that tourists like me can get a photo of themselves straddling it.

Jukka buys me a lapel button of a moose, then gets me a certificate to say that I have crossed the polar circle. Another gig, another certificate. The blurb on it waxes lyrical: 'The sun shines here for an uninterrupted period of 720 hours in midsummer. Then there is an abundance of light and warmth and the rhythm of life pulses excitedly.' And in the winter it's twenty-four hour darkness and half the population commit suicide.

It's a bit surreal; temperatures in the high twenties, and everywhere Christmas paraphernalia. As we leave the Santa Shop and cross the courtyard under the sweltering sun, 'Silent Night' is wafting out of the discreet speakers.

I've been set up good and proper. The organisers of the festival have secretly asked Jukka to make sure he gets a photo of me and Santa. I shuffle around in the grotto feeling foolish, keeping my sunglasses firmly on. 'Come on over,' says Santa beckoning me up to sit at his side. We shake hands.

'Must be pretty boring sitting here all day?' I suggest.

He shakes his head with a twinkle in his eye, then talks a bit about the festival, and asks, 'What was the name of that band you had in the seventies?'

Knock me down with a sleighbell—Santa knows a thing or two about punk rock.

He puts his arm over my shoulder and we pose for the photo. 'You want to keep the sunglasses on?' inquires Santa. 'Sort of a trade mark, is it?'

'Yes,' I lie.

Santa's helpers—disappointingly not dressed as elves—develop the shot at lightning speed, slip it into a souvenir wallet and bring it over. Santa signs the back 'for my friend Tim,' then gets another copy printed for himself, which I sign 'to my old friend Santa.' He asks for a record, but I don't have any with me, and say I'll try and get one to him.

We drive back the pretty way, Rovaniemi visible in the distance over the stunted arctic trees. 'The trees get shorter and shorter the farther North you go,' Jukka tells me, 'but in Lapland they say, The smaller the tree, the bigger the dick.'

The plan for tonight is that Punk Lurex will play before me, then join me at the end of my set for a few numbers together. We're hoping to rehearse them at the soundcheck, so I take my guitar and bags down to the Tivoli promptly at 7:00, which is when we've been told to turn up. Soundchecks are running on Lapland time, though, and an hour later we get a chance to try just one song before the doors open. In front of the stage a troupe of acrobats and fire eaters are running through their routine.

I need to get something to eat, and there's nothing vegetarian in the backstage, so one of the organisers walks me over to a pizza place a few blocks away, where I ruminate over a baked vegetable dish and cabbage salad, with a lot of coffee to try and keep my energy up.

Back at the Tivoli, Punk Lurex ask where I've been—they all went for a swim in the Kemijoke and wanted me to come too. Narrow escape.

The latest estimate is that I'll be on around two in the morning. Backstage I'm pacing around trying to keep focussed when a woman comes up and says, 'What's the matter with you?'

'I'm just trying to prepare for the gig, keep my energy up.'

'No, there's something wrong with you,' she says. 'Too much salt, too much sugar, maybe.' Suddenly she gives me a power stare straight in the eyes. 'You should relax. Life is a beautiful thing, you know that, don't you?'

Boy, people up here sure get weird all of a sudden.

Outside, on a makeshift stage, the Helsinki crew are preparing for an acoustic gig. They have stuck silver gaffa tape on their lapels and, to a cheesy beatbox backing, perform a Finnish-language version of David Bowie's 'Starman.' Then they strip off the jackets to reveal Abba T-shirts and proceed, totally straight-faced, to sing a selection of Abba hits, complete with all the movements, specially translated back from English into Abba's native Swedish. Because the Finns think Swedish sounds ridiculous, everyone is falling about with laughter.

After this performance finishes, I become aware of some commotion by the entrance. Over the bouncer's burly arms, a pair of eyes trained to spot a single berry across miles of tundra fix on me. 'Tim! Tim! They won't let me in, they say I am too drunk. Make them let me in!' I give a helpless shrug. He tries to push forward and is restrained. 'Let me in! Tim! Help! HELP!!'

I retreat discreetly indoors.

Backstage, a very drunk girl sits next to me on the couch and proceeds to speed-gabble at me in Finnish. I try and stop her. I'm English, I say slowly. She looks uncomprehendingly at me, and carries on talking. I stop her again and try out one of the few Finnish phrases I know—'Puhutteko englantia?' (*Do you speak English?*) She glares at me. 'FUCK OFF!' she spits, then turns her back.

I have a word with Punk Lurex, who will be playing before me and also joining me for a couple of numbers at the end of my set. Looks like it's going to be 2:30 before we start, still quite a few bands to go. Wander outside, but Berry Picker is still hanging around there, and starting to get aggressive. He points at me across the crowd, and with an angry look on his face shouts, 'Tim...why are you so CRUEL AND STUPID?' His hand closes into a fist, with one knuckle nastily protruding. He lifts it towards me slowly, then falls over, taking a bicycle down with him.

Only a couple of bands still to play. With luck we could be on soon. Punk Lurex finally get to take the stage shortly after three in the morning and play a short set. I walk straight on as they come off and get right into it. I've been pumped up and ready to go for about eight hours, so it's a relief to finally play, but after half an hour one of the organisers waves me over and says, 'Just time for one more, and two with Punk Lurex.' I'm speechless. We've been running on Lapland time all night, but at 4:00—everything's got to stop.

I take my guitar and bags upstairs to stash in the tiny room above the venue that Punk Lurex have been given to sleep in. It's pretty obvious no-one's going to be sleeping though:

fifty or sixty people have gathered in the yard outside the venue to trek down to a nearby field where the annual festival football match between North and South Finland will take place. We all wander down there, through the quiet streets in the crisp night sunlight and arrive to find various people limbering up on the field, some of whom unaccountably have no clothes on.

We sit down on the grass and a bottle of spirits that smells unpleasantly of tar is passed round. 'Try it, though,' someone insists, 'the flavour is really smooooth.' Yes, but it still tastes like something you would waterproof a fence with.

Someone else explains to me that there are no old buildings in Rovaniemi because the Nazis burned the old city down when Finland changed sides during the war. Even up until the seventies, shopkeepers here would refuse to sell German tourists boxes of matches.

I get into another conversation with someone who explains what the minus forty degree temperatures were like this winter. One morning, he tells me, he went down to the bakers in a puffa jacket and by the time he arrived it had frozen solid and he couldn't move in it to pick up the bread. The baker managed to bend one of the arms and the jacket shattered.

Eventually the football match starts, but before long a police van pulls up to the edge of the field and we're told that there's been a complaint about the noise and we all have to leave. As we wander back up the road. Sami and Riitta from Punk Lurex are coming the other way, heading for the station to get the 6:15 a.m. train. We say our goodbyes, then carry on to the club where we split into two groups: most go to find another pitch to carry on the football match; the rest of Punk Lurex, a couple of the Helsinki crew, and a few other new friends sit in the basement under the Tivoli finishing off a few beers, passing around the tar spirit and chatting whilst one of the night's victims snores dramatically on the sofa, an unlit cigarette planted firmly in his mouth.

At 7:00 we call it a day. I go back to my hotel and doze for a couple of hours, then take a shower, pack my bags and walk over to the Rio Grande, which is providing breakfast up until midday. Everyone I left a couple of hours ago is there, sitting round an outside table nursing coffees and beers.

After another round of goodbyes, a car comes to take me to the airport, and Hessu jumps in to accompany me. Halfway there I realise I forgot to give Santa a copy of the record. There's still just about time, so we take a short detour to the village. Hessu suggests that there could be more than one Santa—I can't believe this—but I edge past the queue of children snaking into the grotto and sure enough it's the real one. I wave the CD at him.

'TV my friend! You remembered!' He beams and ushers me forward. He asks me how the gig went as he leafs through the CD booklet to find a place for me to sign it, then passes me a pen. 'Do you have an e-mail address, TV?'

I start to write a dedication, then pause. 'Sorry to call you Santa,' I whisper confidentially, 'but I don't know your real name.'

'That's O.K.' he reassures me, 'I *am* Santa. Now then, you want another photo, this time without the sunglasses?'

While I'm signing the record, Santa chats to Hessu in Finnish. As I cap the pen, he tells me, 'I was just asking your friend what his involvement is, but he tells me he's just a fan, an engineer by profession. Engineering is a boring job, though, eh TV? Engineers need some rock'n'roll in their lives.'

I nod seriously. 'Everybody needs some rock'n'roll in their lives, Santa.'

I've got to be quids in next Christmas.

12. TWO ONE-OFFS

PUNKAID

18th September

I try and steer clear of these punk festivals, I really do. But this one seems a bit different: organised by a group of people raising money for some hand-picked charities without any of the profits getting lost in directorship costs or mysterious 'expenses' and at the same time promising to promote the diversity of the punk music and spirit, it sounds like a worthwhile project. I've decided to go for it, and am planning a set based almost entirely on the Adverts' 'Crossing The Red Sea' album.

One of the organisers is Mark P, the 'Sniffin' Glue' fanzine founder who still plays with Alternative TV today. He's already in Westcliff-On-Sea, just outside Southend, where he was overseeing the opening of the three day event yesterday. I'm meeting up with the rest of his band in London to travel up there with them.

I get to the flat on time at 1:30, but the band, and about six people coming with them, are sitting around wondering where the driver and van are. We're all a bit unsure about how much we want to be associated with punk rock, the term is so devalued these days. I'm reminded of it even more when Rufus arrives from where he's been hanging out in the flat upstairs. Rufus is a stylish young punk with spiked hair, a pierced lip and a great attitude. Last time I saw him was a few weeks ago at a gig I played with A.T.V and Menace at the Borderline in London. He was at the front as usual, and my set was going well, except that I kept getting interrupted by an aggressive, tattooed girl shouting, 'Play Gary Gilmore!' and 'Do the old stuff!' between every song. There was a short break while I changed a string, and Rufus mentioned to this girl that the rest of the audience wanted to hear the new songs too. There was an invective-filled response, then she swung out—her fist covered with rings— and decked him. He was carried away to the dressing room, face streaming with blood.

Well, this is the kind of attitude we're a bit worried about facing today, and we all start to take the piss, raising our fists and croaking 'Anarchy!' ,'Destroy!' in old man voices. John, A.T.V.'s drummer, tells us he had to ask his neighbour in Brighton to switch his stereo down last night 'because I've got to get up early for a punk festival tomorrow.'

We all have a nice cup of tea.

The driver arrives, and we lug out the guitars and some cushions into the back of the van. There's room for three in the front, the rest of us spend the two hour journey crammed together watching the world go by through the two little windows in the back doors.

First stop in sleepy Westcliff is the off-licence, then on to 'Club Riga' which disappointingly turns out to be just a smallish room at the back of a pub. The weather is cool and Autumnal as we unload our gear and stand with it outside the venue because the paranoid security guys won't let us in until we have our official passes. Word has it that the chip shop opposite is closing at nine, in case of trouble!

Indoors, a couple of hundred punks are milling about in front of the stage The dressing room upstairs is almost entirely filled by a boxing ring.

I bump into Spizz and we reminisce about how we used to sign on every week at the same dole office, not acknowledging each other because we didn't want anyone to find out we were musicians. Special Duties are about to go onstage, and the singer comes up to tell me that they're going to do a version of 'Gary Gilmore's Eyes' and would I like to sing it with them? I decline.

I watch a bit of their set from the back of the club, and when it gets to 'Gilmore,' the singer says, 'We asked TV Smith to come up and do this wiv us, but he says he's concentrating on his solo career these days...'

I bump into 'Fear And Loathing' fanzine writer Andy P. and we slip out of the venue and walk down the road to the Pavilion Café, set high up on the cliffs overlooking the murky grey Thames estuary, where we have a nice cup of coffee and a chelsea bun.

When we get back to the Riga, Jock Macdonald is just taking the stage with the Bollock Brothers. There is supposed to be a guest appearance in their set from 'rogue trader' Nick Leeson, for some reason. I go outside again where I bump into Mark P's partner Annie, and Rufus. They're looking for somewhere to get a coffee and something to eat, so I take them back down to the Pavilion Café. Dusk is falling, and the lights are coming on in the numerous nursing homes along the way. Outside one of them we all stand rudely staring in at the sight of one old woman who sits in her wing chair unattended, her neck bent in a monstrous sideways U so that her head flops onto her chest. We gape at each other, shocked.

'A good reason to have children,' says Rufus, 'is that you can instruct them to shoot you if you ever end up like that.'

Outside the Pavilion Café, the singer from Menace and a fan who's traveled over from France are also escaping the noise back at the club. There's a fierce chill wind barreling in from the North Sea. It's enough to whip the foam off your cappuccino.

Back to the venue in time for a great set from A.T.V., then pretty soon I'm on. Fears about being the only acoustic act at a punk festival are unfounded; the audience are with me all the way, even enjoying a newer song when I slip it in between all the Adverts numbers.

Now fifteen of us cram into the van—fifteen, ye Gods—and drive back to London. We can't find anything on the radio and end up listening to Classic FM. Once we hit the suburbs, we have to drive around for hours dropping everyone off and I end up back at my place at four in the morning.

Ah, just like the old days.

WOMBLESTOCK

9th October

I'm heading to Liverpool Street for the train to Oulton Broad, near Lowestoft, where 'Wake Up' fanzine writer and dentist Dave T., affectionately known as 'Womble,' is holding his annual party which involves lots of friends and musicians going on a boat trip through the Norfolk Broads with unlimited supplies of food and alcohol, playing and getting pissed.

Get to Oulton Broad on time and notice a couple of other people carrying sleeping bags also leaving the train—likely suspects for the party, I reckon.

Just down the road is the hotel that Womble has booked me into, so I check in and drop some of my things off there before walking down to his large house and dental surgery where festivities have already started. As I arrive, Attila has just finished a set in one of the downstairs rooms and Womble is at the microphone announcing imminent plans for us all to go down to the boat.

A shambolic bunch of about eighty people carrying guitars, flagons of ale and bottles of wine, straggle through the streets of Oulton Broad where the boat, hired by Womble for the day, awaits. We swing gently out into the broads, past the holiday yachts and canoes, and various small boats who cut kamikaze-style across our bows. You have to have some excitement in Oulton Broad.

Ten singer/songwriters, a couple of poets and a band are due to play over the next six hours, which includes an hour's stop at a pub in the evening, just in case anyone feels there's not enough opportunity to drink on board. Downstairs, an attentive audience is crammed in along benches up the side of the boat and at tables and chairs in the middle. The bar is doing brisk business.

I take a break from the music, and wander up to the open top deck and watch the reed banks slip by. Despite the fact that it's early October, the weather is mild and dry, and now and then the sun peeks out briefly from behind the clouds. A heron glides by, wings brushing the rushes, and all is still apart from the chug of the boat's engine and the muffled sounds of music and merrymaking below.

It's dark by the time we reach the pub. While everyone troops off, I take the opportunity to attempt a soundcheck, but am completely baffled by the P.A. system and go over to the pub to get a drink too. When we're all back on board I plug in to start my set and discover I've only soundchecked the monitoring system—there's no sound going out front at all.

Once that's sorted out though, an extremely enjoyable gig. Talk about a captive audience.

We dock at 9:00 and all stagger over to the Indian restaurant across the road which Womble has booked exclusively for us—veggie food all round. It has to be said that many of our party are now looking somewhat the worse for wear. Some wobble out during the course of the meal and are not seen again.

Great meal. Those of us still functioning wander back to Womble's place for some more impromptu music. At two in the morning, about fifteen survivors gather in a downstairs room. Me, Joseph Portar, Wob, Murray Torkildsen and a few others take it in turns to play a few songs acoustically while the rest of the house slumbers. It really is, as Womble says, before he too wanders off to collapse, 'one of those magic moments.'

Long live Womblestock and all who sail in her. Let's hope there's plenty of dentistry to be done in Oulton Broad over the coming year to pay for the next one.

13. TWO BACKSTAGE QUICKIES

HULL

23rd October

I'm sitting on my own in the dimly-lit dressing room directly behind the stage at the Adelphi while the support band, 'Santa's Bugger Boyz,' play. Don't know what my old mate Santa would think about this name. I'm trying to compose myself and get an idea of what songs to put in my set tonight, but it's too noisy to concentrate. Onstage, the band are in full grunge mode, and one of them has taken an angle grinder to a car bonnet; a hideous screeching rings out, and a fan of sparks arcs through the open doorway, showering over where I am sitting. There's no way out of the dressing room except onto the stage. As the cacophony reaches its climax the band turn their smoke machine on: unfortunately they forgot to take it out of the dressing room before the gig started, and for the next ten minutes it puffs insistently away around me, filling the air with a choking smog.

BERLIN

6th November

In the office that is being used for a backstage room there is a large placid black dog who sits quietly on his rug for most of the time, but growls aggresively at any new arrivals coming into the room until they are introduced to him by the people running the club. After the gig, I'm playing with the dog when the girl who owns him comes over and asks if I'd like to see the one trick he does. Then she looks into his eyes and quietly says 'Sid Vicious.' With a very sad expression, the dog sinks slowly to the ground and lies motionless until we all make a big fuss and he jumps up happily again (unlike the real Sid).

14. GENERATION Y2K

18th November

As we pull out of Euston station, the pleasant voice of someone who sounds like he's auditioning to be a television weatherman floats out of the speakers: 'Seating for customers with unreserved seats can be found in coach C. Now, unfortunately coaches C and D have had to be switched, so that whereas coach C would normally be next to coach B, it can now be found between coaches D and E. Hope that makes sense.'

A sign on the window says, 'Not for public use,' but by then it's too late—I've already looked out of it.

I'm on another stop-start tour of Britain, and I'm going to be staying with Chris from Ozit records for the first three days. Driving back from Hartford station towards his home in Northwich, Chris points out all the posters for tonight's gig he has been painstakingly putting up over the past couple of weeks. Some have already been pasted over with posters for the local disco. 'It does rather piss on yer chips when they do that,' he grumbles.

The first gig is in Manchester. Not too many people in, but they come up close to the stage and it's a good gig. Afterwards I have a quick chat with Owen, a teacher from a primary school near Preston. He has arranged by e-mail for me to go and speak to his class tomorrow morning as they've been studying a song of mine, The Day We Caught The Big Fish. In the afternoon I'll play a concert for the entire school of two hundred 4—11 year olds. Owen wrote in his original e-mail, 'as payment I can offer you a packet of Ginger Nuts, as much chalk as you want, and the sight of a roomful of beaming cherubs.'

We're back at Chris's shortly after 2:00 a.m. and after a couple of slices of toast head for bed. The good news: his sons Thomas and Mathew are sleeping in the bunk bed in Thomas's room, so I get Mathew's single room. The bad news: it's also the cat's room. 'That won't be a problem though, will it?' says Chris, unaware of my cat allergy.

2:45 a.m. I've coaxed the cat out of the room, the first bout of sneezing has subsided and I'm just getting off to sleep when Butch, Chris and Angie's tiny elderly Yorkshire terrier, starts barking. From the next room I hear Chris getting up to let it out.

3:02 a.m. Just getting off to sleep when I feel the cat on my feet padding around ready to settle down. How the hell did it get back in? I grope around in the dark for the light switch and get up to shoo it back out, then stack my bag against the door.

19th November

6:36 a.m. The alarm goes off—Mathew set it for his paper round yesterday and forgot to switch it off.

8:00 a.m. Outside I can hear Chris starting up the van to get out flyposting. Must get up for this school gig.

8:20 a.m. Have a shower. Hot and cold water come in a slow cycle so you have to keep stepping back out of the way. During one of these manoeuvres I knock the porcelain soap dish over and it smashes in the bath.

8:45 a.m. Put new strings on guitar.

9:00 a.m. Angie gets up to make some breakfast. I apologise about the soap dish. Chris arrives back with a frozen thumb. He'd left the paste pot outside overnight.

10:10 a.m. Chris is running up a speaker cab in the middle of the kitchen, trying to get a rudimentary P.A. working for the school concert.

10:20 a.m. P.A. still not working properly. Chris is looking for an impedance changer.

10:41 a.m. Everything is up and running. We carry the gear out and load up. Thomas decides to come with us.

10:52 a.m. As we leave, Angie hands us a thermos of coffee through the van window.

10:54 a.m. Thermos is broken and leaking everywhere. Thomas runs back to the house with it. I am due at the school in six minutes—it's about fifty miles away.

11:05 a.m. Use Chris's mobile to ring the school, but there's no reply. Sign on motorway says 'congestion ahead.'

11:28 a.m. Ring the school again. The teacher who answers says that Owen has been getting 'a bit jittery.' I reassure them that I will be there soon—'We're just passing Preston now,' I lie.

11:55 a.m. Bundle into the school and straight into the classroom where about thirty kids are waiting expectantly. Owen looks relieved. They ask if I'll play 'Big Fish' for them first, so I do, then they ask me lots of questions about the song and what it's like being a musician. A photographer from the local paper arrives to get some pics of me with the kids.

12:30 p.m. The dinner bell rings, and while the kids go to the dining hall, Owen, Chris, Thomas and myself stay in the classroom eating a veggie school dinner; Owen behind his teacher's desk, the rest of us lined up in front of him at tables, hunched down into kiddie chairs. Owen hands me a suggested set list for the afternoon's concert: all the gentler songs, with an encore of Runaway Train Driver ('slow version!') Underneath is a further reminder, 'slow and not too loud, so you don't scare the five-year-olds.'

1:05 p.m. While the tables are being cleared away in the dining hall I have a quick soundcheck through the little P.A. Chris and Thomas have set up. The volume knob hardly leaves zero.

1:20 p.m. All the kids file in, the older ones on benches at the back, the infants sitting in rows on the floor at the front. With one last piece of advice from the deputy head to cut it short if they start fidgeting and looking restless, we're off. They love every minute of it. When I get to 'Big Fish' the whole hall sings along. I finish off with quite a fast song and try a few leg kicks to see what happens. Each time I do it all the kids roar with laughter.

The deputy head walks up to the microphone and says, 'I think we'd all like to hear TV play his 'Big Fish' song one more time, wouldn't we children?'

2:15 p.m. Now it's time for a hymn. A teacher sits at the piano and starts playing, while all the kids sing, 'Old man Noah he built an ark...' then I'm invited to help with this month's school awards. As each child walks up to the front I shake their hand and give them their certificate. At the end there is a special award for me—a packet of Ginger Nuts.

2:30 p.m. Playtime. I sign 300 autographs.

3:00 p.m. Back to the classroom to listen to some poems written by the kids around the theme of the song. I congratulate each of them, and Chris gives away a couple of C.D.s as prizes for the best ones.

3:25 p.m. Head back to Northwich. Very tired.

4:00 p.m. Unload the P.A. and sort myself out for tonight's gig in Coventry. Angie is making pizza, a veggie one for me and one with salami for Chris. We relax briefly and eat some of that, then she wraps the rest up for us in case we're hungry later, and fills a new thermos with coffee.

5:47 p.m. Finally get out of the house and on the road, Chris and I both totally exhausted and talking bollox to keep awake on the motorway.

7:47 p.m. There are approximately seven thousand roundabouts on the road into Coventry.

8:00 p.m. Soundcheck.

10:15 p.m. Onstage.

11:30 p.m. Offstage. I apologise to the promoter for having to leave straight away, and explain that it's been a long day. 'You should be back in Northwich in an hour at this time of night,' he says cheerily.

12:06 a.m. Seven thousand roundabouts later we are on the M6.

12:47 a.m. We are stuck in stationary traffic queuing up at roadworks on the outskirts of Birmingham.

12:55 a.m. We get out the pizza. I have a U.M.M. (Unexpected Meat Moment)—it's the salami one.

1:00 a.m. We have moved about two hundred yards in the last twenty minutes. Both dead tired. Break out the coffee.

1:15 a.m. Through the roadworks and moving again, still only just leaving the outskirts of Birmingham. Have to keep on opening the windows and letting in blasts of freezing night air to stay awake.

2:06 a.m. Reach Northwich. Chris goes straight to bed, while I sit in the kitchen for a while and drink a glass of wine.

2:10 a.m. Butch starts barking, I let him out.

2:20 a.m. Butch starts barking, I let him in.

2:50 a.m. Go up to the bedroom. Remove cat from bed. Put my bag against the door.

20th November

Wake up around 9:45 and spend a very boring day sitting around while Chris is out trying to rig up a P.A. for tonight's gig.

Early evening, Angie takes me down to the venue. There are speakers everywhere and Chris is on the stage with a soldering iron, joining cables together. Gig time approaches, but when I start to play, the guitar is virtually inaudible and there's some kind of phasing problem across the two monitors in front of me so that there's a delay between the one on the left and the one on the right. I'm having to hit the guitar so hard that I soon break a string, and while trying to change it in the dark on stage I accidentally replace it with the wrong one. Twice. Then the monitors stop working altogether, so everyone can hear what I'm playing except me.

There are a bunch of lads from Liverpool here tonight who always seem to come to the gigs where everything goes wrong. They've told me before that these are their favourite ones, and are loving it as the concert descends into chaos. I start taking requests from the audience and talking a load of bollox between songs. There's a lot of good-natured heckling, and we all have a great time.

We pack up the gear, then Chris, soundman Foggy and I travel back in the van, stopping briefly because Chris has seen 'a really good bit of wood by the roadside,' which he throws into the back with the P.A. speakers.

A few people gather back at the house, and two of them decide to treat us to a cassette of their first mushroom trip at high volume, winding forward frequently to 'the good bits.'

Much later it all breaks up and I head towards the bedroom. As I reach the door, the cat comes streaking out. It's obviously beginning to get the idea. It has left a legacy of cat hair, though, and I'm soon snuffling once I switch the light out. I grope around in the dark for my handkerchief which is lying somewhere among my clothes scattered on the floor by the bed.

Hmmm. Something not right about this. I switch on the light and find I have blown my nose in my sock.

21st November

End of round one.

25th November

I drive up to the Garage in North London through bad traffic and soundcheck around seven. The manageress hands me a large envelope. It's from a woman in Scotland who wants me to write out the lyrics to Gary Gilmore's Eyes on the enclosed piece of card for her to frame and give to her husband on their wedding anniversary. The age of romance is not dead.

I play a couple of hour-long sets, then pack up the gear, exhausted, and drive back. Traffic has got even worse.

Home 1:30 a.m.

26th November

There's a nice atmosphere in the Steamboat Tavern in Ipswich. It's just a small pub, with a couple of speaker boxes and an amp for a P.A. system, but everyone is friendly and it has all the makings of a good gig. So it turns out—a packed and enthusiastic crowd drives me on to play for nearly two hours again.

Afterwards I'm sitting having a drink with a few of the audience. One of them tells me that he is in a group 'The Rists,' who sometimes do gigs where they play only food-related songs, usually throwing around the food in question while they play. 'Doughnuts Make Your Brown Eyes Blue' was one of the messier ones, with the Shakin' Stevens classic 'Behind the Cheese Straws' a close second. They ask me if it would be okay if for their Christmas gig they did 'Gary Gilmore's Mince Pies.'

Just time for a quick word with Dave T—the rock'n'roll dentist and fanzine writer who organised the Womblestock boat trip a couple of months ago—before he heads back home to Oulton Broad. He'd said I could stay overnight at his dental surgery if I needed to, but I tell him it's okay as I'm being given a room above the pub. Two minutes after he's left the room a large filling falls out of one of my back teeth.

27th November

Wake up to find the orthopaedic pillow I have been sleeping on has moulded itself irrevocably to the shape of my head, no amount of shaking or pounding will bring it back to pillow-shaped. Downstairs, landlady Val makes me a cup of coffee and drives me to the station. I promise her I'll be back for another gig next year.

Back to London on the train, home to pick up the car, then I drive down to the south coast where I'll be playing a gig organised by Attila The Stockbroker at his local venue, The Barn Theatre in Southwick.

Tonight is the first night for a new P.A. rig, which sound good, although rather quiet onstage because the monitors were stolen recently after the local amateur dramatic society left the cupboard unlocked.

After the gig, I spend the night at Attila's place. A couple of days ago I phoned up to check it was okay to stay there: he said, sure, no problem as long as you don't mind sleeping in the same room as the tarantula.

28th November

End of round two.

1st December

I had expected to have a couple of days rest, but ended up rushing around catching up with stuff around the house and getting my tour clothes washed for the next leg, plus fitting in an emergency dental appointment which has left me with a large temporary crown.

I'm into Durham station shortly after six, and within a few minutes Craig arrives in his small van loaded up with the P.A. for tonight, and we drive over to the venue, a little pub called 'The Angel' where a birthday party for a student is in full swing. While we set up and soundcheck, there is much noisy merriment and dancing and singing along to the jukebox which is pumping out Abba songs at high volume.

Most of the birthday revellers leave before the gig starts, probably a good thing. Those that have come for the concert are a bit more reserved but still give me a great response. Unfortunately the manager of the pub is extremely drunk and keeps on staggering around in front of me miming on air guitar while I play, at one point asking me if I can 'do Blitzkrieg Bop.' Afterwards he very nearly gets into a fight with some of Craig's mates—not a good idea as he is very tiny and they are very large—and the two parties have to be held back from each other in traditional male sparring fashion.

Quite glad to get out of there and back to Sunderland, where we have a couple of beers and something to eat in peace. At 2:00 I'm back in the bunk bed, the kids are sleeping in their parents' room again. I put my bag against the door and drop off to sleep shivering with the cold. The Topsie Tippee Panda thermometer on the wall says that the temperature is 'just right.' I beg to differ.

2nd December

I can hear Dean and Daniel, Craig's two kids, arguing outside the door over who is going to get to see Uncle Tim first. Sharon's voice roars up the stairs, 'You're NOT seeing him before you go to school, now get down here and LEAVE HIM ALONE!'

I spend a quiet day indoors, and when Craig arrives back from work late afternoon we load up the gear and take the hour's drive into Northallerton. This is the fifth time I've played this venue and it's a great success again; I play two sets and it goes down a storm. Someone comes up afterwards and reminisces about seeing me with the Adverts years ago. 'I once touched Gaye Advert's leg, you know,' he says shyly.

'Really? Where was that,' I ask.

'Ohhh...' he gestures at the back of his thigh. 'Round about here.'

Back to Craig's place for a couple of beers and some pizza, in bed 3:30.

3rd December

Two hours later I'm woken by my wisdom tooth trying to come through, on the opposite side of my mouth from the recent dental work. I can't go downstairs to the kitchen to search for painkillers because Craig put the burglar alarm on overnight, so I pace up and down the small bedroom (3 paces) clutching my jaw in agony for the next two and a half hours watching dawn creep slowly over the rooftops.

As soon as I hear Craig and Sharon get up I rush downstairs, where I let two paracetomol dissolve over my gum. Dean and Daniel stare at me with big eyes, scarcely able to believe I am up so early.

'There, at least now you've seen him,' says Sharon tartly.

It's wild weather outside. First snowfalls of the year in the Northeast, and a wind so strong that when Sharon walks the kids to school, Daniel gets blown out of her hand. When she gets back she tells me she had a dream about me last night: I was demanding that I needed my bleach-spattered tour jeans cleaned. 'You can clean them here, man, we've got a washing machine,' she told me, but, no...I insisted they had to be *dry cleaned...*

She cooks me a nice meal around midday and halfway through it the temporary crown falls out. I'm a dental disaster.

It's just a short drive down the coast to Seaham, where Craig has booked me into a venue I've not tried before. I'm worried about getting an audience here, and not feeling any more confident as we arrive in the town. It is totally deserted, and a wind that could rip the flesh off your bones howls across the seafront.

By the time I go on there's only Craig and four friends, the manager and his wife, the sound guy and a couple of bar staff in the room. The disappointment is tempered only by the fact I was told earlier that Boo Hewardine played here a couple of weeks ago and got ten people in, as did John Otway shortly before that.

In the van with Craig, we start to see the funny side as we drive back out through the deserted windswept streets. 'Look!' I cry at one point, gesticulating excitedly out of the window, '...a PERSON!!'

As we leave the town we see two empty taxis driving in. Oh how we laughed.

4th December
Day off.

In the evening, I go with Craig and Sharon to see The Sixth Sense at the local cinema complex. We've all desperately been trying to avoid anyone telling us the much-touted surprise ending. Craig certainly gets a surprise; he jumps out of his skin when Sharon nudges him during the final credits and he realises he slept through the whole thing.

5th December
There is some inane daytime quiz on the television.

'Who said,' asks the questionmaster, "*I have a dream*'?'

The contestant looks panicky. 'Er...Boyzone?'

Down to a pub called the Borough right in the centre of Sunderland early evening to set up the P.A. in a corner of the bar, no stage or lights. But after the last gig it's a relief to see people coming in, and despite the basic conditions and the nasty little cold I've gone down with, a really fun gig.

One of the four people who was at the Seaham gig chats to me. He was knocked out with it and has been playing the album non-stop all day.

6th December

End of round three.

11th December

Near the end of the U.K. tour now, and I'm in Berlin. Eh?

I'm supporting a Toten Hosen cover band at a one-off gig in a tiny bar with a tiny stage, which feels a bit strange as a year ago I was here in a big club supporting the real Toten Hosen.

Luckily, lots of my fans have turned up and the gig is great. Berlin crowds are the best.

13th December

Back in London for a last-minute date put in by Chris from Ozit, to help promote his new band Mr Blonde, who I'll be supporting. I played the official London date a couple of weeks ago; now I'm back as unpublicised 'special guest' to a band no-one here has heard of, in a venue—The World's End—I've never played before.

I travel in a crush of Arsenal fans to Finsbury Park to find quite a nice little venue. The only thing bothering me is that around the time I'll be getting on stage, the match down the road will be finishing and two hundred drunken football fans are likely to pile into the pub.

Good gig. Only a few from the match turn up in the end and seem to enjoy it. As I leave, someone who was dancing at the front says, 'What part of Ireland are you from?'

'Er—I'm not from Ireland.'

'Then why do you speak with an Irish accent?'

'Er—I don't.'

Walking past Chris's van, where Mr Blonde are packing up for the drive back to Manchester, Angie leans out and gives me a tangerine. Which reminds me, tomorrow I have to get that wisdom tooth out.

Back home, I put the tangerine on the kitchen shelf next to the unopened packet of Ginger Nuts awaiting my full dental recovery.

18th December

Heading up to Hartford again, where Chris is going to take me up to Birkenhead for the last date of the tour, and my last date of the millennium. I am finally no longer in pain from having the tooth out, but I've eaten nothing but bananas and yoghurt for the last three days, and have a packet of emergency swabs in my pocket in case I burst the stitch in my gum and start haemorrhaging when I'm singing tonight.

After waiting for an hour on platform five at Crewe station for my connecting train which is running late, its arrival is announced at the last minute on a different platform, so I have to grab my guitar and bags and run up the steps and over the footbridge to platform eleven. Stitch doesn't burst.

We're at the Royal Castle, situated on a traffic island in a desolate area of Birkenhead, just over the Mersey from Liverpool. Inside, the three other bands who are playing tonight and all their friends fill most of the back room before it has even opened. There is no stage and no lighting. An awful little P.A. system is rigged up, complete with a mixing desk that, as Chris says, 'looks like it cost about forty quid,' and battered cheap microphones. No monitors. Promoter Richie can't understand it. 'Last time I used this P.A., in Llandudno, there were monitors right across the stage,' he says.

The guy operating the mixing desk is clearly not that familiar with it. 'Which two inputs should I use for the sequencer?' I ask.

He shakes his head. 'Nope. You're talking a foreign language to me now.'

I ditch the sequencer and decide to play with just guitar. 'Just switch it up as loud as possible.'

Just before the gig, Richie hands me a piece of paper with a suggested set list, consisting of seventeen songs. Underneath he's added, 'Medley of Cheap and Adverts numbers that have not been covered by the above. Any order, I'm not fussy.'

Seconds into my first number, the left hand P.A. speaker stops working, and for most of the rest of the gig someone has to crouch behind the stack holding the jackplug into the socket.

I concentrate on Adverts songs for the early part of the set, then start getting shouts for 'new stuff.' Soon the place is jumping. Amazingly, in this horrible little pub with a broken-down P.A. in the middle of a roundabout in Birkenhead, I seem to be pulling off one of my best gigs of the year.

Finish off by getting the spare microphone switched on and half the audience up with me singing along to One Chord Wonders. What a way to leave the twentieth century.

19th December

I get home and open my post. There's a Christmas card from the school; all the kids have signed it and written little messages saying thanks, and wishing me a happy Christmas. Also in the envelope is an article from the local paper, with the headline: 'Punk hooks pupils with Big Fish.' It begins, 'Former 60's and 70's punk rocker TV Smith went back to school to spend an hour with the Year 6 Class...'

60's? Oi!!!

15. ONE CHORD WINTER WONDERLAND

21st January

I'm flying to Finland on the Swedish airline Scandinavian Airways, where business class stretches almost the entire length of the cabin. Then there's a little curtain, and behind it about seven economy class seats crammed in across the aisle from the toilets and the galley.

After take-off a glamour girl stewardess appears from behind the curtain and starts preparing the business class meals under our economy class noses. Luckily I had the foresight to order a vegetarian meal in advance; I get handed a stapled brown paper bag with an attached label: _Spesial Meal. Type of Food—Fr 3. Note—ML_. Inside the bag is a sachet containing a lemon-scented hand-cleaning tissue, a cellophane wrapper with another paper tissue, a plastic knife, fork and spoon, a wrap of sugar, salt and pepper...and one green apple.

We land at Tampere airport at nearly one in the morning, and Jukka is there to meet me. 'It's expected to reach minus twenty in the next few days,' he says cheerily as we crunch across the snow to the taxi.

22nd January

Breakfast with Jukka, then we walk into the centre of Tampere to meet up with Punk Lurex O.K., who I'm here to make a four track EP with. Spend the rest of the day in the rehearsal room with them, then get taken to where I'll be staying for the remainder of my visit, a one-room flat on the other side of Tampere kindly being loaned to me by guitarist Kukka's girlfriend.

Then I go over to a bar across the road called "Doors Of Dublin" to meet with Riitta and Tiina, guitarist and bassist from the band, and drummer Sami, and we have a couple of beers. Riitta and Tiina reveal a plan to take me to a karaoke bar a couple of streets away. Sami cries off, but I show willing and tag along. It's a depressing place full of serious drunks who keep approaching our table and sizing me up—the English guy sitting with two Finnish women— to see if there's any chance of a fight.

Riitta's phones her tee-total cousin, who drives over and takes us to a bar on the outskirts of town. The bar, named the Pispalan Pulteri ('The Big Stone of Pispala') is a much nicer place than the last one, with a friendly atmosphere. We sit round a large wooden table with some more of Riitta's relations and have one more beer. Tiina tells me she knows something about me: Punk Lurex have been covering 'Gary Gilmore' at some of their gigs, and when she declared it to the Finnish copyright society, they sent her a letter saying 'Is this TV Smith the same Talbot Wayne Smith we have on our records?' She thought she'd found out my secret name, and said yes. I have to show her my passport before she'll believe it's not.

23rd January

A mercifully short day in the rehearsal room. We've prepared about as much as we can and now just want to get into the studio tomorrow.

Everyone leaves and I walk the length of Tampere main street back to the flat. I'm starting to develop the staying-upright-in-snow trudge, feet planted heavily on the ground at each step so that after ten minutes your thighs ache. However, I have no doubt I will end up falling flat on my arse at some point during my stay here.

24th January

10:00 a.m. Meet up with Sami and Riitta at the rehearsal room, where we load some of the gear into Sami's car and head up to the studio.

It's a nice studio, and sound engineer Jani is right on the ball. He's using a computer recording system called Pro-tools, and likes it so much he's had the logo of the company tattooed on his arm. The session goes well and we have all four backing tracks recorded by early evening. A cartoonist called Kivi, who has come to the studio to make some sketches for the record sleeve, can't believe how good the atmosphere in the studio is. 'How come it's all going so easily?' he asks, 'what's the secret?'

Seems the English guy has to try a sauna, so one has been booked for us all this evening. It's a twenty minute walk.

Outside, the temperature has dipped to minus 25° centigrade. On the first hill an alarming thing happens: I can't stand up. While the rest of our group power on, I'm skidding and slipping over the snow-covered pavement, my arms wheeling like an out-of-control puppet. Kivi looks critically at my shoes when we reach the sauna, and shakes his head. 'Doctor Martens. They freeze over.'

Jukka and his wife Merja have already arrived, and in the room next to the sauna cabin Merja is laying out some food on a central table. We all sit down and have a little salad, and some bread and cheeses, then Jukka pours us a glass of Russian liqueur and toasts the 'great Finnish tradition of the Sauna.' The only thing missing, apparently, is a certain kind of fine-leaved tree branch—*vihta*—that you're supposed to slap each other with when you get in there. The markets were closed today, so Jukka couldn't get any. Jani gets on the mobile phone to see if any of his friends are able to provide some, but no luck. Imagine my disappointment.

It's not really the English way to sit naked in a small steamy wooden cabin with a bunch of men you barely know, but it turns out to be quite pleasant. We chat and relax to the gentle hissing as Jani spoons water over the coals, getting out to shower every so often, then climbing back onto the wooden slat benches. Jukka brings a few bottles of beer in and we sit there supping that.

We get dressed, then sit round the table in the traditional post-sauna state of zen-like calm while the women take their turn. There seems to be an awful lot of giggling going on in there. Jukka tells me that normally they would have a mixed sauna, but they thought they'd better spare my delicate English sensibilities. Probably a good job: when the women come out, Tiina tells me they were laughing about the idea of five hairy men crammed into that tiny cabin.

Hey, not *that* hairy!

Time for just one more beer at the Doors of Dublin on the way back to the flat.

25th January

A good morning in the studio. We have a lunch break in the nearby Telakka bar, during which Riitta decides to read my horoscope from the local paper. 'Hmmm, this is a bit difficult to translate,' she says, 'but it's something like this: *Aries. You are scared a rabbit will jump into your trousers when someone comes near you.*'

Kivi turns up at the studio, scratching away madly on his sketch pad while we record. The record is going to be called 'The Future Used To Be Better', and he comes up with a pretty good rough cartoon of me and Punk Lurex gazing out of the shadows into a bright future for the cover.

After recording we reckon we should all get a good night's rest, but I figure there's time for just one beer with Kivi in the Telakka. He tells me about his last record sleeve job, for a band he didn't like very much. They told him to do anything he wanted as long as it 'captured the essence of the band,' and he drew a solitary cow standing on an ice floe in the middle of the ocean. They didn't like it very much.

Before going back to the flat I drop into the Doors of Dublin and have a quick flick through the local entertainments magazine to see if there are any bands on tonight in Tampere worth checking out. Among the possibilities are 'Deep Space Sex Change' and 'Eternal Erection.' Looks like an early night.

26th January

Another smooth-running day at the studio. By mid-afternoon we have one track finished and mixed, and are having fun adding some linking pieces between the songs.

I'm out of the studio just too late to buy any beer, as the shops here aren't allowed to sell it after nine. Spend a long, boring evening at the flat drinking fruit tea and watching a German news programme on the TV go round and round again.

27th January

Last day in the studio, and it's an easy job to get the last few tracks mixed and compile the record so that everything runs together with all the linking pieces working properly. Jukka rings early afternoon to say someone from a newspaper wants a photograph of us: they'd heard about the record and are going to write a feature on the crazy record company guy who had the idea of inviting an old English punk rocker over to record with his band. Half an hour later, Jukka arrives at the studio. We sit him down in front of the speakers and play the record through to him, anxious to see what he thinks. As the last note dies away, he spins slowly round to us in the chair and pronounces, 'Yes. It sounds very...*wide.*'

The photographer arrives and takes a few shots of Jukka pretending to work the mixing desk while I look on approvingly.

A couple of hours more work and it's all done. We're intending to celebrate with just one beer in O'Connells, the Irish bar where I'll be playing a solo gig tomorrow, when we remember we still have some equipment to take back to the rehearsal room, so between us we lug it over there. As I'm struggling along trying to stay upright while carrying a Marshall cab over the ice, Tiina turns to me and says, 'Hey! We made a record!' We certainly did.

28th January

It's warming up. The temperature now is just a couple of degrees under, and with it comes the snow, falling in increasingly heavy flurries throughout the day. I watch it out of the window of the flat as I run quietly through a few songs to prepare for the gig tonight.

Sami is taking the night off to get some rest before the lengthy drive we'll have for tomorrow's gig together, so Tiina takes her car to the rehearsal room and we load up the P.A.—actually Sami's home stereo—and the guitar amp, and drive it over to O'Connells.

Shortly after soundcheck the Helsinki crew arrive. They check in to their hotel then we all go down to an Italian restaurant and catch up with each other over pizza.

Back at O'Connells the place is packed. I play two long sets, and it's a blast.

Hang around chatting to the Helsinki crew for a bit. Tommi tells me that his band have been doing a song called 'Jukka Tolonen's Hair'—a version of 'Gary Gilmore's Eyes' with slightly altered lyrics. Jukka Tolonen was the notoriously long-haired guitarist in a seventies rock band from Finland. In Tommi's version of the song, a young punk rocker wakes up in hospital after a car accident to find he has long hair and realises to his horror that it has been transplanted from Jukka Tolonen. The chorus goes, *'I'm combing through Jukka Tolonen's hair....'*

29th/30th January

We all meet up in the driving snow outside Tampere's Russian-style onion-domed church, where Jukka is going to take some shots for the record sleeve. A couple of days ago I'd had the idea of all of Punk Lurex dressed in summer clothes while I shivered in full winter gear for the photos, but now at the last minute realise it would be funnier the other way round, so I strip down to my T-shirt and stand amongst the band in the blizzard pretending not to notice the cold.

We wander down to the Telakka to take a few more photos then Sami goes off to hire the van. By the time we leave Tampere, we're running late. It's dark, snow is swirling across the road in the strengthening wind, and we have a four hour drive to Seinäjoke ahead of us.

I'm pleasantly surprised to find a large-ish smart venue in the Seinäjoke youth centre. There are six bands playing tonight. Punk Lurex O.K. have been put on in the middle and me at the end, so now we have to negotiate to get our sets put next to each other as we're playing some songs together. The organisers agree and start rewriting the timings on all the posters around the club.

Another advantage of changing the timings is that we get a chance to go over to Riitta's flat for a few hours—she recently moved here and had been hoping we would have time to visit her new place. As soon as Hessu—tonight's sole representative of the Helsinki crew—arrives on the train, we dress up and head off up the road, leaning against the snow, which is bowling down now in massive flakes, settling as soon as it lands. Under the night sky everywhere is milky white, and there's no sound except the howl of the wind.

We shake the snow off our clothes and tramp up to the flat, where Riitta opens a couple of bottles of wine and heats up some food. We put our record on the stereo to play to Hessu and feel pretty pleased with ourselves.

By the time we leave the flat, our footprints leading in have already been covered by new snow. At the venue, there are chaotic scenes as one of the bands shouts and screams from the stage while young punks fling themselves about and slam into each other. In the dressing room, broken bottles litter the floor, and people stagger around in various stages of drunkenness. The good news is that the event is running to time and pretty soon Punk Lurex get onstage. The audience take a little while to warm up, then start throwing themselves around again, spilling over onto the stage area, knocking microphones and monitors over, etc. etc. Shortly after midnight Punk Lurex finish and after the shortest possible break I start. All the punks sit down on the floor and stare at me.

About half an hour into the set a few people have dared to start dancing. Seems to be going well. Then Punk Lurex get up with me and the place goes wild.

We're out of there and loading into the van by two. We say goodbye to Riitta. Hessu takes her place in the van, and we drive South, hammering through the still, snow-packed roads, forests looming up ghostly on either side.

Hours later, as we reach the outskirts of Tampere, the snow is turning to sleet. We unload the gear into the rehearsal room and drop off various members of the two bands around town, then Tiina, Hessu and Kukka come back to the flat for a farewell drink with me as light starts to show on the horizon. At around eight in the morning everyone has left and I doze for a couple of hours before taking a shower and packing my bags, heavy in the heart at the thought of leaving this beautiful country.

Dear Diary: went to Finland. Made a record. Didn't fall over.

16. ANOTHER DAY, ANOTHER COUNTRY

3rd March. Kleinweiler Hofen (Germany).

I've been feeling like I need a holiday, and this could be it: four gigs over the course of four days in four Alpine ski resorts, supporting my old friends, German supergroup Die Toten Hosen.

Of course, holidays require some travelling, so I'm out of the house before nine in the morning to take the tube to Heathrow, where my flight gets me into Munich mid-afternoon. From there I get in the mini-bus with the band and crew for the four hour drive to Kleinweiler.

The venue is tiny; normal for me, but strange to think of stadium regulars Toten Hosen playing it. Upstairs there are a couple of rooms being used for a backstage, where I meet up again with Vom, the English drummer who was a roadie for the band until their regular drummer developed back problems and Vom found himself suddenly in the band. It's his first gig tonight, and he is looking understandably nervous as he gets into his stage clothes and crimps his hair. Looking at the heavily repaired and dangerously frayed electrical cable coming out of the crimpers, we speculate as to whether he'll live long enough to play the gig. Imagine the headlines: *New Hosen Drummer Killed In Bizarre Crimping Accident*, or *He Died With His Crimpers On.*

Downstairs, the venue is crammed, hot and airless. I'm gratified to find that the Hosen crowd take to me, and enjoy playing to such a packed venue. At the end of my set, the band come on and play Gary Gilmore and One Chord Wonders with me; good fun.

Holidays can be stressful, and I must be more stressed out than I realised: no sooner am I offstage than I'm crippled with heartburn. I talk to some fans after the gig with what must be a peculiar expression on my face as bile burns its way up my digestive tract, then wander out into the car park in the misty rain to try and find 'the red bus' that I've been told is going to take us to the hotel in Füssen, thirty minutes away. I stare in confusion at the line of identical buses out there, parked up for the two hundred competition-winning Hosen fans who are accompanying us on this jaunt (all expenses paid by the band), then work my way down them, burping generously until I locate the right one.

Finally in Füssen at three in the morning, I stagger gratefully up to my room, but not before receiving the unpleasant news that we have to leave the hotel before nine for a proposed visit to the ski slopes tomorrow.

The hotel room is enormous. I close the door behind me and walk down a corridor past a toilet and a shower room to a cavernous living room and bedroom, where I dump my coat, bags and guitar in the middle of the floor to try and create some comforting clutter.

I get into bed, only to discover there is no light control by it, which means I have to get up and take the long walk back to the door to switch it off. In the subsequent pitch blackness I lose my way trying to get back to the bed. It's the first time I've ever got lost in a hotel room.

The alarm will be going off in a couple of hours. You can't expect to get much sleep on a holiday.

4th March. Ischgl (Austria).

Breakfast: mint tea.

The convoy of coaches heads off up the autobahn for a mass ski-ing appointment at midday in Austria, and immediately gets caught in a traffic jam on the only road across the border into the Alps.

Surprisingly, we still get to Ischgl with a few hours of the afternoon left, but everyone is so desperate to get on the slopes that they dash off furiously for the ski lifts, leaving virgin skiers such as myself down below without a clue what we should be doing. Eventually I go in a cable car with Hosen guitarist Kuddel—excused ski-ing due to ankle injury—and a couple of his friends to the top of the mountain to see what goes on up there.

This is all completely new to me. Wherever you look, packs of earnest skiers, snowboarders and tobogannists are dashing past each other; there are shops, equipment hire places, training schools and *apres-ski* restaurants.

We go into a restaurant for a little *apres-ski* without the *ski*.

I'm probably not going to be able to escape having a go at this ski-ing lark tomorrow, and to boost my confidence Kuddel tells me about his first time on the slopes: finding himself ski-ing out of control he grabbed the only thing he could—a small boy—to slow himself down, and dragged the startled child fifty metres down the hill before he eventually came to a stop.

By the time I check in to the hotel my indigestion is back so I decide to lie down for a couple of hours. I'm drifting off nicely despite the pumping disco music from the restaurant below, when an ear splitting volley of explosions starts up from outside. Peering over the balcony I can see a wide strip of firecrackers running the length of the street, banging and flaming away while a crowd gathers round cheering. I guess that's it for the sleeping idea. Things don't always go the way you plan when you're on holiday.

I'm still worried about the indigestion as I sit in the backstage room with gig time approaching, sipping on another mint tea. To cover all angles, I also consume:

* a Vocalzone tablet (containing peppermint oil, menthol and myhrr—yes, that's what they use myhrr for!)

* a phial of liquid calcium and vitamin C, given to me by Kuddel.

* a bottle of isotonic energy drink ('healthy body plus healthy mind equals power.')

* oh, and just before going onstage, a very strong cup of coffee, with a lot of milk to cut the acidity, and a lot of sugar for energy.

The gig's great!

Afterwards the pain has completely gone, and I sit in the dressing room feeling relaxed and happy, watching the snow outside whirling brilliant-white in the spotlights. The only stressful moment comes much later when I go back to the hotel and my credit card-style plastic key that should let me in the front door doesn't work until I push it in for the fourth time. The old couldn't-get-into-hotel-so-had-to-sleep-in-the-snow scenario.

5th March. Vals (Italy).

Today is going to be the day. Out of the hotel before nine again, and winding our way through the Italian valleys, I'm told that Vals will definitely have instructors for beginners, so there's no excuse. At the resort Heike, the tour manager for our coach, hands me a ski pass and points me in the direction of the hire shop where I'm clipped into a pair of rigid plastic boots and handed a pair of skis, which I don't even know how to carry. By the time I'm fitted out, the rest of the handful of first-timers have disappeared. As I stand around looking lost, Heike returns with a snowboard and travels up in the ski lift with me. Suspended high over the mountain heading for the top station, she is telling me about the difference between snowboarding and ski-ing when she suddenly stops in mid-sentence and breathes '...Mein Gott!!'. Following her gaze downwards, I see someone cartwheeling helplessly down a near-perpendicular ski-run far below, in a flurry of flailing limbs and clouds of kicked-up snow.

Out of the lift at the top station, where packs of Hosen fans have gathered to watch their heroes swish elegantly past down the trails. I clump unsteadily over to the ski instructor, where I join a lesson already in progress, and am shown how to put on and release the skis, then we move off down the idiotically shallow training slope. At the bottom, you grab hold of a moving rope which pulls you back up so you can have another go.

Needless to say, the process involves a great deal of falling over. I fall over as soon as we start off and fall over again a number of times going down the slope. I fall over trying to turn round to reach the rope lift at the bottom, and fall over when I finally manage to grab it. I fall over whilst being pulled back up by the rope, and fall over again when I try and let go at the top of the slope, causing an interesting logjam of skiiers behind me, who all fall over as well.

I grit my teeth for a second run. The ski instructor skis backwards in front of me, shouting out instructions in a heavily-accented German which I can barely understand, then halfway down the slope he disappears after a trendily-dressed female novice and streaks off down the mountain with her. Before teaching me how to steer.

I glide gently into a snow bank and fall over, then after I've hauled myself up find I'm heading towards an unpleasantly steep bit and make myself fall over in order to stop. At the bottom of the slope I try and turn around again for the rope lift and a ferocious gust of icy wind batters me, lifting off my cap and sending it bouncing down the mountain. As I watch it fly into the distance and realise that there is no way I will ever be able to reach it again, I become aware that my headgear is not the only thing to have been caught by the blast: I too am moving gently—backwards—down the slope which is about to drop away below me like a cliff. Oh God.

When in doubt, fall over. And if your humiliation isn't complete enough, there will always be Toten Hosen fans on hand to take your photo as you lie sprawled there, panting and covered with snow.

A short coach ride to the hotel for an hour's rest, then out to the venue. And guess where it is...back up the mountain to the ski restaurant by the top lift station. The entire audience will be coming to the gig by ski lift, and a few are already shivering outside as we go in to soundcheck. Given the arctic conditions, tour manager Kiki decides to let people come in as they arrive (always a downer when half your audience dies from exposure before a concert).

I get up onstage for a quick soundcheck in front of the rapidly-filling hall, and am alarmed to find my voice has diminished to a tiny squeak. In the stuffy, overheated dressing room downstairs, I gulp down a sandwich and coffee, change strings and panic. Ten minutes to showtime.

Push through the crowds to get onstage, still not sure if I'm going to be able to sing. Maybe an afternoon's exposure to freezing air is not the best thing for the vocal chords. Well, I shout a lot rather than singing and just about get away with it. By the time I get back on with the Hosen for the two Adverts songs, my voice has degenerated further, and comes unexpectedly out in a tuneless demonic howl...rather good, actually.

Back down in the cramped dressing room after the show I'm worrying again. Tour doctor Faust gives me a few sips of *Fenchel Hönig*—and I drink some medicinal Sekt. Meanwhile, the band have to do the publicity thing—a television crew comes bursting unannounced into the room, floodlights spring on, and suddenly an interview is taking place.

Eventually the TV crew leave, and things get a little raucous. One of the Hosen team is taking photos for their website, and Vom poses for him by dropping his trousers and holding a smoking cigarette in his foreskin. I guess he's got over the first night nerves.

They're sweeping up the floor of the venue as we leave in the early hours, skidding up over the brow of the mountain to the dark and deserted ski lift, where we haul all our gear into a cable car and glide gently down the mountain to the waiting coach.

6th March. Davos (Switzerland).

A long drive through the valleys across the border into Switzerland, where we pull up into a rest stop for a mass photo shoot of all two hundred fans and the band in the car park, then hang around chatting in the spring-like sunshine.

We wind up into the Alps again through picture-postcard Klosters, where sagging blankets of snow lay a metre thick on the rooftops, and watch the sun go down spectacularly over the mountain tops, pulling into Davos just after dark. The coach fails to make the incline up a narrow road to the hotel, so we all get out and carry our bags the rest of the way, then half an hour later take a mini-bus to the venue.

It's a small club again, but with a nice atmosphere to it; I feel comfortable in this size of venue. To my intense relief, when I hit the stage I find my voice is in great condition and have an extremely enjoyable gig, best of the tour.

The Hosen concert, too, is the best of the run; loose, energetic and great fun. By the end I'm at the side of the stage gagging to get back on and do 'One Chord Wonders,' and 'Gary Gilmore,' which Campino has generously decided to close the night with.

Churlish to resist the schnapps which is being offered by the people who run the venue. Or the wine and beer, come to that. It's getting on for four in the morning when I realise that just about everyone I know in the club has left, and I don't know how I'm supposed to get back to the hotel. Fairly confident I can find my way on foot, I grab my guitar and bags and set off through the snow only to have to face the fact that I actually have no idea where I am. Retracing my footsteps to the club, I find a group of Hosen fans getting into a taxi, and they cheerfully invite me in with them and take me back to the hotel. There are two and a half hours left before the coach back to Munich in the morning.

At 8:45 a.m. I go down to reception to find a ragged bunch of hardcore crew members who obviously haven't had any sleep at all passing round a bottle. I clamber onto the coach with about thirty others also going to Munich airport. There are no delays and we get there by three in the afternoon, which means a six hour wait until my flight goes.

Like all good holidays, after this I feel like I need a holiday.

17. BIGFOOT

12th April

Out of the house at 9:15. Have bought a rucksack to see if it'll make it any easier to carry all my gear around the country, but now as I struggle down to the tube I get the feeling everyone is thinking, oh look—he's going camping. And he's taking his _guitar_ with him. Hippy.

10:30 a.m. Been waiting for quite a while for the train to move off when there's an announcement. 'We will be subject to delays. This is while we wait for an engine.' Everybody picks up their mobile phones and starts shouting 'I'M ON THE TRAIN! THEY'RE LOOKING FOR AN ENGINE!!'

I'm back on tour in the U.K.

At Coventry station, Martin from Attrition picks me up. I'm playing just down the road tonight, but first we're going to do some recording for an idustrial goth metal version of Gary Gilmore's Eyes.

Early evening, the rain starts. Good turnout despite that, and a nice start to the tour.

13th April

I take a stopping train to Wrexham, rain beating drearily on the windows all the way. Get a cab to the gig, and the driver boasts that it's just been announced over the radio that 'Wrexham is Britain's biggest boom town.' I give him a 50p tip.

I like the idea of this venue in booming Wrexham, but ten minutes before showtime there are still only twenty people in, and it doesn't get much better.

Chris drives us back to his place, where I'm to sleep in the bottom bunk in his son's bedroom again. Crawl towards it feeling my way in the dark past the speakers and boxes, and slip under the quilt.

There is a cheese knife in the bed.

14th April

Back to London.

16th April

Get up at 7:30 to catch the only train that will give me a cheap fare. Chris picks me up at Crewe and we go back to his place where he sits at the kitchen table making up leads for the P.A. for tonight's gig in Burnley. His wife Angie says, 'Never happier than when he's got a soldering iron in his hand.'

Pasta for lunch. Have a U.M.M.

We arrive at the Talbot Arms in Burnley just as the football—which is being shown on a huge TV occupying the stage—is into its last ten minutes, then shove the TV out of the way and set up the P.A.

'ONE, TWO!! ONE, TWO!!' mimic the late drinkers at the bar.

Encouraged to see that the room is starting to fill and I recognise a lot of faces, shaping up for a good gig.

Which it is.

Back to Northwich, the rain slashing down incessantly. 'Weather's just practising for the Easter holiday next weekend' says Chris.

17th April

Back to London.

20th April

The tube to Liverpool Street station is held up at Bank due to 'delays behind.' Still make the train for Ipswich. Looking forward to this one—played the Steamboat Tavern a few months ago and had such a nice gig I booked in another straight away.

It's another fine and very long concert. After the gig I sit by the bar while my guitar gets taken over and used to lead some impromptu singing, starting with 'Whole Wide World' (good), then 'American Pie' (Hmmm), and finally 'Nellie The Elephant' (Gak!). Stand up any self-respecting punk rockers who would start such nonsense...that means YOU Red Flag '77.

Later that evening after a few more drinks Rikki Red Flag tries to persuade me I should come back to Ipswich in a couple of months to guest on the band's tenth anniversary gig. I say 'Yeshh.'

21st April

Checking through my pockets on the train back to London I find a piece of paper that reads, <u>BIG REMEMBER</u> JUNE17th (SAT) PLAYING AT RED FLAG ANNIVERSARY FOR TRAIN FARE & A LOT OF FUN! HOORAY!!

23rd April

Mid-afternoon drive down to Brighton after the Easter bank holiday traffic has died down, to the Evening Star pub, where the manager has asked me to play because it's his birthday. He sits at the front grinning for most of the show while I make comments about his advanced age (actually, he's younger than me).

24th April

A quick walk up the pier with the rest of the Easter Monday crowds. Then drive back to London and wash the seagull shit off the car.

26th April

Back in Northallerton for one of my favourite gigs, the Tanner Hop. I'm out of the train at around 5:00 and haul my rucksack and guitar a mile down the road to the venue. Soon my mate Craig arrives from Sunderland in his little van with the P.A. loaded into the back. We lug the gear up the stairs and go about setting it up and soundchecking.

Slightly lower turn-out for the gig than the last couple of times I've played here, put this down to the fact it's Easter week. Great atmosphere, though, and I play for nearly two hours.

Dismantle the P.A. and load it into the van, forty minute drive back to Craig's in Sunderland, then I'm back in the bunk bed in the kids' room. It has a new 'Thunderbirds' duvet.

27th April

Er. When I booked these gigs I forgot to take into account that it's the school holidays. Dean and Daniel are home all day, they have a new Playstation and they mean to use it. The sound of car crashes and gunfire fills the house. Dean works the joystick until his 'hands are out of breath.'

When Craig finishes work we set off for nearby Chester-le-Street. I've been worried about what this venue will be like, and am pleasantly surprised to find a beautifully restored chapel with a great atmosphere. Looks a bit empty until about ten minutes before I go on, then suddenly a few familiar faces turn up, and there's a comfortable crowd.

28th April

I get up and do some work on my laptop, to the kid's great interest. Dean is at the age where one minute he is learning computer skills with astonishing speed, the next creeping up behind you and firing a cap gun next to your ear so that you spill your tea down your crotch. In the afternoon I change the strings on my guitar, and both of the kids take it in turns to get in the guitar case—'It's nice in here!'

Craig finishes work, and we load up the P.A. to the sound of gunfire from the living room. It's a half hour drive to Felling, and a pub called the Jekyll And Hyde.

By about nine the place is crammed, and the atmosphere is great, even though I'm way above the crowd on a kind of railed balcony. Being up so high gives me a chance to make some cracks about looking down on all the old punks' bald spots.

Load up the P.A., drive back to Craig's place, unload the P.A. into the hallway; pizza and beer. Craig switches on the Playstation. When I go to bed, he has reached a level with the instructions, 'Kill anything that lives.'

29th April

After lunch Craig and I head off through the Tyne tunnel to a small town out in the countryside where a mate of his is getting married. The bride is early and waiting outside the church when we arrive. She looks somehow familiar.

'I know you, don't I?' I ask.

'Yes, you do,' she says. 'I was the one at your gig in Sunderland last year who sat at the front talking to my friend all the way through until you told me to shut up.'

In the church there is a punk version of 'The Wedding March' playing through the sound system which seems to rather shock the elderly organist, then a trendy smiley vicar performs the service, after which we all adjourn to the pub.

Soon Craig and I escape back to Sunderland for something to eat before tonight's gig. Wonderful, this Northern hospitality: I always get well fed here, and Sharon now scours all the labels for the 'vegetarian' sign so I don't get a U.M.M. We won't mention the notorious 'Gravy Incident' a couple of years ago.

Early evening we load up the P.A. and go for soundcheck at the Royalty, near Sunderland city centre. It's another venue that only fills up five minutes before I'm due to start so I have to leave it to the last minute. Then, moments after I finish we're being hustled out of the venue by the management—dismantling the P.A. and lugging it down the stairs still dripping with sweat. Oh, the glamour.

30th April

Train back to London.

3rd May

Last chance to book cheap advance train tickets for the three gigs that Chris has set up for next week in the North West, so I e-mail him to ask what time I need to arrive. He e-mails me back to say that the Liverpool gig has changed from Friday to Saturday. Bit annoyed about this as I've already mailed out 250 newsletters with the other date. Send him an email back complaining about it.

4th May

At Kings Cross station, I find out that I was given the wrong times for the train to Peterborough over the phone yesterday. The person at the information stand on the concourse advises me to 'take the later train, because it gets there earlier.'

Mark is on the platform, apparently unphased by the fact I'm nearly an hour late, and walks me to the venue—a black and mirror-walled disco with a seventies feel to it and scaffolding rails barricading the front of the stage. After a quick soundcheck we go to a nearby fast food joint called 'Mega-Bite' where I have a cardboard veggie-burger, and he explains that this is only the second gig they've tried promoting at the venue, it's basically him and a bunch of mates trying to get something going in Peterborough.

Looks like Peterborough needs it; after Mark's gone back to the club, I walk around the strikingly deserted streets for a while, past the bland rows of closed shops, no-one around. Eventually I stumble into the cathedral area, a tiny pocket of character just off the shopping centre. I bet the town planners wish they could have pulled it down and built a nice car park.

I'm due on at 11:00 but there's a rumour that there's a bunch of people on the way from another club, so I'm persuaded to wait another half hour. Not a bad turnout eventually, and a good gig, seem to have made a few new fans. I'm sitting on the stage afterwards, trying to sell a few CDs, when a woman comes up and says 'Excuse me, TV, but would you mind signing my arse?'

Funnily enough I bought a new signing pen with me today—the 'Sharpie Fine Point PERMANENT MARKER.'

Back at Mark's place the cats cuddle around me until I point out my allergy and they are removed to the kitchen.

Four in the morning, I get into the sleeping bag on the sofa, and drift off to the sound of the cats jumping at the handle to try and get in.

5th May

A brisk twenty minute walk down to the station to blow out the cobwebs. Just time for coffee and a cardboard croissant in the station café before the next London train. There is a man in the café dressed in a lion costume playing the gambling machine. No-one takes any notice.

Get home to find an e-mail from Chris complaining about my 'whingeing last e-mail' and saying he's going to pull all three gigs.

I think Chris must be under a lot of stress at the moment.

8th May

I'm going to do the gigs one way or another whatever's bugging Chris, so I ring him up and try and sort it out. He sounds just like his old self and by the end of the call agrees we should do the gigs. But that evening I get another e-mail saying he's decided to pull them again.

I don't understand what's going on here, but now I'm getting angry. I get on the phone to the three venues and tell them that whatever they hear from Chris, I'm coming. In the course of the phone calls I find that he's arranged two of the gigs via another promoter and that the date of the Liverpool gig was changed five weeks ago.

I phone the other promoter, Eric. He says he'll take over the gigs and offers to let me stay at his place. Later in the day Chris phones Eric to say he's doing the gig after all—he's sent off the £80 cheque for the P.A. hire in the venue and is still the official promoter.

I'm not feeling in a very positive frame of mind for the last section of the tour.

9th May

Have a bad feeling about Liverpool. If Chris hasn't actually sent a cheque for the PA, the club will definitely cancel the gig. I send off a cheque as well, just in case.

10th May

Upstairs at the Garage again, now my regular London venue, and I put in a set lasting over two hours, fitting in a big spread of material including lots of new songs. Very nice atmosphere.

11th May

Head up to Ashton-under-Lyne, near Manchester, on the train. This is the first of the gigs that Chris originally booked, and I'm worried that we're going to have some kind of confrontation, but when I arrive the people running the club tell me to that he rang up to cancel support band Mr. Blonde two hours ago and isn't going to turn up himself. The club has just booked a different support, and I see them bringing their gear into the venue as I soundcheck. This is a great little venue, there's a quality PA and lighting rig and some of the bigger bands on the circuit often play here. Everything now seems to be back on course and I'm really looking forward to the gig.

It goes well, and afterwards I head off with Mick, a friend of mine who used to be in a band called Harvey's Rabbit. I'd originally intended to go back home for the weekend, but because of the mess up with the Liverpool date I'm going to stay with him and his wife Bev in Manchester for a couple of nights.

Just before I crash out on the fold-out bed in the front room at four in the morning, Mick warns me that his two and a half year old son James might be in at six thirty to watch Sesame Street. Ah.

12th May

Day off.

13th May

Today is the Liverpool gig. There's a very strong chance that things are going to go wrong today, so I resolve to be as professional as possible.

But somehow I end up hanging around indoors and not getting the bus into Manchester city centre to catch the train to Liverpool until just after five. Should be okay though—I said I wouldn't be there for soundcheck until around 6:30, and the venue doesn't open until nine. Get off at the wrong bus stop and trudge with my guitar and baggage for fifteen minutes over to the station which is in the middle of major rebuilding works. Eventually I find the right platform for the Liverpool train and get on board. An hour later I'm getting worried—

we should definitely be there by now, but we keep pulling into these little stations I've never heard of. A while later we arrive in Preston. I'm on the wrong train.

Half an hour later I'm on a very slow stopping train, which goes back past most of the stations I've just been through and then some, while I stand awkwardly with my guitar and baggage, unable to get a seat, fuming about how late I'm going to be. Rushing out of Lime Street with twenty minutes to go before doors open I take a brisk pace to O'Neills bar, and dash in to find Eric looking relieved that I've turned up. Oh yes, Mr Professional. He tells me that Chris phoned up this afternoon to say he's not doing the gig or providing any support bands. The cheque he sent wasn't signed, so they used mine. There is no publicity for the gig. There are two O'Neills in Liverpool, and most people would assume it was the other one. And my newsletter said it was yesterday.

Apart from that, everything's going very well.

Downstairs to the venue in the basement, where I soundcheck, only to discover one side of the P.A. isn't working.

Back in the bar there are about ten people who've turned up for the gig. I find myself in the peculiar position of having my audience try to persuade me I shouldn't play. 'Don't bother, TV—it'll be embarrassing for all of us.'

After a quick discussion with the manager of the venue, I arrange for everyone there to be given their money back, then I play an hour set anyway, with my small audience providing most of the chat between numbers and requesting songs. Really good gig actually, and it only cost me eighty quid.

I take a cab with Eric through the Mersey Tunnel and on to his house in Wallasey, where I'll be staying the next three nights.

Eric tells me about the motorcycle accident he had when he was a courier a few years ago, shows me the scars up each of his arms where the bones are pinned together and gets me to put my hand on his inner arm so that I can feel all the bits scrunching around in there. He tells me that even longer ago he used to have a normal job and wear a suit and tie. Then he went to see 'Woodstock' at the cinema and his life changed. He went back to see it thirteen times.

To go with the Emerson Lake & Palmer cap Eric wears, every wall in the house is covered in Emerson Lake & Palmer posters. There are shelves full of Emerson Lake & Palmer—and every other prog rock band you can think of—videos, and a stack of Emerson Lake & Palmer CD's as high as a man. It's a punk nightmare!

14th May

Stuck in Wallasey with nothing to do.

When the football comes on the television, I go for a walk and soon find myself on the banks of the Mersey looking across to the distant silos and gantries of dockside Liverpool, a holiday feel to the riverside path in the warm sunshine as Sunday families promenade. Low tide, and shirtless men are turning over rocks on the beach, collecting shellfish in plastic supermarket bags, while far away on the river jetskiers in wetsuits churn the murky water. I walk westwards along the bank a mile or so to New Brighton, where an old fort guards the mouth of the Mersey, ice cream vans park up, and a few amusement arcades are doing a slack trade. Just round the corner you look out to the open sea, darkening now to a murderous grey under the gathering clouds. I sit for a while with a book, then head back to Eric's before the rain comes down.

Waste away the evening watching a few programmes on the cable channels, and get bitten on the foot by an enormous mosquito.

15th May

Wake up to find my foot has swollen to twice its normal size. Hang around the house until 5:30, when one of the Liverpool fans Richie and his brother Paul arrive to pick Eric and me up. It's a short drive to Chester and we get to Alexander's to find a smart, intimate venue with a café vibe to it. Bit of a panic when I check the pieces of the P.A. stacked up in the dressing room and realise half of it is missing, but after a phone call to the engineer the missing bits are located and I go about setting it all up. Mr Blonde were supposed to be headlining tonight, but Chris cancelled them (surprise!) a few days ago, which gives me the opportunity to play longer. Thirty-three songs in and the audience still won't let me leave the stage. A good way to end a tour.

Eric, Richie and I travel back in Paul's car. Somehow a discussion starts up about vegetarianism, and Richie says, 'if God didn't mean people to eat cows, why did he make them out of meat?' This is the scouse sense of humour, happily not beyond taking the piss out of scousers: when we pass the rusting hulk of a submarine on display in front of one of the old Birkenhead shipyards, Richie says, 'Look a' tha'...even tha's up on bricks!'

Back at Eric's I finally get to take off my shoe and release my swollen foot. It's monstrous. I am bigfoot.

16th May

I take the bus into Liverpool Lime Street (Third prize, Best Station Award 1986) and as I hobble up to the departure boards to check that I am getting the right train I can feel my foot kind of sloshing about inside my shoe.

By late afternoon I'm finally on the tube in London and heading for home. A grey-suited businessman is eyeing me up, probably thinking I am a hippy who has been camping with his guitar. Eventually he leans towards me and points at my guitar case. 'Is that a violin?' he inquires.

It would have to be a bloody big violin.

'No, it's a guitar,' I say.

'Well, do you know where I could buy a violin?'

'I'm sorry, I don't know anything about violins, I play the guitar.'

He's quiet for a moment, but I can see something is turning over in his mind. 'So that's a bass guitar in there, is it?'

'No, no, it's just an ordinary six string acoustic guitar.'

He looks at me as if I have taken leave of my senses.

Wake up TV. The tour is over.

18. GETTING THERE

6th June

Sixth of the sixth and I'm up at six o'clock. Surely no bad omens to be read into that?

I have a day's journey to Finland ahead of me, due in to Tampere at 3:00 in the afternoon, with an interview scheduled for five, followed by a rehearsal with Punk Lurex O.K. for a short tour.

The flight is delayed because of fog, reducing the time to catch my connecting flight at Stockholm airport to minus ten minutes. I ponder on that as I eat my delicious pre-booked vegetarian meal: a plastic dish with slices of orange, kiwi fruit and melon, with for dessert a half-size plastic dish of slices of orange and grapefruit. Plus a plastic cup of orange juice. And, mysteriously, a plastic pot of marmalade. Ooh, we vegetarians love our oranges and plastic.

After a ten minute run through Stockholm airport I find that my connecting flight has gone, the next one is full, and I'm going to be put on a flight to Helsinki instead, where a flight to Tampere will be waiting for us. We're gently coasting down to Helsinki airport when there's a sudden roar of engines and the plane lifts sharply upwards and roars away. Five minutes of sweaty palms later and the captain explains that he had to abort the landing because there was another aircraft on the runway. We circle for a while, then make another approach and land without incident, but the connecting flight to Tampere has gone.

The good news: I've got a place booked on the next Tampere flight. The bad news: it's in three hours. I'm sent over to another desk where I find another five people who are as annoyed as me, and the airline staff start trying to calm us down by promising to book us a taxi to Tampere—a two hour drive. They have no idea where my luggage or guitar is.

At this moment I realise I should be at the interview, so I use the airport phone to call Tiina from Punk Lurex.

'Hey Tim! How are you?!'

'Fine! Er...but I'm in Helsinki.'

So six of us end up in a plush airport mini-bus taxi travelling up the motorway to Tampere. As soon as we arrive I run into O'Connell's and bump straight into Jukka, just heading the other way to see if there's any sign of me. He takes me into the side room where the journalist and all the band are waiting. The journalist says this is the longest interview he has ever done—two hours and it hasn't started yet. Jukka hands me a 'welcome back' present—a quarter bottle of Lihona vodka and a kilogram bag of carrots. Probably an old Finnish tradition.

After the interview there's still time for a quick rehearsal. Just as we're about to start, the airline phones to say they've found my luggage. I'm getting there.

7th June

I meet the band at their rehearsal room at five. We load up the gear into Sami's car and take it in two trips up to the club. After soundcheck, we drive out to a rental place on the edge of town, but the van we're hiring is having the brakes fixed and isn't ready yet. Sami agrees to go back and pick it up after tonight's gig.

By an unfortunate coincidence, Pelle Miljoona, one of the most successful punk bands in Finland, is playing the Telakka, just across the courtyard from our show, and it's still worryingly empty in the Tulliklubi an hour after doors have opened. Punk Lurex go on to about fifty people, and during their set the club slowly starts to fill, so I end up playing to about a hundred—comfortable, but not exactly bursting at the seams. The audience are slow to warm up, but by the end, after Punk Lurex and I have played some songs together, they explode into life, clapping for so long they force us back for an encore even though the house lights have come on, but by then the power to the stage has been cut.

We pack up the gear and Sami arrives back with the van. The brakes still aren't working properly so he's going to have to do them himself tomorrow before we leave for Helsinki.

The rest of the band and some of the Helsinki crew who have come up to Tampere for the gig head with me down to the legendary *Doris* nightclub. The first time I played in Tampere the *Doris* wouldn't let us in; this time they've invited us in for free. Either we're getting more famous or they're getting more desperate.

8th June

Go to meet Jukka in the morning and on the way bump into staunch Helsinki crew member Hessu. He peers at me curiously: 'Don't you *ever* sleep?'

Jukka and I go to see tour agent Haari to talk about organising some gigs for next year. Jukka puts my bad luck about playing the same night as Pelle Miljoona in context: he tells me about a band he knows who recently played a gig in the north of Finland. One person showed up. Gamely, the band played anyway, then a few numbers into the set the police came into the club, arrested the single member of the audience and took him away because he'd failed to report on a drunk charge. Now *that's* bad luck.

Meet up with Punk Lurex an hour later outside the Tulliklubi. Sami was under the van in the mud this morning sorting out the brakes, and we're ready to go. So it's back past the miles of fields and forests and lakes to Helsinki, on the way discovering that the van has a leaking coolant pipe which has been dripping onto the floor and soaked through Tiina's bag, so that she has to hang all her clothes out to dry on the curtain rails above the windows and we arrive in Helsinki looking as if we are in a laundry van.

There's a very narrow alleyway to reverse down to get into the Semi-final club, but Sami paces it out and reckons he can just about get the van through. He's inching into it when there is a loud crunch. The width was okay, but he didn't think to check the height.

A promising soundcheck where everything sounds great then I go into a nearby bar for a quick interview with radio presenter Hilu, who loves the new record I've made with Punk Lurex. Recently she was in London for a Chumbawumba gig at the same time as my journalist friend Dave Thompson, who was over from Seattle. By chance they got talking at the gig. Finding out Hilu was Finnish, Dave said to her, 'I only know one Finnish band— Punk Lurex O.K.'

Hilu replied, 'I've interviewed them. They've just made a record with an English guy called TV Smith.'

Dave said, 'I'm staying at his place tonight.'

I watch from the side of the stage as Punk Lurex play a storming set that goes down well with the packed crowd. I'm itching to get started, and have an exciting gig, the audience with me all the way. The only negative point is when I walk off stage at the end and whack my head on the low ceiling, raising an interesting bump.

Much later, we get back Tommi's flat, where we'll all be staying. Riitta hits the record decks, choosing a selection of Finnish artists doing kitsch covers of sixties hits, most memorably the remarkable Freddi—a bewigged moustachioed hearthrob who belts them out in a reedy tenor. Tommi once had a band called 'The Freddis' that played only Freddi songs, and everyone in the band dressed up like Freddi, complete with the appropriate wigs and moustaches. There is some talk of a new image for me.

I drift off to sleep on a mattress on the floor around 4:30, daylight streaming through the window, to the sound of Riitta and Tiina giggling on the other side of the room, feeling as if I have strayed into a girl's sleep-over party.

9th June

Today I play on an open-air stage in a music festival in Turku, and by some miracle it's a beautiful day and the sun is shining for first time since I arrived. I'm playing at around four in the afternoon, so the band and me along with Tommi, his girlfriend Anastiina and Hessu, pile into the van and set off mid-morning. Riitta has a newspaper and reads me my horoscope: 'Er...let's see...*Aries—Don't leave home...*'

We're barely out of the city centre before we notice a rather disturbing noise coming from under the van, and pull over to discover the exhaust pipe is hanging loose and dragging along the road. Hessu to the rescue: he works at the Finnish technical research centre in the university, just a kilometre or so down the road, and knows someone who could fix it. We limp over there, and one of his colleagues comes straight out and gets to work.

It's a couple of hours drive to Turku, and as we reach the outskirts a spring on the accelerator snaps, causing the engine to rev up alarmingly every time we slow down. But, hey, we're getting there. Eventually we crawl, engine roaring, through a crush of people along the riverside to find a little bandstand-style stage, where I play a short solo gig. Somehow it doesn't really feel right: people amble past in the sparkling afternoon sunshine, not paying me much attention. The band I can see playing on the huge canopied stage further down the river aren't faring much better — their nearest audience is 30 metres away on the opposite bank.

It's time to get down to the serious business of enjoying ourselves. Shops aren't allowed to sell alcohol in Finland after nine, so we do some panic buying, then after some co-ordination with mobile phones our entire party meets up on a woody, boulder-strewn hillside looking out over the river, the sounds from the many stages reverberating around the valley. The sun never quite sinks below the horizon. We open a few bottles of wine, including the ones we were going to save for tomorrow. Jukka tells me some Finnish colloquialisms for getting drunk, including one which translates literally as 'putting your arse onto your shoulders.' We all pretty much have our arses on our shoulders by the time we make our way down the hill later in the evening to watch a few bands in the clubs in town.

During the course of the night quite a few people come up to me and say how much they'd enjoyed the gig in the afternoon—more people than I'd thought had actually seen it. It's very gratifying. One guy hands me a scrap of paper with a special message he has written for me. I find it in my pocket many hours later back at my hotel room, and it reads, 'HOPEBIRDS, ENJOYEING TANKS AND BOREFARE...MULTIMASSIVE...'

Er?

10th June

Have an appointment with Jukka and his wife Merja to look round the 16th century castle, just a short walk from the hotel. Strolling across the grounds towards it, I can't help noticing a small boat in the harbour proudly bearing the nameplate 'Fart.'

Over to the venue, a school hall on top of the hill over the river, transformed into a gig for the festival. Punk Lurex are to play soon, at three in the afternoon, with me following straight on from them. When we arrive there is no one in the hall except for one man asleep by the mixing desk. Eventually a sound engineer turns up, and suprisingly the place starts to fill.

Punk Lurex were probably very good. Unfortunately I went out of a door behind the stage to tune-up as they started and got locked out of the venue. When someone finally comes and lets me back in, the band are into their last couple of numbers and I'm just about due on.

After the gig we get in the van and head back to Tampere, hatching a plan to go to Sami's place and get his authentic wood-burning sauna going.

We unload the gear into the rehearsal room, then drive out into the forest, where Sami and his wife live in an old railway station. Sami gets to work loading wood into the boiler, then he and Jukka carry some huge containers of water over from the house to the sauna cabin to start heating. It's going to take a good hour for it to come up to the right temperature. I follow Merja and Tiina out into the woods, where they select the most suitable young branches from birch trees to make up the *vihta*, which I will have no option but to try this time. The bundles of birch are tied together with strips of bark then left to soak, ready to slap ourselves with once we're in the sauna.

As the moment arrives, Sami's wife laughingly points out that the cabin is only tiny and that there's not really room for three men's arses to squeeze together on the bench.

'Mmm—that is okay,' says Jukka, grabbing a case of beer. 'I can put my arse on my shoulders.'

So here I sit, way past midnight, sweating out the stress of the last few days, the smell of woodsmoke in the air, the gentle rumble of the boiler, the crackle and spit as the logs burn and collapse. I slap myself gently with the *vihta*, releasing the sweet smell of birch, my skin tingling.

'Harder,' says Jukka, '...my father always said, the harder you hit yourself, the better it feels.'

11th June

I have the whole day free in Tampere before my flight, so I decide to go to the Sara Hildén art museum, set in parkland on the edge of the town. Since the last time I was here, a huge tourist complex has grown around the area and I end up lost in a children's zoo, unable to find my way to the gallery, even though I can see it in the distance. I have to ask the man feeding the chickens.

A couple of hours later, I make my way back to Jukka's place, stopping off at the waterfront, where an outdoor karaoke session is taking place at a bar. Rather than the pop songs I would have expected, a succession of mournful traditional numbers are being attempted by middle-aged Finns all dressed up in their Sunday best. Despite the warm sunshine and holiday atmosphere as the boats bob on the waterfront, I find myself being drawn into these melodies full of melancholy and longing, and trudge the rest of the way back feeling strangely moved and disquieted. Somehow, even though I didn't understand a word of it, there was poetry in these songs.

SAS airlines, too, have discovered the power of poetry. The label on the cardboard box containing the snack on the flight back says, '*A taste...A sigh...A feeling of satisfaction...*' and the sachet of salt inside bears the legend, '*The colour of snow...The taste of tears...The enormity of oceans...*'

Good job the sick bag's handy.

19. LIKE A HOOPOE

PART ONE: German TV

15th September

I'm changing flights at Stüttgart airport, en route for Berlin. As my luggage goes through the X-Ray machine a clutch of officials gather round the screen and throw glances in my direction. I'm already running late because I was hauled out of the crowd for a bag search while I was checking the departure boards, now I see my chances of catching the flight slipping away altogether as one of the women approaches me, a serious look on her face.

'Could I possibly have your autograph?' she says.

I don't really have any illusions that the X-Ray team in Stüttgart airport know who TV Smith, so there is an uncomfortable silence.

Finally she says, 'You *are* in the Rolling Stones, aren't you?'

Aha! She thinks I am Keith Richards!

Anyway, celebrity is fickle. Just a few weeks ago I was invited to play a couple of songs with Tom Robinson at an Ian Dury benefit concert at London's Brixton Academy, along with a lot of people much more famous than me. Ten minutes after the applause from three thousand people had died down after our performance, we were being thrown out of our dressing room so that Robbie Williams could use it, and having to stack our gear in the corridor.

Viola, a fan who comes to many of my German gigs, is at Berlin airport to meet me. I've accepted her offer to drive me round on this tour, on the theory that she'd be going anyway, so why not pool resources. Rush hour, Friday afternoon, and it takes more than two hours to get across the city to the Wild At Heart, my favourite Berlin club.

My pilot friend Holm pops in to say hello after soundcheck. He won't be able to stay too late because he has to get up at 5:00 a.m. and drive to Bremen to take part in an aerobatics competition. We drive back to his flat for a coffee and get back to the venue at around 10:30. The place is packed and the Berlin crowd as enthusiastic as ever. What a great way to start a tour.

5:00 a.m. I have forgotten my toothbrush.

16th September

Last time I came to Klub Südstadt in Cottbus, on tour with Attila, it took us a bad-tempered hour of driving round the city before we found the venue, so this time I come prepared. I have three faxed maps of directions from the promoter, and Viola has a book of city plans. I just hope the gig turns out better than the last one, where only about fifteen people showed up.

It's not looking good by start time, just a few young punks hanging around in the club. If it's disheartening for me to play a solo set to a sparse crowd, it must be even worse for the headliners tonight, a ska band called the Tornadoes: after a full power energy-charged set, the nine of them come offstage to the sound of three people clapping once.

17th September

A long drive up to Ratzeburg, where we hop into the tourbus of the 5 Kleine Jägermeister, who'll be supporting for the next few nights, and continue on to tonight's gig in Kiel.

I am the only one in the minibus to laugh at the motorway sign to 'Wankendorf.'

Hadi, bass player for the Jägermeister and also a surgeon, studied medicine in Kiel and so is able to direct us straight to the venue. Even though we're playing in the smaller of the two halls in the 'Traumfabrik' it's still enormous, and as we wait for the technicians to get the huge P.A. set up for soundcheck I'm worrying about the turnout; it's my first time in Kiel and the gig's not been mentioned in any of the local press.

In the dressing room Hadi splints up guitarist Babe's finger, which he broke during onstage high spirits at a gig a few days ago, then they go on stage to good applause considering the place is relatively empty.

I can feel the songs going down well when I'm on stage too, and afterwards everyone's keen to tell me what a great gig it was so I feel pretty happy.

It's already late by the time we get back to Ratzeburg, where 5KJ singer Andi is putting me and Viola up for the night in his two kids' rooms—they're staying with relations. Then we have a few beers and—oops—it's 5:00 a.m.

18th September

When I eventually get up and out of the shower, Andi is just arriving back with the kids, then we have a leisurely midday breakfast. Andi isn't in the best of moods. As a day job he runs a small business supplying and operating scoreboards for sporting events, and has just heard that the deal for a board he needed for an upcoming tennis championship has fallen through.

Oh, the problems of day jobs—as time to leave for soundcheck approaches, it appears Hadi is still in mid-operation at the local hospital. We have to wait until he's through, then we drive by and pick him up.

Looking forward to this gig—have played the Knust club in Hamburg before a few times and there's always a good atmosphere. Usually get hopelessly lost trying to find it, but this time the Jägermeister drive us directly there; it's just a few paces away from a rehearsal room they use. Must tour with a local band more often.

The club is slow to fill up, and when the Jägermeister go on it's still only half full. Unfortunately, what starts off as a good-humoured gig degenerates as Andi can't hear himself in the monitors. Frustrated, he cuts short the show and walks off the stage.

Now I have to really work to get the good mood back and end up playing for two hours. Luckily, everything sounds great onstage and the audience aren't shy about letting me know they're enjoying it.

The atmosphere in the van is a little sour during the drive back to Ratzeburg due to the Jägermeisters' curtailed performance and back at Andi's we commiserate. It's been a bad day for him and he feels worse about it than anyone, but he just let the stress get to him.

Oops. Nearly 6:00 a.m.

19th September
Day off.

20th September
The bad news about this tour is that I couldn't find any gigs to fill the middle three days; the good news is that it's given me a chance to spend a day singing some backing vocals on the new Garden Gang album. Viola and I make the eight hour drive down to Bavaria and arrive at the little village where singer PamP and Andi live at about seven in the evening. PamP is just back from today's recording session and still hyped up from the studio coffee. To calm down, he pours us each a *Dünkelweizen* beer — a ritual which is even more complicated than pouring a Guiness. Too fast and it's too frothy, too slow and the yeast which gives it its characteristic flavour sticks to the inside of the bottle. We eat a delicious meal Andi has cooked from local organic ingredients, and drink another *Dünkelweizen* and...

Oops! 5:00 a.m. As I drop off to sleep I hear the whine of a mosquito around my head. Now can I be bothered to get up and catch it...?

21st September

Eech! Aark! 9 mosquito bites!

The rain is sheeting from the skies as we drive into Munich but we're soon in the hermetically sealed comfort of the studio. Lying on a shelf next to the mixing desk is a compilation CD entitled 'Americans and Brits attempt to sing in German.' Unable to resist, we listen to snippets of a few hilarious tracks until settling on Sandy Shaw's German version of 'Like a Puppet On A String,' performed here as 'Wie ein Wiedehopf im Mai,' which fits phonetically but translates back into English as 'Like a Hoopoe in May.'

Then we listen through to the new Garden Gang material, and I get going on the backing vocals—only sporadically interrupted for a few rounds of *'Wie ein Wiedehopf im Mai.....pom, pom, pom, pom...tralalalala...'*—and a lot of good work gets done.

Late evening when we re-emerge the rain is still relentlessly tipping down, and we drive back out into the countryside through a gloomy blur of spray. Back at PamP's again we have an evening meal and a *Dünkelweizen* and...

22nd September

It's true, I could be more organised. I have the address for the gig in Ulm, but no directions, and the phone number I have doesn't work. Don't know what time soundcheck is either, but figure that if we leave around 4:30 we should be fine for a soundcheck at six. It's past five by the time we get ourselves ready and into the car, but, yeah, should be fine.

Near Ulm we stop off at a petrol station to buy a town map, but the street we're looking for isn't on it. We miss the autobahn exit and have to drive another 26 kilometres before we can turn back. We drive helplessly around for a while, not even able to find the town, let alone the club, then phone up the Jägermeister — who are playing tonight too—to see if they can help. They say that to get to Ulm we have to follow the signs to Blaustein. There are no signs to Blaustein. Ten minutes later a car pulls up beside us as we pore over the map at the lights, and the driver gestures for us to wind our window down. 'BLAUSTEIN!' he shouts, pointing to the road off to the left. Brilliant! Although slightly weird that he knew what we were looking for. We follow his car when the lights change, and pull over into a layby next to him to find that he actually shouted 'BLAUSTEIN?' He's lost too.

Get a call on the mobile from Klaus, who runs my website, and is coming to the gig. He's lost.

7:00. We've found Ulm. Now all we need to do is find the club. After many phone calls and much driving around, we spot the correct street, right on the outskirts of town, by complete chance. The Jägermeister are already there, standing around waiting for the second support band to arrive because they are hoping to share equipment and make a quick getaway after the gig—they are going to drive the ten hours straight back to Ratzeburg as soon as they finish.

I'd kill for a cup of coffee right now, but they don't have any. Hardcore punk blares out from the DJ booth, and the DJ himself, obviously an old punk, keeps on wandering over and *looking* at me. There is a tiny band area curtained off, but the only place to escape the noise is out in the rapidly cooling night air, where various members of our party have gathered. Hadi is applying a new dressing to Babe's finger.

Klaus arrives, complete with new haircut and for a second I don't recognise him. He claims he is actually Klaus' brother Günter, and has killed Klaus *'that little shit'* and buried him under his floorboards. Hmm, getting a bit worried about my website manager.

Soundcheck actually doesn't sound too bad, but I'm tired and cold. With two bands to play before me there seems little chance I'll be on before one in the morning.

A few bedraggled punks are wandering into the club as I wander out with PamP and Andi to drive into Ulm to find some coffee. It's 10:00 now, and we aim to be back by the time 5KJ start at 10:30. After a few wrong turnings we find ourselves in the city centre. Ulm is neat, clean and characterless and all the cafés are closed. We walk around for a while through the quiet streets full of closed shops and eventually come across the cathedral in the central square, which is breathtakingly beautiful. Underneath it, in an incongruous modern building—a café. Two expressos later, I can once again imagine playing a gig tonight.

Out of the café, and suddenly it's misty. The top of the cathedral towers are no longer visible, shrouded in thick fog which has appeared from nowhere in the last half hour. No stars, and an unnatural hush swallowing up our voices.

In the car, we get lost trying to find the way back to the club. Out of town, on the wrong side of town, and the fog is hiding all the orientation points. By the time we're back at the club the Jägermeister have long ago finished their set and the other band is belting out their last couple of numbers to a thin crowd.

At last I get onstage, and get a pretty good response, apart from one of the hardcore punks in the room who shouts out, *'Too melodic!'*

At past three in the morning, Klaus crams into the car with us and we head off at a crawl through the mist and out of Ulm. At 5:30 we're back at PamP's and it really is time for bed. Andi says she is going to set the alarm for 6:30 because she wants to go down to the village to buy fresh bread rolls from the monastery bakery when it opens.

Klaus turns to me. 'They must be really good rolls.'

23rd/24th September

Just past midday and summer is back in Bavaria, so we sit out and have a pleasant breakfast in the back garden. Actually, they really are good rolls.

Today's gig is in a tiny organic restaurant in a village just a few kilometres from here. PamP will be playing an acoustic support set with a couple of friends, and we're expecting a good crowd from around the area. No stress, just for enjoyment.

Mid-afternoon PamP and I head off to the Garden Gang rehearsal room in a barn way out in the countryside, pick up a rudimentary P.A. system—actually the old stage monitors from the sadly-missed local venue 'The Ballroom'—and take them over to the restaurant in Asbach. As a few customers finish lunch, we start setting up the gear and moving tables out of the way. PamP practices some songs with his two bandmates, and I stroll down a lane to sit for a while in the weak sunshine by a stream which has overflowed its banks in the last few days of torrential rain and is sweeping over the fields, lapping up to the edges of the tarmac.

It's so rare and fine when everything goes as planned, as it does tonight. People come in right on time and the place is crammed full by the time PamP starts his set. He's on great form. The P.A. sounds good, and everyone is enjoying themselves. People are packed into every inch of the little room, and crushed into the hall outside, crowding around the doorway, trying to see in. I start my set and play for two glorious hours, a great way to finish the German leg of the tour.

When we get back to PamP's there's really no other option than to drink a few *Dünkelweizen* and talk bollox for a couple of hours until it's—oops — 7:00 a.m. and we force ourselves to get some sleep. When my alarm goes off at 10.15 I drag myself out of bed and knock on PamP's door to wake him up so he can take me to the airport. Running late. No time for breakfast. We're out of the house and speeding through the country lanes towards the autobahn. Less than an hour to go before my flight as we pull into Munich airport. Into the departure lounge just as my flight is called, just time to grab an expresso as I join the queue. Then I'm in my seat and on the way back to London.

PART TWO: TV Swiss

6th October

Zurich airport. The uniform standing behind the table in the customs hall beckons me over, tells me to open my guitar case, and starts questioning me about what I'm doing in Switzerland.

'I'm a musician,' I explain.

'Playing some concerts here, are you?'

It suddenly occurs to me: Switzerland isn't in the EU. Maybe I need a visa or something. Maybe if I say I'm playing gigs here they're going to throw me out...

I'm standing guiltily in front of him with my mouth hanging open, and realise I'd better come up with something quick before he starts suspecting I'm an international terrorist and drug smuggler.

'I *said*, are you playing some concerts here?' he repeats slowly, looking hard into my eyes.

'Er...yes?'

'Okay. You can go.'

René is at the airport to meet me. We drive through the Friday rush hour traffic to Bremgarten for tonight's gig. Bremgarten seems a very smart, clean, typically Swiss town. As we drive in I see only one building that looks run down, dirty and covered in graffiti: tonight's venue, of course, the KuzeB. The venue is a typical example of the youth centres you find in Switzerland and Germany: independent, underfunded; run and staffed by unpaid volunteers doing what they can against the odds, often the only place in town that will put on a gig. The front door opens into a cold, dusty, airless cellar, no-one about except a few members of the support band. Eventually we find out there's a café upstairs, so we all go up there away from the smell of damp to wait for the guy who's doing the sound.

Two hours later he turns up and we get into soundcheck, but there are technical problems: first of all nothing works, then it starts working and sounds horrible. The engineer explains that it's the last night of the old P.A. system before they install a new one.

René's partner Mariann arrives on the train, and we all go upstairs to eat, then I mope around shivering from the cold and worrying about the sound. At eleven o'clock I'm onstage. Sounds pretty terrible in the monitors, but the crowd are responding, in fact they're responding a lot. I'm getting requests for songs! I play for over an hour and a half! It's a good gig!

René, Mariann and I get into the car and head back to their flat in Winterthur. Mmm— heated car seats.

7th October

Yuk. Nose full of black gunk where I was power-breathing dust during the gig in that cellar last night.

In the kitchen area of their open-plan flat, René and Mariann have laid out a breakfast of Swiss specialities: *bircher* muesli, *gipfeli* (croissants), wedges of potent mountain cheeses, locally baked bread, and honey from René's uncle's bees. He grinds some coffee beans and brews up a delicious expresso, henceforth known as *va va voom!*

After lingering over this for an hour or so, we head off for tonight's gig, one of my favourites, the Café Mokka in Thun, a couple of hours drive away on the edge of the Alps. We've been asked to arrive by about four so I can play a couple of numbers at an afternoon wedding reception for one of the barmen.

Club manager Beat, immaculate in black eye liner and a 'Too Old To Die Young' t-shirt under his suit (it's his birthday), is standing around outside with a few of the other guests as we pull up to the club. He takes us upstairs to the dressing room and I'm pleased to see it's still as kitsch as ever, walls and shelves crammed with everything from model aeroplanes to plastic flowers, from guitars to theremins, all lit by lava lamps and Christmas lights. There's a TV set with little illuminated model planets spinning round behind the screen. I spot the new Café Mokka flyers, proudly announcing 'Musik ist scheisse.' Yes, everything is much the same at Café Mokka as last time I was here, hurrah!

In the courtyard I stand in front of about fifty people all dressed up in their wedding best, and belt out a couple of songs that I think will work acoustically out here in the open air. Maybe I should have thought about the lyrics as well: afterwards Mariann pulls me aside with a disbelieving expression, *'Gather Your Things and Go??'*

Early evening, we get back from checking in to the hotel to find Viola waiting outside the club—she's taken the ten hour train journey from Berlin because she enjoyed it here so much last time. Expectations for tonight are running high; it's going to have to be special. Happily, soundcheck goes well and by mid evening a fairly young crowd is streaming into the venue.

It is special, extra special. Up on the stage, between the model pelican and the vase of sunflowers, I play for two hours and give everything, only slightly disconcerted when halfway through I begin to notice a rather pungent aroma, finally identifying it as one of the strong cheeses I ate this morning vaporising through my pores as I pump out sweat. Lucky for the audience the stage is reasonably high. Must remember to go easy on the cheese for the rest of the tour.

After three encores I am physically unable to play another song, so I run upstairs to the dressing room where I sit heaving for breath and drinking water.

When I've recovered a little I go back down into the club and talk to some of my new fans. A local band give me a CD they've just recorded in the basement here at Café Mokka. 'We hope you like it,' they say, 'and we hope you will invite us to come and support you on a big tour of England!' I don't have the heart to tell them I can barely get gigs in England for myself.

Later René, Mariann, Viola, a new fan called Toby and I sit upstairs for a while, eat some of the delicious home-made pasta cooked by the venue, and work on emptying the well-stocked refrigerator.

The time comes to walk back to the hotel. Turns out Viola is staying in the same place as us, but Toby has to take an early train and is going to spend the night in the railway station. He says it's okay, as he wanders off through the chilly streets of Thun—it's only a few hours, and he has a good book.

8th October

Meet up with René and Mariann at eleven, and we take a walk up the picturesque river that runs through the middle of Thun and sit outside a café in the weak sun sipping a coffee while the lasts wasps of the summer buzz drunkenly around us.

Walking back to the car, I get the first suspicions that I'm going down with a cold; irritated nose, head spinning and a raging thirst. But at least today is a day off—I have until tomorrow evening to get rid of it. In the meantime, before heading back to Winterthur, we check out the map and decide to drive up to the top of one of the hills around Thun to a good viewpoint. Half an hour later we are standing in the crystal air high over the Thun lake, looking out across to the Alps, notably the black thumb of the Stockhorn poking above the the surrounding peaks, the spindly matchstick supports for the cable car—which we rode up last time we were in Thun—just visible against the skyline. All around us and down into the valley placid cows with large bells hung around their necks gong gently as they graze, like a living Swiss Tourist Board commercial. I break the mood with a volley of explosive sneezes.

9th October

Not far to go for tonight's gig in Zurich so I have the day to rest and consume huge quantities of vitamin C to hold back this cold. I confuse my hosts by asking if I can wash my handkerchiefs, but get the German word for 'handkerchief' mixed up with the word for 'tablecloth.' By the time we leave late afternoon I'm still feeling dizzy and blocked up, but running on adrenaline.

Tonight should be interesting: I'm playing a double bill with an American country singer called Katy Moffat so it should be an eclectic mix. The club flyer lists all the famous names Katy has worked with, then describes me as an old punk, nowadays perhaps *ein bischen müde* (a little tired).

Katy hasn't arrived yet but club manager Viktor suggests I play first so all my punk fans can leave if they don't want to hear her. So much for eclectisism. I do a quick soundcheck then take a walk around Zurich to clear my head and prepare for the gig as I'll be playing in about an hour.

When I get back to the club, just about ready to start, Viktor tells me tells me that Katy has just arrived and wants to do a soundcheck. She would also like to play first. I mentally stand down and set my gig alarm back two hours.

Trouble with the soundcheck. It's a new P.A. system and Viktor is having trouble making Katy's guitar audible. In desperation, he fetches me from where I'm standing up in the balcony to see if I can help. A mixing desk is a bit like a car with the hood up: groups of men with no idea of how to fix it will gather round and say things like, 'you could try pressing *that...*'

I join the cluster and accidentally hit on what the problem is, a couple of buttons muted. Suddenly Katy's guitar rings out through the speakers. Her German assistant comes over to me scowling and snaps, 'Hey! Can't you get rid of that low-mid boom on the guitar?' Oooh, I am the sound man.

As it turns out I'm pleased to be onstage later as people are still coming in as I start and the place ends up pretty packed. The set goes well, I forget about my cold for ninety minutes, and now I feel great, ready to go up to the restaurant in the balcony with René and Mariann, drink some wine, have something to eat, and talk bollox for a couple of hours.

10th October

No gig today, but René and I head off early to Schaffhausen where I'm going to be interviewed and play a couple of live songs for a two hour show at an independent radio station. Hanspeter, the DJ, seems to know quite a lot about me. We're just discussing my song about mobile phones,'The World Just Got Smaller,' and I'm saying how people use the technology to talk more trivia than ever, when there is a strange noise through our headphones: it's interference from someone sending Hanspeter an SMS message.

He plays a record and takes a call off-air. It's a listener ringing up to say that he's enjoying the interview, but doesn't like the way every time I finished saying something, Hanspeter replies, *A-ha.* 'Must try and stop doing that,' he says.

Microphones back on. 'OK, let's see just how trivial mobile phones really are,' Hanspeter announces brightly. 'I just got an SMS on my phone, let's find out what it says.' He proceeds to do so, without checking it first. It's from a friend of his who has been becoming increasingly depressed and drug dependent over the past few years since his last relationship broke up. He has finally decided to do something about it and is checking himself into a clinic to get his life back in order once and for all. '*I do not want any more contact with the outside world until I have sorted this problem out,*' Hanspeter reads aloud. '*After this message, I will be throwing my mobile phone in the river.*'

I say, 'A-ha.'

After lunch, Mariann arrives on the train and we embark on the tourist programme for the day. First, a stroll around the town and a quick stop at a posh delicatessen to try some type of biscuit which claims to be a local speciality. We all agree: not so special. Then up the many steps to the Dürer-designed fortress high over Schaffhausen. Dürer's plans were already one hundred years old by the time it was built and so it was completely useless as a military installation. Looks good though! Next stop is *the* Schaffhausen attraction, a broad stretch of rapids and waterfalls a few miles out of town.

While all the other tourists queue up to pay, René leads us down a back route through the woods to the river's edge where we stand for a while watching the crushing mass of water hurtling down towards us, little rainbows arcing over it from the spray.

Unfortunately all those positive ions don't seem to be clearing my head much. I'm still feeling ill, and quite glad to be on the road back to Winterthur to rest for the evening. On the way out of the car park there is a sign for *Das Mais Labyrinth*—literally 'The Maize Maze'— but right now even that cannot tempt me.

11th October

Just down the road for tonight's gig in Winterthur's 'Gaswerk.' Since the last time I was here, the venue for music has been moved to a much more suitable room inside the building. The P.A. and lights are excellent and soundcheck goes well, so far my voice is fine despite this cold. Now all I have to do is hope some people turn up—last time I played here it was virtually empty. René tells me that a few months ago when Nikki Sudden played only thirty people came, so for the next few hours I pace up and down the dressing room repeating to myself, '*more than Nikki Sudden...more than Nikki Sudden...*'

Turns out to be a great gig. Lots of familiar faces are here—Toby, Hanspeter, some of the audience from the Zurich gig, plenty of others I don't recognise...more than Nikki Sudden, in fact the room is nearly full. I play for two hours.

In the backstage area a young guy tells me he thought the gig was fantastic. He is really pleased because when he saw me backstage beforehand he thought I looked a bit of a *komisches Vogel*—'a strange bird.'

But I am a strange bird! I am a *Wiedehopf im Mai*.

This kid was also slightly confused by the flyers that said 'Gary Gilmore's Eyes Are Back!' on them. He thought it was going to be a solo concert by Pink Floyd guitarist Dave Gilmour.

12th October

A couple of hours drive down to the shore of Zurich lake to the small town of Stäfa, and the tiny Rössli bar. With room for about four tables and chairs and a few bar stools, this is going to be an interesting little gig. Just wish I felt better. Apart from the gathering tour fatigue, the cold has left me aching all over, with a nasty tightening at the back of my throat. Have to get on my own to try and focus on how I'll approach tonight's gig.

Out into the cool, quiet night. The tourist season in Stäfa is over and there is no-one about. I walk through the deserted streets for a while, then wander down to the water's edge and look across the choppy black expanse of the lake to the twinkling lights in the far distance on the opposite shore, breathing in the fresh air whipping off the surface of the water.

A peculiar gig. Those that can't squeeze into the bar area hang around in a corridor. Most of those that were lucky enough to get one of the few tables spend most of the concert rolling joints and barely respond at the end of the songs, despite the fact I'm standing a few feet in front of them belting it out at full power. Yet when I come off stage ninety minutes later, many of them tell me it was brilliant, one of the best gigs they've seen.

Backstage, I'm very dehydrated and ask for a litre of still water. They bring me fizzy, but I'm so thirsty I drink it, then spend the rest of the night burping.

13th October

Friday the 13th and a full moon, surely no bad omens there?

A few *va va vooms*, then René, Mariann and me get into the car for the drive through the rain down the banks of the Rhine and across the border into Germany, where we arrive at the Café Irrlicht—another youth centre—in Schopfheim by early evening.

It's going to be a late one tonight, no question, but at least I feel a bit more myself today, think this cold is finally shifting. I get the feeling tonight will be pretty punky. Already at soundcheck, while I'm running through some songs and trying to deal with some technical problems, a couple of young punks who have arrived early are dancing, and cheer me off the stage when I've finished.

Upstairs, the venue has cooked a very tasty meal of tofu paté, garlic bread, new potatoes and a mushroom casserole. As an *aperitif*, they offer a Kir Royale.

I hear that someone from a fanzine is downstairs and would like to do an interview, so I invite him up. A group of five people arrive, one to do the interview, the others to watch. The guy is a big enthusiast—saw me for the first time at Bremgarten the other day and now wants to do a piece in his fanzine 'Toilet Talk.' My heart sinks a little when he pulls from his pocket three sheets of questions written in close-lettered red ink.

An hour later we are coming to the end of our chat and the questions are getting more and more bizarre. 'I just have a few personal ones now,' he says, 'which it's up to you if you want to answer or not...'

He checks the bottom of the last sheet of paper. 'TV—why do you carry on?' Mmm. Leave the easy ones until last.

'TV—why are you so RIDICULOUSLY THIN??' Errr.

'TV—you're old, but not *that* old...why is your hair SO GREY???'

The gig is good, very punky. The crowd love it. Every now and then between songs one or other of them jumps up onto the stage and kisses me.

Two hours later I am splashing around in a puddle of my own sweat, reaching my limit. After three encores I retreat to the dressing room and ask for some water. They bring me fizzy, so I pour it over my head, then drink a litre from the tap. Out in the club they are still applauding.

Various members of the crowd come backstage to thank me. A young guy from Switzerland wearing a Union Jack T-shirt bemoans the fact he missed all the previous Swiss gigs and tells me that I have more punk in my little finger than all the other punk bands put together. 'I wish my dad was like you!' he wails.

After I have been hugged and kissed a lot on the way out of the venue (shit life being a musician) René and Mariann and me are back in the car and making our way through the rain across the border to *die Insel* (the island)—Switzerland. As it's surrounded by European Union countries, border controls still exist but we get through without a problem. René and Mariann tell me about a friend of theirs who went to visit a relative in France and was offered some vegetables from his garden. When he got stopped at the border, the customs officials found every inch of his tiny car packed with 55 kilos of potatoes.

As we drive on to Winterthur, the rain eases and every now and then the clouds part and the fat moon looks down at us.

14th October

A long lazy breakfast, then I start packing my things to take with me to tonight's gig—the last of the tour—so we can go straight to the airport tomorrow.

We've all been looking forward to this one. The Safari Beat Club has a good reputation and the town of Chur seems like it will be a nice little place, nestling in among the Alps many hours away to the South East. As we drive into the mountain region, the mist that's been hanging around all day clears and we're treated to a startling sunset over the peaks.

Happily, tonight we have a hotel; I could do with one as I can feel fatigue in every bone of my body. Unhappily, Room Twelve turns out to be the size of a cardboard box. Still, it could be worse: across the corridor in an alcove there is a Room Twelve-and-a-half.

We walk through the streets of Chur to the venue, passing a surprising amount of Sex Clubs, discos and casinos on the way. At the club the poster for the concert describes me as *songwriter-punk-Oldie-Mastermind der Adverts*.

Oldie? Oi!

Actually, I feel pretty oldie looking at how young the support band and all their friends in the audience are. After a pizza in the restaurant upstairs cooked by a chef who has an award for being '2nd best pizza chef in Switzerland' I stand around in the smoke-trap of the rear of the bar, cordoned off as a backstage, listening to the sub-Green Day thrashings of the first band, feeling a deep, deep tiredness wash over me.

Get on stage to find most of the audience are standing well away. I say hello to them and no-one says anything back. Uh-oh.

After an hour of sweat and effort they're beginning to warm to me but it really is an uphill struggle. I'm beginning to lose motivation, missing the high notes, aware of the aftermath of the cold constricting my lungs, feeling my energy ebbing away, unable to push away the thought that I can decide to leave the stage any time I like and this will all be over.

Now they're calling to me across the table blocking off the backstage area where I sit drenched with sweat and gulping water: *TV...it was great! ...play some more songs TV! ....we've waited fifteen years to see you! ...play one more song! ...why not? ...come on TV, just five more songs...!*

15th October

René, Mariann and I are on the road back towards Zurich. Before heading for the airport, there's time for lunch so we drive to a pretty little town on the edge of Zurich lake. It's a clear day with some watery sunshine. The annual town race is in progress. Red-faced runners jog by along the cobbled streets, cheered on by spectators, while an excited commentary screams out of the speakers on every street corner.

We climb up to an old castle and stroll along a walkway overlooking the lake. There's an Autumnal feel in the air. We have coffee and cake, sitting outside a café watching the stragglers huffing past behind the roped-off running course, then drive on to the airport and say our goodbyes. Now I will sleep for a very long time.

Arrive home by evening to find my car has been stolen. Instead of going to bed as hoped, I have had to cycle down to the local police station where an officer is regarding me suspiciously as if I have possibly stolen the car myself in some sort of insurance scam. He tells me to leave the room while he makes some phone calls, then calls me back in to tell me that the car has been found, 'spewing petrol onto the roadway' earlier today. The emergency services were called to deal with it.

'You are the owner, are you sir?' he enquires.

'Yes.'

'It states here in our report,' he says, eyeing a piece of paper in his hand, 'that the owner was informed by telephone this afternoon that the vehicle had been found.' He raises an eyebrow at me.

'I was in Switzerland this afternoon. I only got back an hour ago'

'A-*ha*.' Not only an insurance swindler but also an international terrorist and drug smuggler.

Eventually he gives me the address of where the car can be found. I cycle home, check the address out on the map, then cycle over to it, smelling the sharp reek of petrol from fifty yards away as I approach.

The doors are unlocked. There is a note on the dashboard from the fire brigade: *Your vehicle is blocking the way for the emergency services. Please park more considerately in future.*

Well, anyway the car seems okay. May even be able to stick the bicycle in the back and drive it home. Better check the petrol tank. Oh, someone's nicked the torch from the glove compartment. In the dark, with the freezing wind blowing around me, my sinuses blocked from the cold I wrongly believed I'd shaken off, I lie under the car and brush some debris from the bottom of the tank, including a leaf stalk which I realise—too late!—has been used to plug a neat deliberate hole, now releasing a steady stream of petrol over my hand and onto the road, where it rapidly collects in a deepening pool.

Oh.

Ah.

Something to plug it up. The leaf stalk has floated away and sunk. But if I could just find the right size twig to jam up the hole, that would do it. Yes. Then I could push the car away from the pool of petrol so that it doesn't explode in the night and arrange to get it towed away tomorrow.

A twig...hmm...must be one round here somewhere...yes, like a hoopoe in May looking for nesting material I'll feel around for a little twig...that'll do it...yes, a little twig...

...*pom, pom, pom, pom...tralalalala...*

20. SOUNDCZECH

17th November, 2000

Three days in the Czech Republic supporting the UK Subs—a first for me on both counts. Up until yesterday morning I wasn't even sure I was going—flight tickets had been promised, none had arrived. Then after a phone call to UK Subs guitarist Simon I found out that my ticket had been sent to him.

Early morning flight from Stansted airport. In a very un-punk rock display of discipline all the Subs are there on time and ready to go.

A small triumph in managing to get a vegetarian meal on the flight without having pre-booked it. It's a little salad of finely diced cucumber and onion garnished with cucumber, with a side salad of sliced cucumber. It would be a real hit if you were a cucumber fan.

The plane bumps and I look out of the window to see we've landed. The beautiful city of Prague I've heard so much about is shrouded in such thick fog there's absolutely nothing to see. Promoter Petr drives us to the hotel in his minibus and we see the dreaded sign 'Pension' above it. Two tiny rooms for the five of us. Singer Charlie has to drag his suitcase out into the corridor because there's no room to open it inside. Bass player Alvin attempts to brush his teeth, but then he also has to come out of the room because he's banging his elbows on the walls.

I wouldn't say the room is narrow but I keep on expecting someone to stick their head round the door and say, 'Tickets please!' *Thankyew!*

But at least it's only a two minute walk to the venue.

A chance to get something to eat at last in a bar a couple of doors away. Like me, Simon is vegetarian, so we're both pleased to see there's a special vegetarian section in the menu, and it's in English. Rather disappointed though to find out that all the vegetarian dishes have ham in them. Also decide to pass on the 'Soup with Yellow Eye.'

Nice looking venue, an old theatre, beautifully renovated. Small enough not to be impersonal but big enough to have the full rock'n'roll stage, lights and P.A. I open the evening and play for forty minutes—a stroll in the park compared to some of the marathons I've been playing lately—so I go off like a rocket and do hardly any talking between the songs (not least because I haven't learned a single word of Czech). Offstage by about 9.00 and now there's nothing to do except watch local band Plexis play, then the Subs. Just before they go on I hang around the foyer where some of the local punks have produced some hairspray and are giving their mohicans the finishing touches.

18th November

Seems I have the day free. The venue in Olomouc where we were supposed to play tonight, many hours drive away, has burned down and Petr has had to book us into a nearer venue as special guests to another band. We'll basically be playing for food and beer. But I'm pleased to get some free time, would hate to have missed the opportunity to see Prague.

Before I go out for a walk around the city, I get caught by the woman running the reception desk at the hotel, intent on trying out her English. She tells me a little bit about life before the revolution, when she was a teacher. After the revolution she got cancer and would have died because health care had become so expensive, but some of her former pupils who had become doctors pulled some favours and she got treatment. She recovered, but no longer had her job, and as she had no money had to start working in the Pension.

'Before the revolution there was oppression,' she admits, 'but now, tell me—honestly—is it a revolution to be poor?'

The sights of Prague don't disappoint, apart from the endless McDonald's and the swarms of tourists and the souvenir stands.

Unclear where tonight's gig is. 'Plzen' says Petr, who doesn't speak a lot of English, but we've passed Plzen and have now been driving down deserted country roads for more than an hour. Night has fallen. The first jokes about being dragged out into the forest and murdered start going around the minibus.

But no, a building appears out of nowhere, and we troop in to find about thirty people sitting at long benches lined up on either side of a large hall. Before long Brutus, the band whose gig we've bunked on to, arrive and start setting up their P.A. The place starts to fill up with people. The band seem to be soundchecking. People seem to be dancing. Turns out this band don't soundcheck—the gig has started. Petr tells me they're going to do a set, then I'll play for twenty minutes, then the Subs, then Brutus will go on again.

Simon comes up to me, waving a sheet of paper. 'Have you *seen* this?' he asks. It's the Brutus set list, comprising 65 songs.

So there's a bit of a wait. I wander over to Charlie, manning the merchandising stand at the back of the hall. There's a lot of broken glass around. Charlie explains: 'This guy comes up and looks at the sleeve of one of our records and sees there's a cover of a Toten Hosen song on it. He's so impressed he staggers backwards and falls straight through the plate glass window.'

In two weeks I go to Germany to make a record with Die Toten Hosen. Send for more glass.

So two hours later I finally hit the stage. At one point I nearly say, 'It's great to be here in...' Then I realise: I don't know where I am.

I watch from the back while the Subs play. Unfortunately the combination of punk rock and the vast amounts of alcohol being consumed result in some macho posturing in the crowd, and as the band reach their last couple of numbers multiple fights break out on the dance floor.

Next, another two hours of Brutus. As they play on, the drink is flowing backstage. I break off to get something to eat and find the only vegetarian food available—sauerkraut with some slices of white bread.

Brutus play on.

Get talking to a journalist and we have some lengthy difficulties understanding each other until we realise we can both speak German and suddenly we're communicating effortlessly.

Brutus play on.

They're doing some standards, right now it's 'Barbaranne,' and the Subs are taking the piss, boogying together with intent expressions on their faces.

Brutus play on.

Brutus play on.

We're driving forever through the backroads to the outskirts of Teplice, where we have a hotel booked right next to tomorrow's venue so we can sleep all day if we want to. We reach Teplice at six in the morning, so tired we don't care that it's another Pension. At least the place has a toilet and shower in the room, although no soap and no toilet paper.

Have you ever tried miming 'toilet paper' to a hotel receptionist who speaks no English?

19th/20th November

10:00 a.m. Just outside the window someone is cutting up a metal pipe with an angle grinder. His assistant is hammering flagstones with a sledgehammer. The walls are shaking. I crawl out of bed and fetch my earplugs.

Around midday the Subs and I meet up and head over the road to the only place open, a small bar/restaurant we hope will be able to provide breakfast, as we're all feeling a bit delicate after last night's excesses. It's soon clear that the woman running the place doesn't speak a word of English and we have to communicate in sign language that we need food and coffee. We sit down at a table and after a long wait she arrives with a tray laden with glasses of beer. A huge groan goes up.

The woman finally gathers that we want to eat. She takes the beer away and returns with a large jar of what seems to be pickled sausages, but could well be something from the local hospital. After that's been turned down she comes back with some iffy-looking bean soup which Charlie pronounces excellent. Simon tries a bowl, then stops when he finds 'something suspicious.'

I take a look round the venue; Petr's own club, run by him and his wife. Large black room with the floor dropping in steps to a wide stage. Upstairs there's a couple of comfortable band rooms with some beds. I move my gear over from the Pension and settle myself in there. Not that there'll be much sleep tonight, we have to leave for Prague airport at 5.00 in the morning.

The Subs go back to the Pension, and Petr goes to a football match. I take a long walk into town in the late afternoon dusk and send a couple of postcards. Don't know what post boxes look like here. May have posted them in a litter bin.

The evening comes in cold, and I walk back to the club. Pass a bus with the destination, '2 Anger.'

Ten thousand people at the football, but only about fifty in the club as the first band takes the stage to no applause. It's not much better for the second band, and after every song there is a deathly silence. I'm getting a bit concerned, but by the time I start at about 11.00 there's a couple of hundred in and everything goes well. When the Subs come on the whole crowd goes instantly punk rock berserk, slamming themselves all over the dance floor.

Now we have the problem: a couple of hours sleep, or go through? After spending a while in the club bar, where things are getting increasingly raucous as everyone sings along to hardcore Czech punk records blasting through the sound system, I go back upstairs at 4:30 and have a half hour doze on the bed, fully-clothed, until the call comes for us to leave.

Even though it's early, we're still late, speeding through the rain to Prague airport, arriving just in time to dash through the concourse and catch the flight. Before we leave, Petr suggests I come back in the Spring for a bigger tour. Would I say no?

21. CHILD'S PLAY

7th February

It's over a year ago since I was first contacted by a guy called Max to ask if I'd come over to Austria to take part in a benefit concert to raise money for charities helping abused children. Now, after numerous false starts, here I am flying into Vienna to play 'Child's Play 2001.'

Max is due to meet me at the airport. He e-mailed me yesterday: 'Due to the fact you don't really know me, I am always wearing two different Dr. Martens (except at weekends).'

Max drives me straight into the city, where he has found a hotel that will give me a room for free to support the project. It's a huge suite with two balconies and five beds.

We drive on to the radio station ORF for a couple of interviews. You can tell it's a radio station—there's a large sculpture of an ear outside. Then it's straight over to the Chelsea Club for soundcheck. The benefit gig's not for a couple of days, but I couldn't come to Vienna and not play the Chelsea, could I? Max also arranged a couple of other small gigs for me to make the trip worth my while.

While I soundcheck, my hosts Othmar and Rainer—who first invited me over to play the Chelsea a couple of years ago—wander in, and it's great to see them again. Not every gig I've played here has been as well attended as that first one, but each one has been very special, and I've always felt welcome.

Tonight we have a good crowd and I play my longest set so far, over two hours, 32 songs. They want more.

At around three in the morning I lug my guitar and baggage out of the club to find a taxi back to the hotel. As I say my goodbyes, one of the barmen beams at me and says, '*Unser TV*' ('Our TV'). I am so proud.

Back in my suite I realise I've forgotten to eat. Luckily there is a pineapple sweetie on the pillow.

8th February

I drag myself out of bed at 10:15 to get down to the last breakfast at 10:30. I have a heavy sightseeing programme ahead of me before tonight's gig.

I've tried to get to Bosch's 'Last Judgement' twice before when I've been in Vienna and on both occasions time's beaten me, so this visit it's priority number one. I head off on foot past the *Rathaus*, which has an ice rink set up outside it. In a family atmosphere, adults and children skate gracefully round as 'Massachusetts' by the Bee Gees pumps out of the speakers set up on scaffolding among the *Würstel* stands.

On past the imposing parliament building and the museum quarter. So much for all the warm clothes I bought with me anticipating snow and cold—it's a warm day with Spring in the air.

It occurs to me that my recently purchased cruelty-free shoes, made out of rubber, may not have such been a great idea. By the time I get to The *Akademie der bildenen Kunst* my feet are killing me. But you have to suffer for art. And Bosch is worth it—what a great painting. I stare at it for about ten minutes until I notice a Japanese girl giving me a funny look.

I hobble out of the gallery and on to the nearby *Naschmarkt*, full of colourful fruit and vegetable stalls, cafés and shops, and walk straight into the Japanese girl again. Her expression suggests that she thinks the punk who was fixating on that weird picture might be following her. Somehow embarrassed, I duck into the nearest door for a coffee. It's a fish shop.

Across the road to the art nouveau Secession building, where I take a look at the sensuous Klimt friezes in the basement, the atmosphere rather disturbed by the sound of drills and jackhammers as they renovate the galleries upstairs.

I'm back at the hotel in time to be ready for Max, who arrives at five with his girlfriend Jana. Tonight's gig is in her home town of St. Pölten, about an hour's drive away.

The venue, The Underground, is a tiny cellar bar, no stage. I kick off the gig by suggesting that the audience might like to come forward, as they're rather hugging the back wall. As one they run down the little room towards me and I spend the rest of the gig with the front row inches from my face. It's a lot of fun.

After the last song, a girl from the audience askes if she can make an announcement over the P.A. She and some friends then gather behind the microphone and sing a variant on 'Happy Birthday To You' which seems to include the word *arschloch* a lot.

Back at the hotel I finally release my feet and discover my big toe has gone right through my sock and the lining of the boot and the nail has turned black.

Realise I have forgotten to eat. Luckily there is a lemon sweetie on the pillow.

9th February

I drag myself out of bed at 10:15 to get the last breakfast, then head out past the ice rink, which seems to be having trouble coping with the springlike weather, pools of water leaking out around it.

Take the U-Bahn up to the huge Schloss Belvedere to see the two galleries housed in it. The art doesn't inspire me much, but my rubber shoes make a head-turning *skreek-skreek* noise on the wooden floor as I limp through the rooms.

The afternoon has got late, and the cramps are shooting up my shins, so I hop on the U-Bahn and head back to the hotel for an hour. Sure wish I'd bought my old Doc Martens—these boots aren't made for walking.

I get a cab to Planet Music, where Child's Play will take place. Big venue, two other bands playing.

Max is going to be introducing the acts and saying a bit from the stage about where the money raised from tonight will be spent. In the dressing room he is pulling on some pink fake snakeskin trousers which set off his mismatch Docs magnificently. Jana arrives with her mum and dad, and her little sister who has never been to a gig before but likes hip-hop. I'm introduced to Max's friend Flo, who has helped organise Child's Play, and also meet Flo's girlfriend Martina.

As start time arrives the club could be fuller, but we're past 'break even' and will make some money for the charities. Hurrah!

Backstage after the show, Othmar arrives and joins the rest of our little group, more introductions all round, and as we sit in the boxy dressing room I do a lengthy interview with a DJ and journalist called Carlos, in which he asks some very profound questions. Then we take a silly photo of him playing my guitar and me wincing with my fingers in my ears.

Othmar was intending to go home as he has to DJ at the Chelsea's all-night session tomorrow, but somehow he ends up in a cab with the rest of us, speeding across Vienna for an after-show gathering at The Loop, a club literally next door to his.

At The Loop things are comparatively quiet. Carlos is spinning some good records though, and I hang around chatting with all my new friends for a while. But the lure of the Chelsea is too great, and soon Othmar and I are heading back there.

Somehow, much later, I get back to the hotel.

10th February

With practised split-second timing I make it to the last breakfast just as they start to clear it away, then go back up to my room to get my bags packed before checkout at noon.

But we don't need to leave until five. I'm going to meet Othmar at two, which gives me just enough time to take the U-Bahn up to the North of the city centre where I hobble over to the bizarre house designed by Hundertwasser, an architect who believed 'the straight line is Godless' and so didn't include any in his buildings.

Othmar and his partner Andrea meet me in one of Vienna's oldest coffee houses. The Café Hawelka is atmospheric and charming but very, very crowded, so we decide to move on; first to an old restaurant for a plate of traditional and filling *Käsnödel*, then down some precipitous steps to a barrel-lined cellar for a glass of local wine. Then I say my goodbyes and head back to the hotel to meet Max.

Must be the weekend – Max is wearing matching shoes. We head off in a convoy to St. Pölten to pick up the P.A. from a rehearsal room for tonight's gig in Steyr: me, Max and Jana in the car, Flo and Martina in their van. Running late, and Carlos phones us on the mobile to warn us that there's been an accident on the motorway ahead.

After we finally get through the crawl of traffic, Max and Flo drop off the rest of us at Jana's parents' flat and go off in the van to get the P.A. As we watch them drive off I say gratefully to Martina, 'It's great not being one of the guys.'

Jana's mum and dad sit us down and serve us some home-baked sweet croissants and hibiscus tea, then the boys are back and we drive on another hour through the increasingly foggy night to Steyr.

Tucked away under a bridge over the river we eventually find Kennedy's Irish pub. Landlord Eamon points out the tiny area in front of one of the bars where I'll play. Start time is—well, *now*—so we set up the P.A and I get straight into it, playing to an audience of maybe thirty, another few coming and going throughout the course of the set.

Turns out we're staying in Wels, quite a drive away, where both Max's parents and Flo and Martina live. The fog's clamped down and we have to crawl along, barely able to see anything beyond the headlights. Eventually the van splits off along a different road, and soon Max, Jana and me find ourselves at Max's folks' place, where we creep quietly in to the living room. It's chilly. Max and Jana settle into the sofa bed, and I pull a blanket over myself on a fold-out affair on the floor.

11th February

Wake up to the smell of coffee brewing and slouch into the kitchen to say hello to Max's mum and dad. Mum starts making an Austrian speciality for our lunch, mixing up the dough for fruit *knödel*, which she wraps into balls around whole apricots. As I sip my coffee I hear the voice of Jana from the next room, 'I'm never, ever, ever getting out of bed.'

But she does, and Max takes us in the car on a quick tour of Wels, which he explains was once 'the Hollywood of Austria,' and points out the old city walls and towers and stuff. When we get back, the *knödel* are ready and we eat.

Flo and Martina arrive, Martina to say goodbye as she's staying here in Wels today. I say goodbye to Max's parents, then we follow Flo in the van back to St. Pölten to unload the P.A. into the rehearsal room, and say goodbye to him. Next stop, Jana's parents' flat; they're not at home but Jana is staying there so we say goodbye to her. Her little sister comes out to say goodbye too. She tells me she really enjoyed the gig even though it wasn't hip-hop. Back on the autobahn a text message comes through from Jana's parents to say goodbye. They also say, 'it's good to know there are people like you still in the world.'

Through the countryside, and the mist is lifting in swirls to reveal a crystal blue sky, the land steaming in the sun.

Then we're at Vienna airport and Max says goodbye too. That's the trouble with making new friends: all these goodbyes.

Until the next time, Vienna...

22. TROUSERLESS IN TAMPERE

14th March

The last day of three, travelling around Germany on a promo tour for my new album, due to be released in three weeks. The days involve a non-stop round of journalists, phone interviews and visits to radio stations, most of whom tell me that they love the record and believe it will do well. It all has the suspicious smell of some sort of success. Why, when I got off the plane at Düsseldorf they'd even put down a red carpet! Okay, it was soaked in disinfectant to make sure no-one on the plane was bringing foot and mouth disease into the country, but...

Today interviews are scheduled to take place in Enzian, the bar owned by spoof _schlager_ singer Heino in Berlin. Yesterday, when I phoned him up from Hamburg he suggested I play an impromptu gig in the evening, and—keen to play some music instead of just talking about it—I said yes.

So the press interviews are over by late afternoon, and Heino has cordoned off a corner of his bar, set up an ancient mixing desk that looks like it was built shortly after the invention of sound recording, and now finds he doesn't have a microphone stand. All he can come up with is one for a bass drum, about two feet high, which he balances on a bar stool, then sticks the microphone on to the end of it with gaffa tape. It reminds me of my first ever rehearsals in a friend's house, where I had to tape the microphone to the handle of a vacuum cleaner.

But actually, despite the primitive look of it, everything sounds good. I have to make do with a ten minute soundcheck because there is a taxi booked to take me on the long drive out to Potsdam to do a couple of interviews with Radio Eins.

When I arrive at the radio station, I'm surprised to find the DJ holding a copy of the record I made with Punk Lurex in Finland. It turns out he's good friends with Jukka, who runs the label, and can himself speak Finnish. He tells me it is 'easy,' which is rather irritating as I have been trying to learn it on-and-off for the last eighteen months and can still only say, 'One beer, please. Thank you.'

Mid-evening, and word has got around about the gig, even though there was only 24 hours notice. The bar is crammed and I have a good, raucous show, though slightly quieter after the police are called by an upstairs neighbour and I have to switch the volume down.

Despite my early flight to Helsinki tomorrow for a short tour of Finland, I'm not in a taxi back to the hotel until the small hours. Even worse, the taxi driver tells me it's going to take at least an hour to get to the airport in the morning.

15th March

My plan was to catch up on some sleep during the flight, but a very talkative Finnish lady settles into the seat next to me and refuses to let me ignore her. As I gaze deliberately out of the window, she nudges me and says brightly, '*GUTEN TAG!*', then continues rapidly in a Finnish-accented German that I can't understand. I have a German newspaper on my lap and she thinks I'm German. When I finally manage to stop her flow, we clear up who is from where: I'm English and can speak some German and virtually no Finnish, she's a Finn living in Germany who teaches Finnish to Germans and can also speak some English. Her husband looks over and gives me a pitying look.

I have foolishly mentioned that I find Finnish very difficult. The lady scoffs, and opens out her Finnish newspaper in front of us, marking out the syllables in the headlines with a pencil to show how the words are constructed and should be pronounced.

'Now you,' she says, handing over the pencil. 'How would you split *this* word?'

The prospect of sleep seems very far away. I dutifully mark out the syllables. 'Very good!' She makes me read out phrases from the paper. 'Ten out of ten!'

Tommi is at the airport to meet me and together we take the bus to the train station in Helsinki city centre. The reason I'm here is that for twenty years Tommi and some of his friends have been running a record label called 'Ujo' to release anything they like, the more obscure the better (and in Finland that can be pretty obscure). He's planned two anniversary gigs with Punk Lurex O.K. and some other Finnish bands and has invited me to play too. I'll also be playing a gig on my own in Tampere the day after that. This afternoon I'm taking the train to Tampere for a quick rehearsal with Punk Lurex, as they have a new drummer.

As we near the station, I ask Tommi what the sleeping arrangements are for tomorrow. He tells me that he and his girlfriend Annastiina have recently moved to a bigger apartment, so there will 'probably' be room for us all there.

'There is only one problem,' says Tommi. 'Now we have pets. Ants. A lot of ants. All over the apartment, and we can't seem to get rid of them.'

Ants. 'So what you're saying is, I *might* be able to sleep on your floor, and *if* I do, I'll have ants crawling all over me?'

He gives a brisk nod. 'It would make a good headline. Popstar eaten by ants.'

It turns out Jukka is in Helsinki for a meeting, and travelling back on the same train as me. It's a nice opportunity to chat and catch up. I pass on greetings from the guy at the radio station yesterday.

The train is a comfortable affair, with double-decker sections and a strong emphasis on the bar area. On the door of each carriage is a red warning triangle enclosing a symbol of a man in mid-air, arms and legs flailing—*DO NOT FALL OUT OF THE TRAIN!*

The countryside becomes increasingly snowy as we head North towards Tampere. Jukka walks me over to the hotel I'll be staying in tonight. It's warm and comfortable but, bizarrely, the single window in the room looks out not onto the street but directly into a gym in the same building where about twenty people are doing bench presses and pushing weights.

Down to the rehearsal room for a semi-rehearsal: Riitta can't get there for the first hour as she's travelling down from Seinäjoke, and as soon as she arrives Kukka has to leave for a gig with another band, so we never actually all rehearse at the same time. I'm struggling anyway, so tired I can hardly sing, and as soon as possible we retire to the Telakka club to meet Jukka and Merja for a beer.

A couple of hours later, as Jukka and Merja head home, I make the mistake of mentioning to Tiina and Riitta the karaoke bar we visited last time I was here, and before I know it I have been whisked around the corner to a similar place, where the two girls join the twelve other locals in the bar taking turns to sing those heartbreakingly melancholic pop songs the Finns specialise in, all done to a *dinky-dinky* synthesiser backing track.

Lucky for me there are no English songs in the selection, although I'm almost tempted to have a go at the Finnish language version of Penny Lane, or perhaps 'Moottoripyörä on Moottoripyörä'—'*A Motorbike is a Motorbike*'.

Riitta is going to do another song now, and Tiina has told me we are going to dance. Despite my struggling to remain seated, she drags me up off the bench hissing, 'if there is ever a place where you can dance a tango and no-one will ever know, it is *here*.' Riitta has started crooning the lilting 'Pieni Mies'—'*Little Man*'—and, oh God, I am dancing a tango in Tampere.

2:00 a.m. Forgot to eat. Luckily there is a butterscotch sweetie on my pillow.

16th March

Eight hours sleep. Fantastic, can't remember the last time I was able to sleep for so long. I draw back the curtains to see if it is snowing outside and—*AKK!*—twenty sweaty fitness freaks pause in their exertions and stare back at me from the gym. I snatch the curtains closed again.

I spend the morning wandering aimlessly around the streets of Tampere, enjoying the snow in my face, then meet up with the band again for another attempt at a quick rehearsal—with everyone there this time. The band cram into Tiina's car with half their gear for the trip to Helsinki, but there's no room for me so I get back on the train, then take a cab from . Helsinki station to the venue, in the Technical University in Espoo, some way out of the town centre.

Most of the loyal Helsinki crew are there to greet me. The significance of this venue is that the people involved in UJO first met here while they were studying, and this is where they began to play in bands and formulate plans for the label. In the hall, before the bands start playing, slides are being projected showing old photos of those involved in UJO over the last twenty years.

They're not allowed to sell any alcohol in the venue, so Hessu and Kivi take me down to the campus bar.

By the time we arrive back, the first of a varied selection of UJO bands are playing. Alcohol mysteriously starts appearing out of bags and coat pockets and it's starting to feel like a party.

Tommi shows me a book he has received as an UJO anniversary present—a 'How To Make It In The Music Business' type of thing. The back cover has a complicated diagram on it: a large central bubble with the words *one simple strong idea* linked to a network of smaller bubbles containing words like *'manager'*, *'touring'*, *'making a video'*, *'getting played on the radio'*, *'launching a press campaign'*.

Tommi points at the central bubble. 'Well, anyway, we got that one right.'

A band is playing whose songs all last less that twenty seconds, some only around three seconds. On a couple of them, the count-in is longer than the song. In ten minutes the entire thirty song set is over. The band stand around for a while congratulating themselves and slapping each other on the back, then launch into an epic encore, lasting about a minute. Afterwards, many in the audience are saying, 'Great! But the last song was too long...'

I catch Tiina telling Kivi about my attempt to tango. Kivi writes a regular gossip column for Finland's biggest music paper. How hollow those words seem now: *'if there is ever a place where you can dance a tango and no-one will ever know...'*

I grab a quick chat with Kivi myself. He tells me that he has recently moved out into the countryside, many hundreds of kilometres north of Helsinki. Life there is a little different. To get around the fact that you're not allowed a driving licence until you're older than sixteen, many kids in the area have taken to buying tractors, which they can legally drive. It's become something of a cult; some of these machines are enormous and can cost up to half a million for the very top of the range with all the customised extras. It's quite something, he tells me, seeing these sixteen year olds out cruising for girls in their tractors on a Friday night.

I'm not playing a set on my own tonight, just joining Punk Lurex as a not-very-surprise guest at the end of theirs. It's great fun and has everyone up on their feet and dancing.

Afterwards, around midnight as the gear starts being packed away, I'm just beginning to wonder where I'm going to be staying tonight, a bit concerned because I don't have a sleeping bag with me. I ask Tommi what's happening.

'I am very sorry. I have booked you a hotel room. I wanted to save you from the ants.'

I feel rather embarrassed about this star treatment. 'I hope it wasn't too expensive...'

'No. Do not worry. It is cheap and nasty.'

It isn't nasty, of course. It's basic, but very pleasant, and it's great not to have to sleep on the floor. Covered with ants.

17th March

Tonight's UJO party is at Helsinki's Semi-Final club which I've played two or three times over the last couple of years since Tommi first had the ridiculous idea of inviting me to Finland. I have the day to kill, and take a walk around the city.

There's a fierce wind and the temperature has plummeted since yesterday. I escape the cold for a while in a smart coffee house, then end up in the Ataneum Art Museum, which is holding an exhibition of Finnish modernism from around the turn of the 20th century. There are quite a few paintings of people fishing in ice holes.

Great to be back at the Semi-Final, despite it having the worst dressing room in Europe, a short dimly-lit stairway, blocked off at the top. Tonight, me and Punk Lurex O.K., as well as two other bands, are all trying to balance our gear on this short flight of steps.

As the first band start to soundcheck I look at their setlist, lying on the mixing desk at the back of the club, and spend quite a few minutes trying to figure out what the titles of their songs mean in English until I realise I am reading their guest list.

The club opens and Tommi gets behind the DJ booth and starts playing a great selection of old punk records. The gig is sold out, but some people are still hanging around in the freezing yard outside in the hope of getting in.

Punk Lurex play, and I slip into the stairway dressing room to tune up. There I make the unpleasant discovery that a bottle of beer has tumbled down the steps and landed on my bag, so that everything I own will now stink of it until I get back to England. While lifting the sodden bag out of the pool it's lying in, I accidentally swipe it across my jeans, which means they will also stink.

Not in the best of moods I take to the stage, but all is soon forgotten. People are leaning against the front shouting things like, 'You are our hero!', 'Just keep on going!', and 'You have a wonderful voice!'

Nightmare!

18th March

In the hotel breakfast room the waitresses are wearing uniforms disturbingly similar to British policewomen. I wait for Tiina and Piise, the new drummer, for a lift back to Tampere. The others had to leave earlier by train so there's space for me in the car.

At around four in the afternoon I take my guitar down to O'Connell's bar. Soundcheck's soon done, and I go for something to eat with Jukka and Merja in a rather upmarket restaurant. As I sit there with my 'Vegetarian Surprise' I become increasingly aware of the unpleasant smell of stale beer wafting up from my jeans and the looks I'm getting from the staff. When I get back to my hotel room, there's still a couple of hours to go before the gig, so I slip out of the jeans and rinse them out in the bath.

Oh dear. Although the room is pleasantly warm, the radiator isn't actually *hot*, which makes it rather difficult to dry the jeans. I jiggle with the thermostat, but it doesn't make any difference. I open the window above the radiator, in the hope of triggering the thermostat into life, but that doesn't work either. Mmm. Hour and a half to go to the gig, and no trousers.

The Corby Trouser Press! A staple of every reasonable hotel room, yet never used by anyone. Your day has come. I drape the jeans in there, as much of them as will fit, and switch it on. Ten minutes later, I check to see how it's going. They are wet, and slightly warm. The Corby Trouser Press has failed me. An hour and a quarter to go.

I remember seeing an ironing board in an alcove on the way to the room. Wearing a long T-shirt I scamper trouserless down the corridor and switch on the iron. As soon as it heats up, I frantically start ironing away. Within moments the cloth covering the board is sodden. The iron is steaming and spitting and seems to be making the jeans wetter than they were in the first place. Everytime I try to switch off the 'steam' feature on the iron, the heat goes off too. An hour to go. This won't do.

Hair dryer! Back in the room, I grab it out of the bathroom and plug it in to the socket next to the window. Draping the trousers over the luke warm radiator, I play the hair dryer up and down them with some success until the overheating mechanism cuts it off five minutes later. But it worked a bit, and a few minutes later, the hair dryer has cooled down enough for the safety cut-out to have reset and I can go at it again. I try tying up the legs and blast hot air down into them so they blow up like the Michelin man. Twenty minutes before

I'm due at the gig, my jeans are only slightly damp and look dry, so no one will know. I dash out of the hotel and hit the freezing wind, which immediately counters the warmth of the hair dryer so that it feels like I am wearing trousers filled with crushed ice.

Mental note: never wash your only pair of trousers just before a gig. Particularly when it's sub-zero temperatures outside.

Another mental note: never play a gig in an Irish pub the day after St. Patrick's day. Particularly when it's also a Sunday so everyone's due at work the next morning. I mean, it's not bad, but—after yesterday's triumph, playing to forty people while wearing damp trousers is a bit of a let-down.

19th March

Meet up with agent Harri in the Telakka bar at midday to talk about the possibility of some gigs in the summer, then set about the complex business of getting home.

2:00 p.m. Fetch my bags and guitar from the hotel.

3:00 p.m. Catch the train to Helsinki.

5:00 p.m. Arrive in Helsinki.

5:20 p.m. Find bus stop.

5:30 p.m. Catch bus to airport.

6:00 p.m. Arrive at Helsinki airport. Hour and a half until check in.

6:10 p.m. Find the check in desk, sit at a cafe near it and make a sandwich and a cup of coffee last a long time. Glad I brought a book.

7:05 p.m. Check in desk opens.

7:15 p.m. Check in, and finally get rid of my guitar and luggage. I'M FREE!

7:20 p.m. Go through passport control, then sit in a bar, making a miniature bottle of wine last a very long time. Glad I brought a book.

8:25 p.m. Flight leaves.

11:25 p.m. Arrive in Stansted. Put clock back two hours.

9:25 p.m. Arrive in Stansted.

9:45 p.m. Pick up baggage. It smells of stale beer.

10:10 p.m. Catch Stansted Express back to London Liverpool Street.

11:15 p.m. Arrive London Liverpool Street.

11:35 p.m. Catch Metropolitan Line tube to Shepherds Bush.

Midnight. No buses around. Walk home from Shepherds Bush.

I drop all the clothes in my bag into the laundry basket, then as an afterthought throw the bag in as well.

Switch on the television, hoping for some news to see what's been happening in the couple of weeks I've been away. The BBC is showing a short public information film called 'Ladder Safety': *'Keep both feet on the rungs at all times!'*

But then, how do you climb?

23. CHALET PUNKS

All the names in this diary have been changed to X.

31st March

A three and a half hour drive down the M4, the M5, then along the country lanes past the burning pyres of slaughtered cattle and sheep through the foot and mouth disease-ravaged Westcountry to a punk festival at Butlins holiday camp in the seaside town of Minehead. It's a three day event, with most of the audience and bands staying overnight in the little chalets usually used for the summer visitors. I'm here for the last two days of the festival.

I pull up to the backstage area at one in the afternoon to be told that my stage time of 2:50 has changed. 'You're on now.'

Somewhat wrong-footed, I get on the huge stage, hidden behind closed curtains from the auditorium, and check the guitar is working. As I'm plugging in, the promoter, X, warns me that the event is 'a bit of a shambles. Last night was fantastic, but everyone's still hungover and staying in their chalets.'

I'm announced and the curtains swish back dramatically to reveal 150 people milling around, dwarfed in the three thousand capacity ballroom. We could all fit on the stage and there'd still be room to spare.

But everyone comes down the front and leans against the unnecessary crowd barriers and we have quite a nice gig, despite the fact I haven't had time to think about a set list and have no idea what I'm going to play next. At one point a Butlins staff member comes to the stage front and hands me a piece of paper that says: *Please do not swear. This is a family venue.*

Then it's over. I feel a bit deflated. My next gig isn't until tomorrow evening in the downstairs venue.

Now I have to get the keys to my chalet. I leave the venue, following the vaguest of directions from X to find 'Guest Services,' through a cavernous sanitised shopping and leisure centre. Under a high-domed roof, video machines roar, a space age Test Your Strength machine clangs and flashes repeatedly, and a mixture of punks and other holiday makers roam around from shop to pub to designer coffee stand. One group of punks has got one of their mates onto the floor outside the supermarket and they are wrestling off his clothes to much amusement all round. Eventually he gives up struggling, and they all run off laughing, leaving him stark bollock naked.

Unable to find Guest Services among the identical ranks of chalets, I return to the complex and bump into X, who is manning his stand selling signed posters, including some Adverts ones. He calls over one of the red-coated Butlins assistants, who offers to show me where I should go.

With nanny beside me, I eventually get to Guest Services, where I join the queue for keys. Ahead of me is X, guitarist in X, who has just discovered that the whole band has been booked into one chalet, two single beds, one double. He is not a happy man.

'Has it got satellite?' his bandmate asks. Oh how we laughed.

Back to the venue, where I watch X play to a good-natured hail of empty plastic beer glasses.

I check out the smaller downstairs venue and immediately get called over by a group of people round a table. One of them jumps up, shouting, 'TV! TV! We've got to have a photo of you with our friend X here...he's a huge Adverts fan. He tattooed himself on the arm with the word 'Adverts' when he was at school...you can still see it,—show him, X!....oh....'

X has nodded off.

Time to find my chalet. My mate, the drummer from X, who is already quite pissed and chatty, gives me a hand with my gear, and we head off following a little map of the holiday camp given to me by Guest Services. A cross shows where I'm staying, in Treetop Boulevard in the Lagoon Bay zone, chalet T1.

It's a bit shabby but at least it's warm. There's a kitchen area, a little living room and three small bedrooms, each with beds with a plastic coating bonded onto the mattresses, sheets neatly folded on top of them. I leave deciding which bed to make up until later, when I find out which room is quietest. Somewhere in the chalets around me are hundreds of punk rockers.

This is my bolt-hole. I warn X, 'tell NO ONE where I'm staying!' He goes back to the bar and I have a nice warm bath.

Refreshed, I return to the venue, and chat with X, who's disappointed that X aren't going to be playing today. Seems they had the same (wrong) timing list I did, and they turned up two hours after they were supposed to finish.

The ballroom is now starting to fill up a little, as evening arrives, and the punks emerge from their chalets. Bump into X again, and we wander around between the two venues, checking out the bands and the drinks. Passes for the band members ran out yesterday evening so I have to blag my way in each time until the security guys start to recognise me and wave me through.

X has stopped being talkative, and is now wearing a stunned expression and swaying a little. A dangerous sign. He's drumming with his band tomorrow morning.

Upstairs to watch my old mates X headline. I pop backstage to say hello and guitarist X gives me a big kiss.

Back in the hall and it's now getting pretty crowded. My mate X seems to have disappeared, but everywhere I go people keep stopping me to say hello or get a photo taken with them, or buy a record, or buy me a drink. Could be worse.

Nip backstage after the gig to purloin a few sachets of coffee for the morning from the dressing room.

At 2:30 a.m. I'm wandering outside through the potentially explosive mix of punks exiting the venues, and the other Butlins crowd—dolled-up disco girls and lads on the pull—going into the conventional night clubs and karaoke bars also on the complex. Amazingly, there's no trouble, just a lot of drunken shouting and laughter.

At 3:00 I choose my room and make up the bed. As I tuck the sheets under and fold in the corners it occurs to me that I am probably the only punk in Butlins actually bothering to do this.

1st April

I consume everything in the kitchen—three sachets of coffee—and struggle out at 10:30 to meet someone from Radio 4 who's asked to interview me.

Walking briskly down between the chalets, dodging the goose shit and—ooh—blood stains. One of the chalet windows opens nearby, someone's head leans out and with a groan he throws up onto the path.

Meet X right on time and we do the interview in her car, the only quiet place. Afterwards, as I get out of the car, X—who plays bass with X—is getting into his van, looking a bit green around the gills. He shakes his head. 'I'm not well, Tim. I was on the voddies at eight in the morning yesterday and didn't stop all day. I'm going to my Gran's in Taunton for a lie-down.'

In the almost deserted upstairs venue I bump into X, guitarist with X. 'Have you played yet?' I ask.

'Yeah,' he replies. 'We were on at eleven. I woke up on the kitchen floor at twenty to eleven.'

Slip into the backstage area of the downstairs venue to see if X is in any condition to drum. He's not looking in good shape. With some relish his bandmates reveal that they opened the door of his bedroom this morning to find him lying in bed covered in his own vomit. Give them credit, they manage to pull off a pretty good set considering, then I wave them off into a taxi to take them to Taunton railway station. They're heading straight back home.

Upstairs, a band called X is playing a fairly ramshackle set to about 50 people. 'Play something you've heard before!' shouts one heckler.

It's about 2:00 in the afternoon. I'm standing around in the sun, chatting with a couple of friends. One of them is carrying a bottle of champagne. His mum's a Butlins gold card member so they get a luxury chalet, with the champagne thrown in. They tell me that X, who should be playing today, have reportedly trashed their chalet and were last seen roaring off in their minibus. Meanwhile X, who arrived too late to play yesterday will probably be playing twice. At that moment we see them come around the corner heading for the upstairs venue.

'But you're supposed to be on the in the *downstairs* venue at *four* o'clock.'

'Nah, we're on next up 'ere' says singer X.

I decide to take a walk into Minehead and see if I can find something vegetarian that isn't fast food. Out in the warm spring sunshine a few mohican punks have ventured onto the crazy golf course.

I stroll along the sea front, among the other tourists, all very British and somehow timeless. In the distance, a steam train pulls into Minehead station, at the end of a few miles of track restored by enthusiasts.

I spend half an hour in a seaside cafe with a vegetable lasagne and a pot of tea.

Back at Butlins, there's a logjam at the crazy golf course. The mohicans are having a bit of trouble on the hole where you have to hit the ball up a ramp and through the door of the model windmill.

I bump into the promoter and he tells me that the story about X trashing their chalet was just gossip and completely untrue. 'X just said it for a joke and it went round the whole camp in about ten minutes. Tittle-tattle. These punk rockers are a right bunch of old women.'

Getting close to gig time now. Everywhere I go people have been saying how much they enjoyed it yesterday and have been promising to come today so I'm looking forward to it. Also, today I'm in the downstairs venue, which has a much better vibe.

Just before going on I pop out to the bar to get a drink and get waylaid by a bunch of lads who want to introduce me to their girlfriends. 'Girls! This is TV Smith!'

'Oooh, Hall*ooooooo!*' they say. 'Wow!'

But their faces say 'Who?'

One of the guys indiscreetly tells me that one of the women has pierced nipples, but she nods approvingly, quite keen that everyone should know. They start talking about orgasms. I only came out to get a drink.

'Right, let's have a photo!'

They cluster round and the woman ducks in front of me. I'm aware of some movement and glance down to see she has lifted up her top and is fingering her piercings for the photo.

FLASH!

'...and here's one of TV Smith looking at my tits.'

Good gig. Quite a few people bought records from me yesterday and have been listening to them in their chalets, so I get some shouts for new songs as well as the old favourites. I feel full of energy and on top of it.

It's back to the chalet to drop off my gear, then back to the venues for the final stretch. Half moon in the sky. People staggering around.

Downstairs I bump straight into the guys again. 'Those girls were a bit forward,' they laugh.

'Those girls? I thought they were your girlfriends....'

'Never seen 'em before. Have a drink.'

Past midnight, and X is going down a storm. I'm at the bar with another bunch of guys who want to find me some gigs in Britain, and keep buying me drinks. One of them says, 'I thought you were supposed to be a star. What are you doing hanging around with us fat middle-aged pissed blokes?'

As the end of the evening approaches I bump into X, who I haven't seen since we toured together in 1977. We laugh about the situation: 'Did any of us back then think we'd end up playing Butlins in 2001?'

Your secret is safe with me, X.

Back to the chalet. Howls, shouts and laughter in the night as I get my head down at 3:30.

WOOOOOOOOOOOOOOOOOO!
WAAAAAAAAAAAAAAAAAH!!
OI—OI—OI!

YAAAAAAAAAAAAAAAH!

24. HERE COMES SUMMER

PART ONE: GERMANY

1st June

The first thing to come up the luggage ramp at Düsseldorf airport is my guitar, with a little yellow Pokemon toy sitting on it. The baggage handlers are having a laugh.

I'm in the middle of a hay fever sneezing fit in the sunshine outside Arrivals when Vom, English drummer with Die Toten Hosen—or, as he calls them, 'The 'Osepipes'—finally finds me. After driving round for twenty minutes through the maze of roads in the airport he dumped the car in the multi-storey and came looking for me on foot. Unfortunately he forgot to make a note of which floor he parked on and now it takes us another twenty minutes to find the car. Vom's just come from rehearsal with the Hosen, where guitarist Kuddel suggested joining in with me on a few songs at the gig tonight. He's put his enormous amp and cab in the back of Vom's tiny car for us to take to the venue, so I squeeze into the front passenger seat with my knees up to my chin. By the time we make it to the car park barrier the free parking time has expired and we block the road while Vom jumps out to find a ticket machine, as does everyone else who drives up. No-one has ever yet managed to get out of the Düsseldorf airport car park in the allotted twenty minute free parking time. Fact.

Driving in to Düsseldorf, we talk about tonight's gig. It's my first tour in Germany since the release of my album 'Useless' with Die Toten Hosen as my backing band, and Düsseldorf is their home town so the omens are good. On the other hand, Summer is coming and everyone has warned me that it's a terrible time of year to tour: people are either away on holiday or sitting around in beer gardens enjoying the warm evenings.

It took some persuading to get Buck Mulligans, a large Irish pub in the old town, to put on the gig. Vom went down there a few months ago and tried to exploit the Toten Hosen connection, but the Irish manager wasn't impressed. He'd never heard of them. Then I spent a few weeks phoning up every other day while he promised to talk to his boss about it. Finally, with a couple of weeks to go before the tour started I told him that he had to confirm by tomorrow or forget it. He phoned up, breathless, at midnight: 'I've just had a very exciting meeting with the boss. He wants you to do the gig. In fact he want you to do *two* nights.'

Seems the boss has heard of Die Toten Hosen.

After soundcheck Vom takes me to the hotel the venue has booked, a ten minute drive away on a small square called Fürstenplatz. The room is small but has everything I need, more if you include the smell of cat's pee. I open the window. Then we go out to an Italian round the corner where I have pasta with a U.F.M. (Unexpected Fish Moment).

Kuddel couldn't make it to soundcheck, but now rings up to say he's at the venue so Vom and me head back and find the place already pretty full with a couple of hundred people. A few chat to us as we walk in. One claims to know me pretty well: 'What was the name of that band you were in...*Erdwerks?*' ('Gasworks')

Vom, laughing, says it was the *Adverts*.

'Oh, of course,' the other guy says. 'Where are you from...Holland?'

There's no backstage, so Kuddel and me practice a few numbers acoustically in the concrete stockroom, while the staff rush past fetching crates, and dumping empties with a great crash over the drain in the middle of the floor.

Klaus arrives from Aachen just in time for the gig. As well as designing and managing my website, he's recently got a car and is going to drive me around for the first half of this tour.

Time to start.

Two sets tonight, a half hour break in the middle. From the first note it's dynamite, with a packed crowd dancing and singing along. In the second set Kuddel gets onstage for eight numbers and the place goes nuts. A wave of people collapse forward onto the stage and all the glasses and bottles that have been placed there get smashed. I'm crunching through broken glass, and the noise travels up through the microphone stand and roars out through the P.A. As it gets too crowded at the front, people are being lifted up over the heads of the rest and carried to the back of the crowd. One of the bar managers struggles down to the stage a couple of numbers from the end and gestures to me. '*Please* ask them to stop swinging from the lighting bars—we need them.'

Then I'm back in the stockroom, exhausted after playing 34 songs. The Hosen come back and hang around. We're all in a good mood and drink a beer or five.

At around two, Klaus and me and a few friends head round the corner to the Q-stall, the small bar I played the last time I was in Düsseldorf. Klaus has told me he could give me a lift back to my hotel if it's anywhere near his brother Gunter's place, which is where he'll be spending the next couple of nights. I've no idea where his brother lives, and at four in the morning – thoughtful of the two weeks of this tour that still lie ahead of me – I take the simple solution, jump in a cab and escape.

2nd June

Wake up too late for the hotel breakfast and walk for half an hour through the drizzle to the main train station to find a coffee and cheese roll. Fortified, I hurry back just in time to meet Clemens, from my record label JKP, who drives me to a radio station for an interview. The rain is now sheeting down and the clouds ominously black.

'In Germany, every low pressure band is given a name by the weathermen,' says Clemens. 'This one is called *Clemens*.'

Back to the hotel. I change the strings on my guitar ready for tonight's marathon then, realising I'm late for a pre-soundcheck interview at the venue, hurriedly throw all the things I need into my bag, grab my guitar and head out. The rain is still tipping down and there are no taxis to be found, so I'm soaked through by the time I get to Buck Mulligans. I sit dripping at a table with three girls from a fanzine who do an interview which lasts about two hours.

I hadn't been convinced I could fill the place for two nights, but there are almost as many people in as yesterday. Another good set. By the half time break, though, I'm getting seriously worried about my voice which is switching all over the place. Got to get an early night tonight.

To the strains of 'Kung Fu Fighting' from the DJ (Buck Mulligans really hasn't got the idea about punk rock) I'm back on for the second set. Towards the end, Vom hops up with a tambourine and joins in.

Uh-oh. As twenty or thirty people pile into the storeroom to congratulate me and ask for autographs I find that my voice has completely disappeared. The manager is getting annoyed about all the people back here, and I try and hustle everyone back out into the pub—not easy when you can't speak. People try and talk to me as I sit at a table in the bar signing records and I just point at my throat and shrug helplessly. Over the last two days I've sung sixty three songs.

Klaus tells me that his friend Markus is going to drop him off at his brother's place and has offered to drive me back to my hotel too. They head off to fetch the car and I slip back to the concrete store room and wait, glancing nervously at the time and worrying about my voice.

The early night is not going to happen. Klaus and Markus couldn't find where they parked, and when they eventually get back with the car they have to leave it a couple of streets away because of the pedestrianised zone. We carry my guitar and bags over to it and I try and direct them back to the hotel but we soon get lost. Finally we pull over and I hand the address of the hotel to Klaus so he can ask someone the way. He glances at the piece of paper. 'Fürstenplatz—that's where my brother lives.' For the last two days he's been staying just a couple of doors away from me.

3rd June

Feels alright. No strain. No pain. I try quietly saying a few words to myself...no voice.

I send a text message to Peter, the promoter of tonight's gig in Iserlohn, to tell him that I've lost my voice and I don't know if I'm going to be able to play. He calls back. 'Try milk, honey, and salty fish. I'll call you again in a couple of hours.'

I say, '*HHEEWWWAHHH HHHIEEEE!*'

Klaus calls to invite me over to Gunter's for breakfast. Out of the window I see him dash out of the house over the road. In ten steps he's at the hotel. We pack my gear together and take it over to the flat where I croak a hello. With some gargling and throat tablets I'm managing to force a little sound out now, just above a whisper. Gunter goes out to buy me some honey from a nearby shop and I drink three mugs of bronchial tea with a vitamin-packed breakfast of fresh fruits.

By the time Peter rings back I've decided that I'm going to go to Iserlohn whatever happens—if I can't sing, then at least I can be there in person to apologise. Whatever happens though, the gig Peter's organised for tomorrow—a low-key acoustic session to open a tattoo parlour, also in Iserlohn—is off.

Gunter packs up the tea and honey for me to take with me then Klaus and I load up his car and head for Iserlohn. As my website master, Klaus knows all the tricks, and has printed up a detailed route plan from a computer navigation programme showing every turn and intersection along the way, so we only get lost a couple of times.

A few hours sitting quietly in the car glugging back water and I'm feeling more confident by the time we arrive. Peter is waiting outside the venue and is sympathetic. He's agreed we should cancel the gig tomorrow. We've also agreed he should cancel the hotel for tonight as there won't be enough money coming in to pay for it, so Klaus and I will have to do the three hour drive back to Aachen after the gig.

In the venue, a pub called the Lindenhof, the P.A. is being tested and there is a great deal of complicated technical stuff going on as they attempt to link it into an internet radio station which is broadcasting live from the back of the room, next to where I'll be playing. When it comes to soundcheck, I cut it as short as possible but I'm gratified that I seem to be able to sing. The manager of the pub comes over. She's keen to open the doors and needs to know what's going on—is the gig happening? I tell her I'll be able to play a short set but she should lower the ticket price in case I have to give up.

A decent crowd comes in. As I start singing, I feel my voice warming up and getting stronger and, safe in the knowledge that I'm going to have a day off tomorrow, I keep going through twenty-two songs, nearly an hour and a half on stage. Over in the corner beside me I can hear the radio presenter doing a little commentary between songs. I say something to the people in the pub about not getting much feedback from the radio audience and from then on the DJ brings over a succession of pieces of paper with email messages from the listeners. 'Greetings from Mannheim, Cologne and Munich.' 'Greetings from Siegen and Bielefeld.' 'Greetings from Berlin and Duisburg.' 'Greetings from Anke...she says, 'you should drink a Sabucca for your voice.''

Klaus and I load into the car. I realise I haven't eaten anything since breakfast so at the first petrol station we come to I buy the only vegetarian option available, some bread and a packet of sliced cheese, slap it together, and sit morosely chewing in the stark blue light of the Aral sign while Klaus studies the print-outs of the route back to Aachen. For nearly an hour we follow it through all sorts of winding narrow lanes convinced we are lost until we eventually hit an autobahn. Klaus says, 'Maybe I will change the settings on the programme.'

At four-thirty in the morning, Klaus installs me into his flat, then goes round the corner to stay with his girlfriend Melanie, leaving me instructions to move his hamster Fletch out of the room before I go to sleep as he will probably start noisily running round his wheel. 'The best place to leave him is out of the draught, in the bathroom.' He gives me a look. 'Please don't mistake Fletch for the toilet and piss on him in the night.'

85 songs so far. I have nearly two days to rest up before the next gig, here in Aachen. Everything will be fine.

4th June

I can speak! We have a relaxed afternoon breakfast in Melanie's flat, then back to Klaus' where he spends a couple of hours updating the website and checking some statistics provided by his ISP. One of the statistics he can bring up shows which search words or phrases were used that brought people to tvsmith.com. The fifth most popular was 'hardcore tv.'

Soon after midnight I return to Klaus' flat and get a comparatively early night. I have the whole day tomorrow before the gig here in Aachen in the evening. My voice is already pretty much back to normal. Everything will be fine.

5th June

Aachen's Irish pub, 'The Wild Rover' might not have been the best venue for the gig; it's not on the punk circuit, and I have a strong suspicion no one knows about the gig. One poster inside the doorway just isn't enough. There's hardly anyone in by the time I start, but I'm so relieved I can sing that I play for ages, enjoying being able to hit all the notes again, and get through another twenty nine songs before calling it a day after four encores.

6th June

Tonight's gig was arranged over the website after someone wrote an email saying, 'TV—if you ever feel like playing a gig in a tiny place out in the country called Nettetal, I know someone who's got a club there who could maybe put you on.'

I said, 'Okay.'

It's just a couple of hours drive, past endless kilometres of asparagus and strawberry fields. Klaus has adjusted the settings and we don't get lost. The venue is a medium sized club, part of an arts centre inside the train station, right opposite the platforms. We drive up on time and Ingo, the guy who wrote to me, is waiting for us. It's the first time he's promoted a gig and he's diligently taking care of all the details. His girlfriend has freshly prepared some healthy food which she sets out on a table for all the bands and crew to help themselves to. I have a U.F.M. with the salad.

People start filling the venue. It's looking good. I get up and play close on to two hours again, the voice totally fine and back to full power, but I make sure I stop after four encores. Then I chat to some of the audience, sign a few autographs and get my photo taken with lots of people. One of them tells me he thought the Toten Hosen might show up tonight as surprise guests—(here? In this little club in a railway station in the middle of nowhere?)—but in the end really enjoyed the gig without them.

Ingo drives us out to the guest house, near his home in Brüggen. His first gig as a promoter went well: over a hundred people turned up, everyone had a great time and when the sums are all added up it's even possible he didn't lose money.

7th June

A long drive to Celle for a gig with the 5 Kleine Jägermeister, who'll be supporting me for a few dates on this tour. The settings work and we get to the venue, the 'CD Kaserne' late afternoon. It turns out to be a large room in a youth centre, with a huge stage and P.A. There are large sliding double doors at the front of the room and when the Jägermeister arrive, they drive the tourbus into the venue and right up to the stage to unload.

While they set up, I wander out front to grab the last few weak rays of sunshine and bump into two Toten Hosen fans who saw the concert in Düsseldorf and liked it so much they decided to come along to this one too. They ask me if any of the Toten Hosen might be turning up as special surprise guests. I tell them it would certainly be a surprise to me. Actually, I'm wondering if *anyone* is going to turn up. The date was switched a couple of weeks ago, and the venue hasn't bothered to change it on the posters so I have my suspicions about how much work they've done on the publicity.

After soundcheck I get a chance to meet up again with Jägermeister singer Andi, who'll be putting Klaus and me up at his house for the next few days. He's in good spirits and looking forward to the dates. Everything's ready for when we get back tonight, he tells me: 'We've got a huge home-made pizza and two crates of beer waiting in Ratzeburg!'

Unfortunately, Ratzeburg is more than a three hour drive away. After a disappointing concert in front of only about forty people, we arrive back at Andi's at four-thirty in the morning.

You can't just go to sleep after a drive like that, so we sit around chatting for a while about how things are going for the Jägermeister. Lately they've been getting more gigs, but they still don't make enough money to live from music, and have to deal with all the complexities of having jobs at the same time as being in a band. Despite the tattoos, chain-smoking and drinking, they have the most un-rock'n'roll jobs imaginable: the two guitarists Babe and Stephan are respectively a florist and a nursery assistant. Most problematic is bass player Hadi, who is an overworked surgeon at a local hospital and always turns up to gigs dog-tired. Today he's had to do a triple-shift and hasn't had any sleep for thirty six hours. On the last shift a mechanic came in who'd severed a finger while repairing a car. Hadi rushed over to the garage and recovered the finger from a pool of grease, cleaned it up and sewed it back on. Then he had to leave for the gig.

The night has slipped away and now the bloody sun is coming up and the bloody birds are singing. As light spreads across the garden, Andi proudly tells us about the 22 varieties of chili pepper plants he is growing out there and suggests we might like to go out and see them. It's six in the morning. I tactfully suggest that we would appreciate them better in full daylight, so instead he shows us upstairs to the two kid's rooms where Klaus and I will be sleeping. The kids are installed in their parents bedroom, and Andi and his wife Tatjana are sleeping in the living room, just as soon as we break up this little party.

168 songs so far.

8th June

Andi and Tatjana's youngest, Genie, remembers me—I'm the one that can't talk properly. But what a great German teacher he is. We wander round the garden and he tells me what things are called—this is a football, this is a tree...

'And what colour is this?' he asks in German, pointing at a flower.

'Blue,' I reply.

He nods. 'And this?'

'Er...I don't know.'

'It's...p-u-r-p-l-e.'

It hasn't quite clicked with him that I usually speak another language. He thinks that I am just a bit slow.

Just a twenty minute drive to tonight's gig. Had trouble filling this part of the tour but one of the Jägermeister found me this solo gig in a pub in his home town of Mölln. We arrive at the venue at six. The pub is right in the railway station (you wait ages for a gig in a railway station and then two come along at once...) with no stage or lights. On the far wall an electronic sign board flashes the message, 'Live music on Friday with TV Smith. Let's go rock!'

The place is still pretty empty so I wander outside and hang around the front door, chatting to people as they come in. Quite a few are wondering what I'm doing playing in Mölln and I explain to them that I'd rather play a gig than have a day off. Someone tells me they wondered if the Toten Hosen might turn up tonight as surprise guests.

After a while the boss of the pub comes out and asks me, rather curtly, when I'm going to start. I glance into the pub, which is starting to fill, and say, 'I reckon in about ten minutes.'

He shakes his head. 'I'm sorry but you won't be starting in ten minutes. You're starting now.'

Great idea! Get me to play a concert in a bad mood!

I sweat it out for an hour and three-quarters and the audience really enjoys it but afterwards the boss doesn't even say 'thank you,' and I feel a bit weird about it. He may be the boss of the pub, but he's not my boss.

We load in the P.A. and drive back to Ratzeburg. Tatjana and the kids are asleep indoors, so we sit around a table in the garden, light a fire in the barbecue to fight off the evening chill, and drink too much.

I head for bed eventually, still in rather a 'what am I doing this for?' mood. For the first time I notice the large rug on the floor of the room I'm sleeping in. The design embroidered on the rug is a scattering of flashily-designed words on a musical theme: POP. RAP. WESTERN. COUNTRY. PUNK. MUSIC. WAVE. EXOTIC. SOUND. DIXIE. RAVE. But where do I fit in to all this? One corner of the rug is covered up by my guitar case; out of curiosity I lift it out of the way to see what's underneath.

T.V. LIVE MUSIC.

9th June

'Woher kennst Du so gut Deutsch, TV?' ('How come your German is so good, TV?') That's been the constant question on this tour so far. I mean, I know it's unusual for an English person to learn another language, but I didn't realise it was *that* unusual. The trouble is, The

Question has now been asked so many times that it's become a trigger point for suppressed giggling and snickering between me and Klaus every time someone asks it.

The other two most-asked questions are, 'What was it like working with the Toten Hosen?' and 'TV, do you *really* know Campino?'

Klaus and I are discussing this phenomenon on the long drive to Hannover in the Jägermeister's tourbus, and he suggests he could perhaps save me some trouble and put up a FAQ page on the website.

Hadi is sitting in the front of the van, looking tired. He leans back over the seat to me. 'I was just thinking, TV, if there's anything you need *doing*...I'd be happy to, you know...' In the last few years Hadi has already performed minor surgical operations on most of the band and their families.

'Well, er...nothing at the moment. But thanks all the same.'

We get into Hannover late afternoon, miss one vital direction on the instructions on how to get to the venue and drive around lost for a while, pulling up to the curiously-named 'Bei Chez Heinz' still in good time for a soundcheck.

While the Jägermeister load into the venue, Klaus and I walk off to a local radio station where an interview and a couple of live songs are planned. The interview goes well, although Klaus and I battle to keep a straight face when the presenter innocently kicks off with two of the three FAQs.

Back at the venue there's a spacious dressing room and some food laid out. A pinball machine helps while away the wait for the show, but it's still long, long, long... Seems I have been on tour forever already and the waiting around is getting hard. The pinball machine has a 'jailbreak' theme and every now and then a panicky recorded voice screeches *I'll never get out of here...!'*

It's a big club, but it's turning into a big audience. As soon as I start I can feel it's going to be a good one. Onstage for over two hours.

It's a long way back to Ratzeburg. By the time we've loaded everything it's past three in the morning, and we power for hours down the autobahn until a red fuzzy sun edges over the horizon. A light sea of mist hovers over the fields. We cruise past the brace of wind generators on a hill near Hamburg, the giant blades static in the morning calm, and a small cheer goes up from those of us left awake as we cross the border into Schleswig Holstein: the last stretch.

10th June

Four hours sleep. I dream that I left my shoes in a taxi.

I'd love to sleep more but downstairs I can hear Andi moving around, and although today is theoretically a day off, he's actually planned to put on a party this afternoon down on the shores of the lake in Ratzeburg, and I want to help him prepare for it. Bleary-eyed, we meet up with guitarist Babe on the edge of the Ratzeburg lake. The plan is for us to rig up a couple of makeshift marquees, bring in some crates of beer to sell to anyone who comes along and play a few songs later in the day.

You would have to say that the weather is not ideal. A fierce wind is whipping in from the lake, which is a deathly shade of black, and waves are slapping wildly against the shore. We stomp around in the unseasonal cold, trying to hitch some string over the high branches of a tree by the lakeside, so we can haul up some sheeting to make some sort of tent, but the string snaps every time we pull on it.

Help is at hand. A request for rope at the nearby lifeboat station leads to an offer of two tents from the enthusiastic young volunteers manning the place. Between us we carry a couple of sacks of metal poles and canvas over to the field where we're planning on having the party, and start assembling them. Half an hour later we have a ragged approximation of two small open-sided marquees, loose canvas flapping in the howling gale, some of the poles bound together with tape where the pieces didn't quite fit. The volunteers then offer us a few more things they think might be useful and we carry over wooden benches and tables and place them under the canvas. We unload the crates of beer from the Jägermeister tour bus, along with the barbecue and the packs of *würst* and bread rolls and sit around in a huddle waiting for people to turn up.

They don't. After a couple of hours there's still only a handful there and none of the musicians feels like playing. We light the barbecue to keep warm, then as the rain starts to drizzle down in the late afternoon we pack all the beer and unopened packs of *würst* away again, dismantle the tents and carry them back over to the lifeboat station, and drive back to Andi's. We go out to a restaurant and spend the evening complaining about how apathetic the people in Ratzeburg are.

11th June

The real day off. I've been telling Klaus how great the Paul Weber museum is and today's got to be the day, so we drive into the town after a late breakfast, park near the market square and wander over to the museum. It's closed. So instead we walk over to the cathedral. On the way we are stopped by a group of schoolgirls, who ask, 'Excuse me, do you know how much the mini golf costs in Ratzeburg?'

We don't.

Ratzeburg cathedral still has cannonballs lodged in the walls from when the region was at war with, oh, the Danes or someone. Ages ago.

Wandering down to the lakeside we are stopped by a group of schoolboys, who ask, 'Excuse me, but do you know what number is on the door of the Ratzeburg sailing club?'

What's going on? It takes a moment before we notice that the kids are carrying clipboards with a page of questions on, for a school test about the town. We can't help with the number of the sailing club, but Klaus takes them over to a nearby telephone box so they can fill in the answer to the question about the local telephone code. They already know how much the mini golf costs.

Back at Andi's in time to meet Lutz at 4:30. He's a photographer and has asked if he can take me away for a while for some photos. His plan is for us to go out in a boat on the Ratzeburg lake. Luckily the weather is better than yesterday. He drives us to his cottage a little further down the lake, loads up with cameras and rolls of film and I follow him down to the shore. When I get there he is baling water out of a wooden rowing boat with a bucket.

Lutz rows us out towards the centre of the lake so that we get into the full light of the sun, which is fast disappearing over the wooded hills in the distance. The choppy water is dancing with light, and there's a stiff breeze. I stand wobbling in the prow of the boat playing my guitar while Lutz leans back at the other end, snapping away. I take off my jacket for some photos in a t-shirt.

'The goose flesh looks good,' says Lutz, encouragingly.

We've been out here for some time now and I can't help noticing that there's more water sloshing about in the bottom of the boat than there was when we started. I point it out to Lutz. 'Hmm, you're right,' he says, carefully puts down his camera on the plank seat and gets back to work with the bucket, which had been bobbing merrily away in the rising water at our feet. 'The boat's been up on the bank all winter, it's not all that watertight.'

As soon as he bails it out it starts coming back in. I can see a rapid stream bubbling up between the boards. 'Er...*how many* rolls of film have you still got to take...?'

The shore seems an awfully long way away, and after stopping to bail out a few more times I'm quite relieved when the final shot is taken and we can start heading back. The wind has carried us far out into the lake and it takes some serious rowing to get to the shore.

We haul the boat up out of the water, then drive over to Lutz's studio in Mölln to do some shots on dry land.

12th June

Just one wrong turn, that's all it takes to get hopelessly lost in Hamburg, but Klaus and I get to see some of the docks before we accidentally find another route that takes us right to the club. The Knust is one of my favourites, a great atmosphere and small enough to make it possible to have a good gig even if not many people turn up. I arrive to be greeted with the news that's there are already 30 tickets sold in advance—more than the entire audience on my last visit—and another 36 press and media people on the guest list from the record company.

By the time I get on stage the club is packed, somehow around 120 people have managed to squeeze in, and I play for over two hours, 36 songs. 267 on the tour so far.

After the Knust closes, promoter Norbert takes us over to a little drinking club near the hotel, where we sit for a few hours. The couple of girl fans who I first met in Celle follow us to the bar, and seem content to sit and watch as me and Norbert chat. Wandering back to the hotel as the sky becomes light, Klaus tells me that the two fans told him he was really lucky to be travelling in the same car as 'sweet' TV Smith. Hah! They haven't seen me after a four hour journey heading for another dark sweaty club and a late night, as I gaze resentfully at the workers in the asparagus fields and grumble, 'Out in the sun all day, regular wages, regular food, regular sleep—I could be doing that...'

Haven't eaten anything except a couple of cheese rolls all day. There is a chocolate-flavoured toffee on the bed.

13th June

My new method on tour is to completely ignore hotel breakfasts, which always seem to get packed away about ten in the morning, and sleep late instead. After all, it only costs a couple of quid to buy a better version of the same thing later, and the sleep is more important. When we're roused out of the hotel shortly before midday, that's what Klaus and I do. While we sit in the Italian café and I satisfy my urge to eat 'something green' with a spinach omelette and salad, Klaus explains an embarrassing incident in his hotel room this morning. Collapsing into bed after last night's late drinking, he failed to notice the chocolate toffee and it melted underneath him. When he woke up, he went across the corridor to shower and came back to find the chambermaids already in his room, gazing suspiciously at the brown soiled sheets.

Unexpectedly we manage to drive out of Hamburg without making any wrong turnings and meet up with the Jägermeister tour bus in a lay-by a few kilometres out of the city. They've driven down from Ratzeburg this morning and Klaus and I are going to travel with them in the bus to an open air festival in Paderborn, picking up the car again when we return tomorrow. Our luck seems to be holding out with the weather: it's a clear blue sky and the sun is beating down, but it means an uncomfortably sticky three hour drive.

The festival is a curiosity. Run by a hotel restaurant, set in fields miles from anywhere, I have no idea what to expect. It takes some time driving around the country lanes before we find the place. We get out of the van and start to unpack the gear into the field. The stage has been set up already and the final pieces of the security fence are being put into place so that access from the rest of the hotel and grounds can only be gained through the one entrance gate at the opposite end of the field from the stage. Beer and *würst* stands are being set up. Cows graze quietly in the fields on the other side of the fence. A small stream ripples gently by behind the stage. Klaus wanders back from the entrance gate where he has been chatting to a few punks hanging around there and has found out that apparently there is a rumour going around that the Toten Hosen will make an appearance tonight as surprise guests. Even though today they are playing in a festival two hundred kilometres away.

After soundcheck we cross the lane to the hotel, where the chef has prepared a top quality meal for us. For the meat eaters it's asparagus soup followed by massive *würsts* and pan-fried potatoes; for the vegetarians it's asparagus soup followed by asparagus. We're shown to where we're going to sleep: the band and Klaus are in two large rooms in a low gabled building opposite the hotel, I'm led up the stairs to a lovely single room under the eaves, where I sit peacefully for a while, listening to the first chords from the local support band as they take the stage in the distance.

Maybe I'm the nearest thing to a famous person they've had around here. I'm getting a lot of curious looks as I wander past the uniformed security guards on the front gate, and a bunch of youths gather round me as I hang around side stage. They keep saying things like, 'TV Smith! Is it really you? I've seen the picture on the album and it sure looks like you!' I'm not quite sure what's going on until Hadi explains that for a joke he has been telling them all that I am TV Smith's double.

As the time to start approaches, the young fans tell me: 'We're really looking forward to it. We'll see you up on the stage later.'

There's no security barrier in front of the stage—in fact right in the middle there are steps leading up to it—and I get the impression that the fans mean *they* will be up on the stage too.

Pretty good atmosphere for an open air gig. Even though quite a few are hanging back by the beer and food stands there are still a few hundred up close to the stage and the avid fans in the first few rows are singing along and dancing.

Sure enough, it doesn't take long for the first visitor to get up with me. I'm joined by a drunken woman who hands me her glass of beer, waves her arms at the rest of the audience, then bumps me off the microphone where she slurs something unintelligible for a few minutes. I stand patiently by until the crowd boo her off, then carry on with the gig.

The dam has broken. One by one during the next song, people dart up the narrow stairway, each one knocking the microphone against my teeth on the way—*CLUNK...!*

CLUNK...! CLUNK...!—and start jumping about on the stage. We carry on like that for a bit, then the Jägermeister join me for two songs and there's a great reaction onstage and off.

I slip away and leave the band to carry on with their own set, which involves much rock'n'roll posing and the handing out of fierce little bottles of *Jagermeister* spirit to the outstretched arms of the front rows. Then it's the early hours of the morning and the crew are dismantling the stage around us while we drink the remaining beers and enthusiastic fans ask me the FAQs.

The sky is getting light. We have to leave early tomorrow because our rooms are needed for the tourists who will be arriving in the morning for a wine festival. We arrange to meet for breakfast at ten and I head off at around five to my luxury private garret, leaving the Jägermeister and Klaus to it, whatever it is.

290 songs so far.

14th June

It's a struggle, but I make it to breakfast. Curiously, I am the only one there. While I get the first cup of coffee down, I switch on the phone to find a text message from drummer Chris, 'We'll have breakfast later!'

I send one back: 'Too late.'

I wander outside and sit at a table in the sun to wait for the Jägermeister to rouse. It's a beautiful day, just a few wispy clouds and a light wind. A bouncy castle is being blown up in the garden beside me.

Somehow our gear doesn't fit in the van any more and we have to unpack it all and lay it on the ground, then repack, while the smart first visitors for the wine festival arrive on bicycles and look on with interest. Then with a round of goodbyes we're off. Returning twenty minutes later when we realise we've left a bag behind.

But then we're off!

It's a long way to Kiel, far up in the North of Germany. Hours in the van with the sun beating down, and some differences of opinion over what should be in the cassette player. After half an hour, Man'O'War is finally voted out; with hands over ears Klaus shouts, *'Diese ist der TERROR!!'* Next up is a spoken-word German language version of 'Lord Of The Rings.'

At Hamburg, Klaus and me switch cars, and follow the Jägermeister van to Ratzeburg, where we'd planned to rest up for a while and get something to eat. But we're running late and there's barely time for a coffee before we're off again for the last hour up to Kiel.

We are all desperately hungry when we arrive, and get some pizzas ordered as top priority before soundcheck. The two women running the place promise to sort it out for us and also tell us that the massive Kiel open-air music festival started yesterday. Although the music is hardly similar to what we're doing—Hot Chocolate, for example—the lure of sitting outside on a warm summer evening could have a serious impact on our gig. Indeed, by the time the Jägermeister are due onstage, virtually no-one has turned up. Neither have the pizzas.

We sit in the dressing room, tired, hungry and irritable. The food finally arrives three hours after it was ordered and ten minutes after the band are due onstage, but unable to play without some kind of sustenance everyone forgets the 'no eating right before a gig' rule and digs in. It's a pretty good pizza but it has to be the slowest fast food in the world. Also there's been a mix-up—one of the guys running the P.A. has accidentally been served a vegetarian pizza instead of the meaty one he asked for (a U.V.M. perhaps?). The rest of the crew are encouraging him to eat it: 'Don't worry, it won't taste as vegetarian as it looks.'

Groaning with food, the band go on to about thirty people and play a fairly short set. I get on straight after them and intend to do the same, but the sound is good on the stage and the thirty people so enthusiastic that I end up playing nearly two hours again. At the end, all the Jägermeister get onstage and we play the two songs together. It's really good fun, shame almost no-one is there to see it.

From the slim entrance money we pay the P.A. crew and there is nothing left.

15th June

The last gig before a couple of day's break back home in England. In the car I get out my laptop and pass the time on the long journey to Berlin by answering questions to an interview I received by email. One of the questions is: _You have a solo career now...who are the members of your supporting band?_

Klaus had planned to drive us straight to Viola's, where we'll both be staying tonight, but we're late for soundcheck, so we stop at a service station and I jump into the Jägermeister van so I can go direct to the gig. We get lost coming into Berlin and drive around a residential area for a while, the gear piled up in the back clunking against the roof as we go over the road humps, then surprisingly everything works out and we follow the computer print-outs right to the Kirche Von Unten. We load the gear down into the cellar, and by the time the Jägermeister do their soundcheck quite a few people are starting to come in, including some I've seen earlier in the tour.

Klaus turns up with Viola and Holm. There is a rumour going round that the Toten Hosen may make a surprise appearance as they are playing in a festival only fifty kilometres away tomorrow. There's quite a crowd downstairs now and the time has come for the Jägermeister to start. They play to a good response and as they near the end I slip into the office that I'm using as a backstage and drink a lot of water and swallow some mineral salt tablets. It's going to be hot.

Within the first half hour I am drenched from head to foot in sweat, no air moving in this cellar. The room is packed with people, including some hardcore punks who stand off to one side of the stage and make a lot of noise. About an hour into the set, I look over to see that one of them has collapsed and his friend is dragging him towards me, where he dumps him on the stage right in front of the microphone stand, the hottest and most crowded place in the entire room.

'Not there, anywhere but there!' I tell him, but he shrugs his shoulders and moves away.

Well, I'm not going to be responsible for a casualty at one of my gigs if I can help it. I take off the guitar, get down from the stage and grab the guy under the arms. He's pretty heavy. Suddenly Holm is there to take the feet, and a way opens up through the crowd as we carry him out to the exit and lay him out on the back stairs. Impressively, despite being unconscious the guy is still clutching on to his beer bottle, although much of the beer has now spilled over me. Holm hurries upstairs to get help and I push my way back to the stage to carry on with the set. I play for a long time, thirty-eight songs, two and a quarter hours in total, my longest ever, finishing off with the two songs with the Jägermeister. Despite being penned in this underground sweat pit for the last few hours the audience goes berserk and as the last note rings out they applaud manically and shout for more. I run through the crowd and into the office where Sid Vicous (the dog) greets me with a lazy wag of the tail, and I sit heaving for breath, my clothes dripping quietly onto the wooden floor.

It's late. We've said goodbye to the Jägermeister, and now we're hanging around outside in the still-warm air, trying to say our goodbyes to everyone else and leave. As we drive through the streets of Berlin a sudden storm breaks out, rain sheeting down and wind battering the side of the car.

We haul the bags and the guitar up the stairs to Viola's flat, then as quickly as it started, the storm is over, the bloody sun is coming up, the bloody sky is becoming light, and the bloody birds are singing.

352 songs.

PART TWO: BAVARIA, AUSTRIA AND SWITZERLAND

22nd June

For the flight to Munich I'm seated in row fourteen, and notice that there is no row thirteen, presumably because it's unlucky. But does that mean that row fourteen is *really* row thirteen, or is row twelve the real row thirteen? And anyway, whoever heard of only one row of seats crashing in an air disaster?

Just a brief moment of panic when I see one of the baggage handlers carrying my guitar across the tarmac towards a different aircraft until one of his colleagues calls him back. They know I have a window seat. They are having a laugh.

I'm flying via Zurich so that I can get a direct flight back when the tour finishes in Switzerland next week. The plane is delayed because of strong winds and I have just twenty minutes to drink a quick coffee in Zurich airport with René, my friend and promoter in Switzerland, then I'm off for Munich, where PamP, singer with Garden Gang, is waiting for me.

We have a reasonably early start tomorrow, it's quite a few hours drive to the gig in Austria, but when we get back to PamP's place late in the evening Andi prepares something to eat, and of course when in Bavaria you have to drink a bottle of *Weizen* beer, oh and also the *Dünkelweizen*, and—oh—PamP introduces me to a variety I've never tried before, and—oh. We agree to skip breakfast tomorrow so we can get a bit more sleep before we leave.

23rd June

Even though we didn't have breakfast we are still a little late—well, over an hour—by the time we get to Garden Gang's rehearsal room in Munich, where the rest of the band are waiting. I meet the new members, bass player Monica and drummer Joe. Joe gives me a banana.

We load the band's gear into the two cars and then we're off. PamP and I go together with the gear in the two-seater van, and Andi drives with the rest of the band in her car. We drive as far as the nearest petrol station then stop to fill up with fuel and check the tires and oil, and drink some coffee and buy some junk food...but then we're off!

The gig has been arranged by Max, who promoted the 'Child's Play' benefit gig in Vienna a couple of months ago. As we cross the border, PamP sees there is a message on his mobile phone answering service. 'That'll be Max,' he says. He listens back to the message and says,'I don't understand—it's just a female voice saying, 'Welcome to Max..."

My phone also has a message saying 'Welcome to Max.' It's the name of the Austrian mobile phone network.

We meet with the real Max at a service station near St. Pölten and drive over to the hotel, the *Schlafgut!* ('Sleep Well!') ten minutes away. It's a nice enough place above a bar on the outskirts of the town. Rooms have been booked for me and the five people in Garden Gang, as well as Max and Jana and their friends Flo and Martina, so they can enjoy tonight too without worrying about having to get home to Vienna and Linz afterwards. We check in, then drive over to the gig in Obergrafendorf, a little country town a few kilometres away. No-one seems to be about, and with the glorious weather holding up it's difficult to imagine people coming all the way out here for the gig. I'm not 100% sure that I am big in Obergrafendorf.

While the P.A. is being set up we sit round a table in the bar and lay into a very large bowl of spaghetti with a very small dish of sauce. Then we're into soundcheck, which seems to take a long time and at the end somehow the sound is still not very good. It's hard to care—I have the distinct feeling no one is going to turn up tonight.

Already suffering from tour fatigue, I go and lie out in a little meadow behind the venue, basking in the still-warm rays of the setting sun, the dry grass rustling around me in the breeze. Pretty soon I notice that there are quite a few ants crawling over me. I am lying on an ant's nest. They bite.

Upstairs from the venue are a few extremely run-down rooms that we can use as a backstage. As night falls, most of us hang around up there. Through the open window we can hear whenever anyone arrives. It's a big club, and every extra member of the public through the door counts if the place is not going to seem too empty.

'Hey!' says PamP, cupping his ear to the sound of voices and footsteps below, 'People are coming in!' He dashes over to the window. 'Oh...no, they're leaving.'

A young local band called Skeptic Eleptic play first, then it's nearly midnight by the time Garden Gang get onstage. There is an annoying reverb effect on PamP's voice and when they finish I go over to the guy mixing the sound to ask him to switch it off when I play. 'Just a minute...' he says, then reaches up and removes a pair of earplugs. 'Pardon?'

Towards one in the morning Max says a few words to introduce me, then I'm on. The reverb is there on my voice and I snap at the sound guy to take it off. Can't see much with the lights in my eyes, mostly just empty floor and some distant figures, and I'm quite glad when Garden Gang join me for the last four numbers and we get a chance to belt out a few songs as a full band.

Upstairs in the dingy dressing room, Max has brought in a large supply of dangerously strong drinks. I guess now we are starting to have some kind of fun. I notice that there is dried spaghetti stuck to the walls.

After a while I go back downstairs to pack my gear away and get on to the stage in the dark to find beer has spilled all over my cables, which I attempt to dry off with an old towel.

'We Will Rock You' comes onto the decks and a strobe light starts up. I've never tried packing my gear away while a strobe light is on before.

We get back to the hotel at 5:30 and arrangements are made to meet for the last breakfast at 10:00, but I say that I will miss it because I would rather sleep.

My room faces the sun, which is already over the horizon. No curtains.

24th June

Never was a hotel more inappropriately named than the *Schlafgut!* At 9:30 they knock on the door. At 9:50 they ring me up and say 'Breakfast is going to be on the table for another ten minutes.' At 10:30 they knock on the door again and shout, 'How long are you going to be?' Then they ring up yet again and tell me they need the room vacated by 11:00.

We all meet up in the car park. Everyone else realised they were fighting a losing battle for sleep and went down to breakfast. Martina goes back into the hotel and charms them into giving me a cheese roll.

We drive back to the venue. While the boys load up the gear I sit outside in the sun on an old couch with Martina and Jana. Jana gives me a pair of sunglasses with yellow lenses so that everything looks ultra-bright. 'Now maybe you will write some more cheerful songs,' she says.

Then it's time for goodbyes. The ten of us had a pretty good party, even if almost no-one else turned up.

A long hot journey back to Munich, where I'll be playing tonight in the Substanz. The name rings a bell somehow, but it's only when we pull up to the venue that I realise it's the same place I played the first time I came to Munich, about ten years ago, and I get a sudden jolt of nostalgia.

No doubt the beer gardens are full on this warm summer's night, but only about sixty people turn up to the gig. All the same, there's a great feel to the venue, the audience are warm and responsive, I feel in good form, and it's a really nice evening, around two hours onstage.

We drive back to PamP and Andi's flat and stay up until the birds start singing.

25th June

Two days off and finally the chance to sleep late. It's well after midday when we rouse, and nearly three in the afternoon when we get round to a lazy breakfast. We spend the rest of the day, well, *off*, and in the evening PamP and Andi prepare something to eat. We sit outside in the dark at around eleven, the moon overhead, fireflies trailing lazily around us. At midnight we go for a long walk. All around are the startling roars and grunts of bullfrogs, and in the stream that runs through the fields below the village, a ghostly white swan drifts by.

26th June

Breakfast at three, then we walk down to the local organic food shop. Opposite is a barn with three doors. Inside the open right hand door a row of contented-looking cows can be seen. The middle door is closed. From the left hand door hangs a thick plastic tube, above it a sign saying: *Milch Automat.*

27th June

To Switzerland! PamP and I in the van, Andi and the rest of the band in the car as usual. Despite René's detailed directions we still get a bit lost, and pull into the Gaswerk to find the rest of Garden Gang already there, along with a few punks hanging around outside wondering if perhaps Die Toten Hosen will make a surprise guest appearance today.

Great to be back at the Gaswerk and see again all the friends I made the last couple of times I played here. The Winterthur summer festival is in full flow and gearing up to its last few frantic days with free music stages, beer stands and fairground rides in the town centre. It's a pleasant surprise to see that quite a few people are in the club by the time Garden Gang play. Perhaps it's something to do with the fact that the weather has broken a little and, though it's still warm, outside it's begun to rain.

It's certainly warm onstage as I sweat my way through twenty-eight songs until curfew, the packed crowd still calling for more. Then Garden Gang go off to their hotel, and I go back with René and Mariann to their flat just down the road, where I will be sleeping in my usual spot—a mattress on the floor of their computer room.

At 3:30 we open a bottle of wine, and René starts making a loaf for breakfast.

28th June

I'm up at eleven and on the balcony looking out over Winterthur. In the distance over the rooftops a giant ferris wheel installed for the town festival revolves gently. The loaf René has baked is also out on the balcony cooling. Garden Gang arrive shortly after midday. It's a day off for most of them today—the stage at El Lokal in Zurich is too small to accommodate the whole band, so PamP is going to play solo.

Late afternoon we head off for Zurich. Soundcheck goes fine. I run through a song or two and when I finish get a huge roar of applause from the people already in the venue, which cheers me up no end. Head of El Lokal, Victor, remembers only too well the last time I was here and had to attempt to make the new P.A. system work for American country singer Katy Moffat. He shows me a large piece about tonight's gig in the Zurich local paper which claims I am an Acoustic Folk Punk Hero and also Katy Moffat's soundman.

Tired, I throw back a couple of espressos and by the time PamP starts at eleven the venue is fairly full.

Then I'm on, and play thirty songs, finally refusing to do any more after six encores. There's nowhere to get away, but the stage has two rather comfortable divans on it, so PamP and I sit up there chatting.

Then we're heading back to Winterthur, dropping the band off at the hotel, then in the lift up to the sixth floor flat where the sound of birdsong rises up to us and outside we can see the sky becoming light.

29th June

René drives us over to the gig, a youth centre in Bremgarten. It's a last-minute replacement for one that got cancelled a couple of weeks ago, arranged by a friend of PamP. Last time I was here I was appalled at how disorganised and run-down the place was, but impressed with the commitment and friendliness of the organisers. This time things seem to have gone downhill: no-one seems to be in charge or able to say what time I will be playing, and there are tell-tale posters on the wall warning that there are too many freeloaders coming in and helping themselves to beer without helping with any of the work.

When we finish the soundcheck a couple of guys set up a projection screen on the stage and ask us to move our stuff back a bit because they're going to be doing 'a bit of theatre.'

Past ten and still no sign of the gig starting. Inside the club the film is in full swing, watched by a small crowd of young anarchists and punks seated on the floor. It's footage shot at various anti-capitalist demonstrations. Our host gives a running commentary through the microphone, explaining what the police are doing and showing their tactics as they mass together to pick off demonstrators and isolate them. We see the tear gas and the water cannons and the mounted charges, the armoured riot vehicles waiting on the sidestreets. The good bits are shown again on a loop at ear-splitting volume. It's like the end of the world.

Outside none of us knows what's going on, when the film is going to stop, when we can start. Tonight Garden Gang are staying upstairs in a tiny room with bunk beds next to the café and have the only key to get up there. There's no access from the venue itself so the only way for the rest of us to get in is to hang around outside the window and wait for one of them to appear so they can throw the key down. Monica says there's no way she's sleeping up there and is laying her sleeping bag out in the car.

Finally the film is over and Garden Gang get to start. Most of the audience went out when the film ended, and they're left to play to about forty people. They're an enthusiastic bunch, though, enjoy my set too, and in the end the gig is fine.

But I feel sorry for Garden Gang having to stay here the night. At 3:30 I'm glad to be making my escape, back to Winterthur, where it turns out there are still quite a few people on the streets, weaving back from the town festival, which shut at 4:00.

30th June

The bells! The bells!

From nine in the morning every church in Winterthur is pealing to celebrate a wedding, and every chime and clang is reverberating around the valley, then rolling up to the sixth floor and through the open windows to batter away at my sleep. Hateful sound.

Anyway, we plan to leave for Lucerne reasonably early. I've never been there before, and it's supposed to be a nice town so maybe we'll have time for some sightseeing before the gig. The sun is beating down and as we set off the car is already hot and sticky so it looks like it's going to be an uncomfortable journey. But no! René presses a button, the sun roof glides back and we have the wind in our hair.

Lucerne is having its yearly festival. There are swarms of tourists on the streets and a large free music stage set up in the centre. It is a beautiful town, surrounded by hills with old fortifications poking up above the other buildings on the slopes. A fast-flowing river that splits the centre is crossed diagonally by a rickety wooden bridge, crammed with tourists. The river widens out to a lake which dog-legs away to the mountains in the distance. Pleasure cruisers sit solemnly in the centre of the lake, while myriads of yachts weave past them, sails gleaming in the sunshine. I wonder, what is the number on the door of the Lucerne sailing club?

We drive out to the club, an old prison now used as a gig and rehearsal centre, up on a hill above the town. Garden Gang are on the stage soundchecking and look rather shell-shocked from last night. But at least this venue has a decent backstage and two tidy little private rooms with beds, where Garden Gang will sleep tonight. The door to the dressing room opens to a breathtaking view of the mountains and a lake.

The organisers set up a barbecue outside, and a couple of the other bands who'll be playing later wander in with some food and sit with us. One of them lays an incense burner on the table and fires it up.

Is anyone going to come? It's—oooh, late—and not many were in the club last time I looked. It's a quite a distance from the town centre where people are lazing around outside at the festival, after all, but PamP is feeling optimistic. 'It's these positive smells!' he sighs, glancing at the incense burner. 'It's going to be good!'

And actually the weather is suddenly on our side—shortly before Garden Gang are due on at around eleven, the rain starts to fall and those hanging around outside hurry into the club. The rain falls very heavily and doesn't stop. There is a crack of thunder and the mountains light up in a zig-zag of lightning.

We are all gathered at the doorway, watching the spectacular display, when René says, 'Did I close the roof on the car?'

As Garden Gang get onstage, the organisers are dashing in out of the rain and dumping the dripping barbecue equipment on the dressing room floor, a rather damp dog dashing in and out between their legs as they try to pack it away. René arrives back with a couple of wet towels from where he has been wiping out the car.

I watch the band's last few numbers from the side of the stage, then one of the organisers gets up and announces the bands that will be playing later, finishing with '...and very soon...TV SMITH!!' At that moment the dog, which has been standing quietly next to me, steps up and wanders out on to the stage.

Not many people, but the sound is really good and I'm pleased with my performance. Another 28 songs, making a grand total of 517 this month, not including soundchecks, more songs than I have ever played in a month before.

Last night of the tour, the storm booming and flashing over the mountains outside and everyone in the dressing room fatigued, but relieved that the work is over. It gets silly. Hasn't taken new member Monica long to get used to life on the road...she is working the coffee pot lid and making it speak. Tom and I find a bolt high up on the wall with no apparent purpose and scratch our heads over it for a while until we find ridiculous things that suddenly become locked when we move the bolt across. Then we play an imaginary game of tennis with some very large spoons.

But, children, it can't go on forever—we've got a couple of hours drive ahead of us. So many friends to say goodbye to and then we're in the only-slightly damp car winding our way down the hillside over Lucerne and along the miles of roadworks on the autobahn back to Winterthur.

1st July

One day's holiday before heading back to England. What do you do on holiday? We get up late, have a lazy breakfast, drive into Zurich and go swimming in the lake, then have a glass of wine sitting by the water. We drive back to Winterthur along the country roads in the early evening, hoping to buy some food from a farm shop so René can cook a meal tonight, but all the farm shops are closed. We set up a table on the balcony then he gets creative with the little food there is in the house. It's amazing what you can do with one large tomato.

2nd July

They are dismantling the big wheel; the cabins have been removed and the bare spokes now stick skeletally out from the rim like a stripped clock. I am at the airport, saying goodbye again.

PART THREE: ENGLAND

6th July

From one holiday to another. A few days after getting back from Switzerland and just before leaving for Scandinavia I'm heading up to exotic Morecambe for the annual Holidays In The Sun punk festival, one of 130 artists including Hate Fuck Trio and Dog Shit Sandwich who are playing on four stages over three days to celebrate this, 'the 25th anniversary of punk.' My partner Gaye, bass player from the Adverts and fellow representative of the original English punk rock scene, is coming with me so we can meet some old mates, watch the odd band and have a laugh.

The plan is to go up the day before my gig so I can see the Boys play, as their drummer is Vom, moonlighting from Die Toten Hosen. The organisers couldn't get Gaye and me the same hotel two nights running so we'll have to do a bit of travelling around when we get there, which means I'm going to have to take the car.

It all goes well until we get to Birmingham, then the traffic slows to a twenty mile an hour crawl and it's seven hours before we reach the first of the hotels, above a pub near Lancaster. The woman behind the bar tells us that there is no room booked for us and the hotel is full. They did have a couple of rooms booked for Holidays In The Sun, she says, but a band called Sham 69 came in earlier in the day, took both the rooms and left with the keys.

Right.

I've been driving for nine hours and it's now late afternoon and we have nowhere to stay. We drive in to Morecambe and hang around the office while the organisers try and find us another room. They check with the tourist office but everywhere in town is booked.

'Sorry, that's all I can do...but the hotel for tomorrow is definitely okay!'

Right.

Someone tells me: 'The best thing to do is head back down the motorway—they might have something in Blackpool...'

I say, 'If I start towards Blackpool, I'm driving on to London and I'm not coming back. Fuck the gig.' I'm not in a very good mood.

Dave, a fan who comes to my Lancashire gigs and writes to me occasionally, wanders up with his girlfriend Claire. 'Awright TV? I saw you just now and I said to Claire, What's up wi' TV? Usually e's got a smile on his face but today 'e looks like thunder.'

Turns out Dave is staying with a mate called Gav who owns a guest house which he's closing down, but right now it's still functional and there's a spare room. Dave calls him up to explain our problem and Gav says we can stay. We drive over there and drop off the bags and guitar in a little attic room, then get back to the venue, where the Boys are already on.

Backstage to say hello to Vom and miss loads of groups while we have a drink and reminisce about the gig in Düsseldorf last month. I tell him about the problem we had getting a room today. He tells me he wasn't happy with his room either—him and John from the Boys ended up having to share a small double bed. Vom lashed out with an elbow in his sleep and inadvertently hit John in the face, giving him a nosebleed.

Vom says he has to leave soon because he'll be getting up at six to fly back to Germany for a gig with the Hosen. Gaye and I cruise around the main venue for a bit, watching a few bands, having a few drinks and getting our photos taken a lot, then head down the road to the Dome, where my mate Craig is drumming in a punk covers band called 1977, and Rikki from Red Flag '77 is running the merchandise stand. We spend the last hour of the night watching bands from the comparative comfort of the merchandising area, quaffing from the tray of free beer.

Did we take a note of the address of the guest house? No. Do we remember how we got there this afternoon? Well, we *think* so...

7th July

In true Northern guest house style, you have to be out of the room by 9.30, but you get a full cooked breakfast for your sixteen quid, and up here they believe in a *big plate*.

We drive straight over to tonight's hotel so we can settle in there. They've been warned that we'll be checking in early and have told us that the room will be free by the time we arrive. It's another guest house, further down the sea front. The landlady welcomes us and tells us that she'll need ten minutes to make up the room but we can go up and leave our bags there if we want. She leads us up to the top floor where the sounds of a television blaring from the room that's supposed to be ours gives her pause. 'They should have left by now,' she says, then after knocking softly on the door a couple of times uses her key. There's no one in there, but the door opens to a scene of chaos: a table lamp smashed on the floor, overflowing ashtrays, empty pizza boxes, red hair dye and blood stains on the sheets... Ah, this was Vom's room.

I turn to the landlady. 'We'll come back in a couple of hours.'

It's a glorious sunny day and the first of the punks are gathering outside the venue, extravagant multi-coloured mohicans fully formed despite the earliness of the hour. The pub is already doing good business. A couple of Germans who came to one of my gigs in the Czech Republic last year ask if they can take some photos. I say yes, and suddenly one of them has ducked behind me, poked his head between my legs and hoisted me aloft.

It's a great view from up here! Out on the fringes of the car park, bandit territory, I can see where Charlie Harper from the UK Subs is running his own merchandising stand, much to the annoyance of the event organisers, who won't get their fifteen percent. I was told yesterday that one of the organisers went up to him as he was putting up the stall and said, 'You can't set up here. What if all the bands decided to do it? That would be anarch.... Oh.'

After a while Gaye and I go back to the hotel room, which has been miraculously cleaned up, fetch the guitar and walk back along the seafront to the Platform, a smaller venue next to the Market Arena. We go backstage where, as per contract, I 'make myself known' to the venue manager, who turns out to be Peter from Peter and The Test Tube Babies. Could be a bit of a problem for him tomorrow when the schedule has him down as stage managing here while simultaneously playing with his band next door.

Wandering from venue to venue I've been getting a lot of people promising to come to the gig and am feeling pretty optimistic about it as start time approaches in the early evening. The thing is, with four other bands playing at the same time and much alcohol being imbibed, it's going to be a gamble whether anyone's organised enough to actually make it. As I get onstage, there's still not many in the hall but by by midway through the first number people are piling in and suddenly the place is packed with about six hundred people. The gig's a knockout.

Afterwards I wander down to the back of the hall, chat with some of the crowd and get my photo taken a lot. Quite a few times people say, 'Where is Gaye these days?' and I reply, 'She's standing next to you.'

Back down to the Dome, which is full to capacity and they're not letting anyone else in. The headline bands on in the Market Arena don't interest us, so we head back into the Platform for a final drink. There's an after-show band on, some young kids playing to about twenty of their mates. Presumably no-one else knows them or is curious enough to check them out, but they go for it anyway, belting out some interesting high energy songs that are completely out of the mainstream and stand no chance of success. Even though I am the oldest person in the room I love them for it. Eventually the bass amp packs up for the second time in twenty minutes and they call a halt, but you know that somewhere soon they'll be back, playing with the fierce conviction of those who believe they have something to say, whether anyone's listening or not. Punk rock: you can't stop it.

PART FOUR: NORWAY AND FINLAND

10th July

Yesterday I didn't know where Oslo was. I looked it up on a map of Norway and said to myself, 'Oh...*there*...'

Now I'm there, and I hope the guy who asked me to do the gig by email will recognise me, because I have no idea what he looks like, in fact I can't even pronounce his name—Trygve. When I get out of the airport it turns out to be the tall guy with the short trousers and longs socks, two kids buzzing around him. He leads me down to the train that runs into Oslo, but after climbing between the barriers and finding ourselves on the side of the train where the doors won't open he admits that he usually goes by bus. By the time we get back up the escalators and down to the correct platform the train is pulling out, and Trygve's daughter bursts into tears.

It's alright, the next one's along in ten minutes. Walking out of Oslo station towards the hotel I try to fix the directions in my mind because tomorrow morning at 6:50 I'll be making the return journey alone on a tight schedule for a flight to Finland. Trygve leaves me at the hotel entrance and points out the venue, just up the road, then heads off to take his kids home, promising to return after the soundcheck.

My sinuses have blocked up since the flight and I take a half hour to rest in the room, but still feel a bit light-headed when I leave for the venue. I spot the person most likely to be one of the organisers sitting at the bar and walk up to him. Bullseye.

'Hello! You must be TV. I'm Kenneth.'

Surely not a very Norwegian name? Luckily Kenneth speaks good English. While we wait for the sound engineer he orders me a coffee and lets me know that a friend of his was at Holidays In The Sun and thought I was the best thing on, which puts me in a good mood right away.

Soundman Michael—surely not a very Norwegian name?—arrives with a large dog and we start the soundcheck. The bar owners ask Michael to shut the dog into the dressing room, but it has obviously figured out how to open the door because it keeps wandering up onto the stage, eventually settling itself down in my guitar case.

Trygve reappears and suggests walking over to a bar near his flat. While his friends there are getting the beers down at impressive speed, I'm holding back, still feeling very blocked up and not wanting to lose my energy for the gig later. I suspect *much* later...it's getting on for eleven when we head back to the venue.

This is Scandinavia so it's still light outside. The venue is suffering from Summer Evening Syndrome, i.e there's hardly anyone there. Even the agent that Trygve persuaded to book the gig is away on holiday. But it's not too bad for my first time in a new country—by the time I get on stage at just after midnight there are about fifty or sixty people in the audience and as soon as I start playing a sudden transformation occurs—they all go nuts, jumping around, singing along, pogoing and, led by Trygve, running up onto the stage to join in on the choruses. It's great.

Afterwards a couple of Trygve's friends tell me how impressed they were: 'It's the first time we've seen Trygve get up on stage since he wrecked a Ramones gig thirteen years ago!'

Trygve wanders over and interrupts me as I am deep in thought trying to remember and write down the list of songs that I played today. 'You're quite into lists, aren't you?' he says. 'I've noticed on the website—lists of gigs, lists of recorded songs, lists of unrecorded songs...'

'Not really,' I counter. 'I only put up all those lists because Klaus asked for them for the site. I'd never even thought of writing them down before then.'

But actually I am thinking: 35 songs tonight, that's 570 since the beginning of June.

Michael comes down from the mixing desk to tell me that the sound was good. Also, I don't need to talk to him so slowly because he is actually American.

It's past three and I have to leave. As I head towards the door someone asks me how long I'm on tour for and I say, forever.

Back at the hotel at 3:30, I gather my bags together for a quick exit and set the alarm for three hours time.

11th July

It hurts. I want to sleep. I can think only of sleep. I get to the station to see the 6:50 just pulling away, but no need for tears—there's another one in ten minutes and I make it to the airport just in time.

Breakfast is served on the plane and my pre-booked vegetarian comes with the sticker *Special Meal. To be served on leg.*

No, hang on a minute, that's—*To be served on leg Oslo-Helsinki.*

It's a banana.

We fly across Norway, then over the sea separating Sweden and Finland, and in the deliriously clear morning skies I can look down and see the scattering of islands that lie between the two countries—some small and deserted, others larger and criss-crossed by threads of roads connecting toy-sized farmhouses and villages.

Get the bus in to Helsinki from the airport and set off up the hill to the hotel that's been booked for me, just a couple of minutes away from the bus station. To my relief, it's a really good hotel. I drop my bags gratefully into a clean, comfortable room, have a shower, rinse out my stage T-shirt and guitar strap and lie down for an hour feeling dizzy and blocked up.

The T-shirt has dried out nicely. I change the strings on my guitar and leave for the venue, only to find I'm an hour early. Also, it turns out that Punk Lurex O.K., who I'd been expecting to support me tonight, actually haven't been booked so I'll be doing a long solo set. Soundcheck over, I go upstairs to the Ilves bar and drink some coffee and do an interview with local music magazine. After that, there's still time to kill so I take a walk to an underground church, which is closed.

Bump into one of the Helsinki crew, Berja, on the way back. I tell him that despite the fact that the Semi-Final is usually one of my best gigs, I really feel that on this hot Wednesday evening I'm not going to get many into the venue. This seems to be borne out when we drop into Ilves and meet someone who tells us he just popped into the club and there were three people in. I start putting myself in the frame of mind for a more intimate Helsinki gig than usual.

When I go down the alley to the venue there are a few more trickling in. Staunch Helsinki Crew members Tommi and Anastiina arrive on bicycles, just back from a cycling holiday in the North, and there are a few other faces I recognise, around sixty people altogether. Despite the low turnout it seems impossible to go wrong at the Semi-final – once again there's a great atmosphere and I play thirty five songs.

Just around the corner a bed in a luxury hotel is waiting. I shall go to it.

12th July

I decide to break the 'no breakfast' regime, and drag myself awake at 9.30 because I figure that this hotel is so good the breakfast is going to be stunning. I immediately regret it. It's a mad scrum down there with people jostling each other round the buffet dishes—most of it meat or fish—and someone's mobile phone ringing repeatedly to the tune of 'Itsy Bitsy Teeny Weeny Yellow Polka Dot Bikini'. No punishment could be too severe.

I don't have a gig today, but a rehearsal is scheduled with Punk Lurex for six o'clock. I take the midday train to Tampere, and Harri, agent for this tour, meets me at the station and takes me over to the hotel—another top quality one which I'll be staying in for the next four nights. I'm up on the sixteenth floor with a fantastic view out over Tampere and the lakes beyond. Did I do something right somewhere, somehow?

I meet my friend and label owner Jukka. He thought I needed a larger label to release my new album in Finland, so we go for a meeting with them. We have a chat about their plans over coffee and muffins and they give me a sheet of paper with my promo schedule for the next few days. Er—two interviews.

Then Jukka takes me over to the administration marquee for the Tampere town festival, which I'll be playing tomorrow, and gets my pass sorted out. It's now five in the afternoon, so he decides not to go back to his day job at the software company and instead we sit with a beer outside a bar by the river. Over on the opposite bank my hotel towers over us, and Jukka points out that I have been staying in progressively better accommodation on each of my visits here. 'Now you are in the best hotel in Tampere, so this will have to be your last tour.'

I meet up with Punk Lurex at the rehearsal room. They say they have more or less learned a couple of new songs we could play together but haven't actually seen each other since the last time I was in Finland. They say they have tried out the new songs 'by phone.'

As usual, after rehearsal we go for a beer, first in a little bar opposite the Telakka, then down to the bar by the riverside I was at earlier, and then in the early hours to a club called the Satellite where I feel rather out of place until I am suddenly recognised by someone who reaches into his jacket pocket and produces a copy of my album for me to sign. His friend, also a fan, comes over and together they start constructing my setlist for the gig tomorrow.

It's past three in the morning and we are being thrown out of the club. A bed in a luxury hotel is calling to me. I shall go to it.

Oops, forgot to eat. There is a mint chocolate on the pillow.

13th July

At three I meet up in a bar with a journalist for the first of the interviews, then go back to the hotel to do the next by phone as the guy is in Lapland. At four I meet with Merja in the hotel lobby and we walk up to the Tampere art gallery where's there's a big exhibition on the Incas, with lots of artifacts on display: masks, weapons, jewellery, some dramatic textiles made from coloured feathers, and an interesting room of erotic pottery—little jugs and statues showing explicit carnal scenes. My favourite was 'Anal Sex Under A Blanket.'

Three bands on tonight. First on will be a Finnish band who Punk Lurex supported on tour last year. Then I'll play, with Punk Lurex joining me at the end, and last on stage will be a fairly well-known old Finnish punk band who are reforming for the occasion.

There's been some kind of mix-up: Punk Lurex had been expecting to borrow the first band's drumkit but they won't let us use it because they will be packing up and leaving straight after their set. I soundcheck alone, still not knowing if Punk Lurex will be able to play, while the venue managers phone around frantically to see if they can get hold of a drumkit. Apart from that, soundcheck goes well. There's a great sound on stage, and the venue itself is a spacious old cinema, with a standing area in front of the stage, then a floor that step up towards the back of the hall with a few tables and and old cinema seats scattered around.

The first band are on, playing an American style of rocky songs that are apparently popular in Finland at the moment, although not too popular with the people here. Someone is carting in all the bits of a drumkit for Punk Lurex and putting them down by the side of the stage. The place is starting to fill up quite nicely and I have a good feeling about this one.

I take the stage and all the people who have piled into the area at the front start dancing and singing along. After half an hour on my own Punk Lurex get onstage and the place erupts.

Afterwards, someone tells me, 'I usually only like death metal, but you were fuckin' evil.'

The band and me get in the back of the ice cream van the organisers found to transport the drums back to the rehearsal room. It's the first time I've been in an ice cream van since getting a lift back from a gig with The Stranglers in 1977.

I'm so tired I'm almost glad when we eventually get to the Satellite and find the queue is so long that it's not worth waiting. A quick beer in the hotel bar and I'm getting an early night at only, oh, 3:00 a.m.

14th July

I dream I am cycling in the village where I grew up and get a flat tyre.

Breakfast in a café in the shopping centre, then back to the hotel room for a string change and to spend a couple of hours on my own before meeting up with the band for the drive to tonight's gig in Turku. Tiina and Riitta have gone to fetch the hire van and will be at the rehearsal room at five.

From up here on the sixteenth floor I can see people below me milling about in the warm afternoon sunshine. Out in the distance a storm approaches across the lakes, and I watch as the forests on the distant shore disappear in a blanket of grey, which rolls across the water swallowing everything in its path. Below me, no-one knows. There is an eerie booming echoing faintly around and the first flashes of lightning dart down to the water, miles away. Then it's over the town. The sky turns dark and people on the streets run for shelter. Thunder erupts, so loud the window shakes. Multiple bolts of lightning zig-zag down and evaporate as they touch the roofs below me; one arcs down over the railway lines and strikes the lightning rod on top of the cathedral.

By the time I take my guitar and bag up to the rehearsal room the sun is shining on the wet streets and people are out again in their summer clothes. It's now six. There's been some problem with the van, putting our start time back an hour, and even though I've been told it's a late gig tonight I'm starting to get a bit worried as we have a two and a half hour drive ahead of us. Punk Lurex's guitarist Kukka arrives and we go to a café for a quick coffee while we are waiting. His English is rather basic. I am a little surprised when he tells me that a friend of his rated last night's gig as 'minus ten out of ten.' Then he explains that he means '*almost* ten out of ten.'

The van arrives at around six thirty, driven by a friend of Riitta's who has the necessary licence. I recognise it as the one that needed new brake pads and then leaked hydraulic fluid all over the passenger area on a previous tour with Punk Lurex. The next time we hired it the exhaust fell off. This time it needed a tyre change, which is why we're running late. We load up and at around seven we're off to Turku. Half an hour later we stop to tighten the wheel nuts...but then we're off to Turku!

We are driving into the glare of a sun that stays obstinately above the horizon. Nearing the halfway mark we stop at a service station in the forest. Outside a scraggy reindeer grazes. I walk up and listen to its leathery lips flapping as it tugs at the grass, velvety antlers tangling in the thistles. In the distance the band are calling to me to get in the van. On through the forest and the fields and the lakes. On one stretch of empty road I notice a handmade sign that reads 'Humppila 6 Kilometres. Mini-golf.' I wonder, how much does the mini-golf at Humppila cost?

For the last hour of the journey Punk Lurex chat and laugh amongst themselves in Finnish while I feel myself floating in a bubble of fatigue. It is the moment for one of the few Finnish phrases I know: *Miksi mina teen tätä?* (Why am I doing this?)

We arrive at the venue just before 10 p.m. and not much seems to be happening. I'm tired, dazed and disconnected. It's quite a nice café bar, but even this late in the evening there are very few people in. The manager says there is another big gig on in town tonight and we should probably wait until just after midnight before Punk Lurex start, with me on at about 1:30. I'd like to get my soundcheck over with as soon as possible but it makes more sense for Punk Lurex to get their gear onstage and go first. After they've finished, the sound mixer says that the pizza restaurant next door is only open for another five minutes and we have to all go there now if we want to get anything to eat. None of us have eaten all day so we troop over, even though I would rather get the soundcheck done. Don't want to piss off the sound guy, though. Never piss off the sound guy. Suddenly I find I'm not hungry and pick at a salad. At the back of the restaurant a baby cries incessantly and I'm thinking, 'He's right.'

I leave the rest of the band in the restaurant and slip back to the venue to do the soundcheck. Then I go out for a walk to try and get focused.

Midnight twilight by the river, and I'm thinking about which songs I'd like to play later. Two young women walk up the riverside path, glasses of wine in their hands and stop to talk to me. They ask me what I'm doing sitting on my own, and start telling me about themselves, suddenly and unexpectedly letting me into their lives. They are two students, friends since childhood and 'spiritual sisters', they say, from the North of the country. One of them has just graduated and is about to move to Turku, and they are both visiting the town together before the split. Actually I know they are two angels descended to drag me out of my depression.

In the venue, Punk Lurex are ready to start. Kukka assures me that everything is running only slightly behind schedule. 'We will play at nine o'clock. I mean, one o'clock.'

They play a short set to a polite audience, then ten minutes later I am on.

How does it happen? One song in, the first trickle of applause, and I am suddenly obsessed with putting everything into this and making it work. The world collapses into these rare minutes when the song and the performance are everything and these people I've never met before will like what I do even if they don't know it yet. And through the next hour and a half they come and are trapped and as time whirls on and the sweat pours off me I look out of the window and in the limpid morning light the clock on the wall of the building opposite shows three, and still people are coming in. And Punk Lurex come back on to the stage and we play this music as if it was created only for now and here and the packed room starts to dance, and the two angels, now wearing sunglasses, appear, push their way to the front and wave at me and join in with the crowd.

Then we drive back into the sun.

Lightning Source UK Ltd.
Milton Keynes UK
UKOW021516210612

194744UK00003B/87/A